Detroit
Reprints
in
Music

Frederick Freedman, General Editor
Case Western Reserve University

*Music
for
the
Bicentennial*

Intended to honor the
American Revolution Bicentennial
1776-1976

# COMPOSERS
# CONDUCTORS
# AND
# CRITICS

BY
CLAIRE R. REIS

WITH
NEW INTRODUCTION
BY
THE AUTHOR

NEW PREFACE
BY
AARON COPLAND

FOREWORD
BY
DARIUS MILHAUD

*Detroit Reprints in Music*
INFORMATION COORDINATORS
1974

Except for the addition of pages I-XVI
and the insertion of a note at the top of page 259,
this is an unaltered reprint of the work
originally published in 1955 by the Oxford University Press.
It is reprinted by special arrangement with the author
and includes a new introduction by the author
and a new preface by Aaron Copland.

Detroit Reprints in Music
A Division of
Information Coordinators, Inc.
1435-37 Randolph Street
Detroit, Michigan 48226

# *Preface 1974*

**While I was a music student in Paris, half a century ago,**
musical events began popping at home.  By the time I was back
in New York (in 1924), a vigorous new organization had been
launched in support of the contemporary composer.  It called itself
the League of Composers, and its executive director was Claire R.
Reis, a staunch supporter of the interests of the living composer.

As a rule, composers are not an easy lot to handle.  They tend to
be over-concerned, edgy, easily disgruntled; no one plays their
music, or if they do, it is poorly performed, or, if performed,
mauled in the press.

Claire Reis proved to be the right woman in the right place.  Her
energy, devotion to the composer's cause, her stick-at-it-ness
through all sorts of musical weather, were what the new movement
needed.  She soon learned how to gather forces together, to energize
them, and to see things through.

The story this book tells concerns itself mainly with the years
1923 to 1948, a crucial time in the development of the new music.
Claire Reis was in the thick of the fight to see to it that the more
adventurous among the new composers at that time be heard.
Those of us who took part in the struggle are fully cognizant and
appreciative of the role she played.  To read the story of those
years brings with it a certain nostalgia.  The scene has changed but
the cause remains the same:  how to make way for the new voice
—the truly creative voice in our contemporary musical world.

As I once wrote, "Anyone who reads Claire Reis' book will get an intimate and personalized view of recent musical history. Her book gives a lively picture of how it was then, with a sense of happy accomplishment in the cause of the living composer."

Aaron Copland

Peekskill, New York
February 1974

# New Introduction 1974

**Twenty years ago when** *Composers Conductors and Critics*
was published about the history of the League of Composers, it was
described as "a chronicle of the Battle for Contemporary Music."
Today we are in a better position to evaluate the germinal work of
this organization about which a legend has developed. The thirty
year career of a society of composers, dedicated to contemporary
music, began in the early twenties and hastened an awareness of an
American cultural heritage. This book tells the story of the crusade
for American composers, the personal struggles of composers, and
the audience reaction to contemporary music performed during the
past three generations.

A wave of experiments in various arts during the twenties and
thirties is remembered by the birth of new theater associations that
discovered talented American playwrights—Eugene O'Neill, Sam
Behrman, Maxwell Anderson, and others. Memorable in the visual
arts was the first great international exhibition of modern painting
and sculpture, a vast collection housed in a huge armory in New
York City. Exposure to these contemporary arts quickly attracted
a new following, ready to enjoy the pleasurable and to profit from
the educational experience of a changing cultural aesthetic.

In musical circles at this time, a few embryonic societies presented
sporadic concerts of contemporary music. In retrospect, their few
years of activity were probably due to a limited horizon of
chauvinistic tendencies, policies of "first performance only," or
programs directed by a composer-team of two young men who
soon found that responsibility for concert management encroached
too heavily on their own creativity.

In the spring of 1923, the seven Founders of the League of Composers announced in their first manifesto that they would present the wide range of contemporary music in their programs—every trend and every nationality, including events of an experimental nature. Embarking on their first season, they quickly realized the importance of crusading for American composers. The Advisory Committee, which included many foreign musicians, soon sent them European compositions. They also contributed articles to the League's publication, *Modern Music* (with Minna Lederman as editor), which became the leading quarterly of contemporary music in America. American composers were not easily discovered, and few publishers were interested in searching for unknown names. This was a critical period in American contemporary music.

Early discussions by our Board of Directors stressed the significance of influential patrons and musicians. They helped us change the general tradition of awarding prizes to that of commissioning composers. Our group was convinced that prizes wasted the time of non-winners, while commissions gave composers confidence as artists chosen by a committee of musicians. Serge Koussevitzky was the first distinguished conductor to encourage us by recommending Béla Bartók and Aaron Copland for commissions in 1924. Soon afterward, I began a wide correspondence with conductors in many cities, offering them a choice of three names we had selected, and emphasizing the importance of conducting a world premiere.

This series gradually reached a record of one hundred and ten commissions, and practically all works received major performances. The commission concept had taken root. Nevertheless, the problem then and today is the follow-up of a second or a third or even more performances of a contemporary work which may require repeated hearings in order to be appreciated or understood.

Today there is less need for ardent crusaders. Many more commissions are given, and the financial outlook has improved: foundations, orchestras, educational institutions, patrons of opera and concert, arts councils, and performers have all shared in establishing important commissions. Recently a unique commission was given (by a small industrial town in England where engines are manufactured) to the Polish composer Krzysztof Penderecki; he will conduct this work in a cathedral in the town of Peterborough. The chairman of the engine company who had brought music there on other occasions gave his reason for the commission: "We looked for what was most lacking in this area, which was good music."

Who could have foreseen that a program in Cooper Union's "Great Hall"—now a National Historic Landmark—would have served as a springboard for the League of Composers? On this occasion, in 1922 (celebrating the tenth anniversary of the Peoples Music League, which gave many free concerts in public buildings), we invited six composers to share a program of their compositions. A capacity audience cheered each composer as he was introduced. They were the first group of living composers to present their own works on the Cooper Union stage. A year later, some of these same musicians helped to create the League of Composers.

Ambition breeds an infectious quality in a pioneering group. Following the concert series which was eventually responsible for performing twelve hundred works, the League added to its reputation and fame by introducing a memorable series of stage works— American premieres of contemporary operas and ballets. When Wanda Landowska arrived in this country, she brought us personal messages from Manuel de Falla as we launched our first stage effort with the New York premiere of his opera, *El Retablo de Maese Pedro*, with life size puppets. It was called a landmark in the theater.

This event was the forerunner of a series of sensational stage works. We did not foresee that the press, patrons and general public would easily attract artists of the stage who voluntarily joined us in New York and Philadelphia to create premieres of contemporary operas and ballets. Among the works presented were: Stravinsky's *Les Noces, Le Sacre du Printemps, Oedipus Rex,* and *Histoire du*

*Soldat;* Schoenberg's *Die Glückliche Hand,* and *Pierrot Lunaire* (dramatized); Prokofieff's *Pas d'Acier;* Shostakovitch's *Lady Macbeth of Mzensk* and an early film, *Odna,* with his music; Douglas Moore's *The Devil and Daniel Webster.* Many of these unique productions were given in Philadelphia and at the Metropolitan Opera House in New York at the end of the regular musical season.

Leopold Stokowski, Fritz Reiner, Pierre Monteux, Artur Rodzinski, Willem Mengelberg, and Tullio Serafin were the distinguished conductors who influenced outstanding designers, stage directors, singers, and dancers, all eager to participate in these exciting presentations. Among them were Jacques Cartier, Martha Graham, Doris Humphrey, Robert Edmond Jones, Rouben Mamoulian, Leonid Massine, Donald Oenslager, and Lee Simonson. With the unusual assistance of three great orchestras—the New York Philharmonic Symphony, Philadelphia and Cleveland—it was not surprising that tickets for every performance were sold out six weeks in advance.

These American premieres were a turning point for new stage lighting effects, and Jones (who had created advanced ideas for contemporary drama) insisted on discarding all the old electrical equipment used at the old Metropolitan Opera House. Stokowski agreed that music and lighting should be in accord with the contemporary works. Thus, it became necessary to put an assistant conductor in the electrician's box, with a score, along with a very confused technician from the opera house. There have been many repercussions from those past events of music and stage. Six years ago, at the Vincent Astor Gallery (Library & Museum of the Performing Arts, The New York Public Library at Lincoln Center) the very knowledgeable Chief Thor Wood, arranged for an exhibition of the League's unique designs, photographs, and programs; also three of the great twelve foot puppets designed for Stravinsky's *Oedipus Rex* (which are now museum treasures). This exhibition provided an opportunity for younger generations to study and enjoy the League's historic memorabilia from an imaginative era of contemporary opera and ballet.

X

During the past years, the New York City Opera directed by Julius Rudel, and the New York City Ballet directed by George Balanchine and Lincoln Kirstein have performed at the City Center's State Theater, and have created extraordinary repertories of contemporary works, many of which have been commissioned. Their productions have been enriched not only by great artists (singers, dancers and directors) but also by new ideas for stage decor and directions which have been added to their standard repertories. Today the New York City Opera and the Metropolitan Opera complement each other in their different approaches. These are not "first" and "second" companies. They are different. There are exchanges of artists from one company to another. There are occasional contemporary operas at the Metropolitan, with memorable performances of Alban Berg's *Wozzeck* and Benjamin Britten's *Peter Grimes*. The list of over fifty contemporary operas presented by the New York City Opera marks a milestone in the history of opera in the twentieth century.

*          *          *

Innovative ideas have produced unusual instruments, and sometimes the inventor has created interesting compositions. In the thirties, the League presented a few special experimental programs which are still recalled: a Mexican ensemble which produced extraordinary intervals on homemade instruments; a modern kithara played by Harry Partch which sent us all back to study our Greek history; and an ambitious program with new electrical instruments which made us consult with a remarkable engineer who had studied music —and helped us to organize a Town Hall concert. A great disappointment, however, followed the successful demonstration, when a commission from an electric organ company offered to the distinguished composer, Serge Prokofieff, was refused by him because his penetrating questions could be answered by neither the keyboard demonstrator nor the factory engineer. A generation after a variety of trials with music and electricity, electronic music moved into the spotlight and has remained there, gaining the vital interest of avant garde composers as well as the cooperation of several leading universities.

An unusual work on a League program was by Henry Eicheim, a composer who had travelled in the Orient and introduced in his orchestral scores temple bells, gongs and cymbals obtained from priests in China.

Today, at the Metropolitan Museum of Art, there is a great opportunity to study an extraordinary collection of instruments from many countries, East and West, and from many historic periods. The erudite musician and historian Emanuel Winternitz, the curator responsible for this permanent exhibition, has included some taped instruments, appealing to the ear as to the eye. These rare instruments may inspire composers to explore the unusual sounds. The visual beauty, especially of the Renaissance instruments, is an added experience for professional artists and laymen.

Among summer schools and festivals, New Music in New Hampshire, recently added a student group as craftsmen to make experimental instruments. Some are planning to enroll later on as engineers in order to learn more about acoustical problems and perhaps to discover answers to those which have escaped, yet haunted, recently built concert halls and frustrated many architects. In this same school the phrases "group activities" and "collective composition" were often heard. At the final festival program, collective compositions were not only played but a social philosophy was initiated in student discussions; genuine concern was expressed for each other in these activities, with less competitive spirit shown in personal relationships than had been experienced in some conservatories.

"Group participation" has had a change of meaning in recent times. The early days of the League produced a keen awareness of the motivating force of the Directors; as a group, there was a constant feeling of each individual's responsibility to study the unknown works of colleagues, often at a sacrifice of time for their own creative work. Altruism has always been an essential quality of success in pioneering efforts.

A radical change in social philosophy influences music, as it does other arts. It is not surprising, therefore, to hear of a concert in Peking where music is composed by a committee. Following a recent program, four composers came on the stage together to share the bows for their communal score.

*       *       *

There are urgent signs today of assistance needed for living composers despite the increased avenues for the dissemination of contemporary music. Educational institutions have added to the contemporary scene through larger music faculties, more students, and composers-in-residence. Libraries, public and private, have enlarged their collections of material on contemporary music; music publishers, record and cassette companies show statistics of greater output, and long-playing records enjoy a large sale today. But what percentage is contemporary music's share?

There are few radio programs devoted to the music of younger composers and rarely is there a major broadcast of music by a distinguished living composer. Televised opera is a rare event. Echoes of the thirties can still be heard. There was a period when the League of Composers gained the cooperation of the National Broadcasting Company and the Columbia Broadcasting System for half hour programs by living composers. Even a few compositions were commissioned directly for radio.

Today, the staggering figure of fourteen hundred orchestras listed by the American Symphony Orchestra League (even if all are not full sized or perform for a full season) represents a musical activity of wide geographical dimension in America. The American Music Center has an enrollment of six hundred composer-members—a greater number of men and women composers than were ever listed in its past history.

But is it any wonder that the time worn verse, "the world is so full of a number of things," can never have the composer's approbation, "we should all be as happy as kings"? It is of no consolation to the frustrated composer to recall the audience behavior of many years ago, when a premiere of a difficult work on a League program produced nervous jitters. People even broke into laughter as a reaction. Some of those very works are now revered! By contrast, the disapproval of an audience today is merely shown by a quiet exodus from the concert hall.

I sympathize with composers who grow discouraged, as I have had an awareness of their struggles for many years. The sensitivity about their careers is often based on a critic's review which they then regard as their Achilles heel. Probably younger critics today feel less committed to a school or a style than heretofore. The University of Southern California was one of the first to develop a program in music criticism. Recently, in Aspen, the summer program added classes in writing led by David Hamilton; seminars with notable musicologists and critics met in Santa Fe to exchange views on the art of critical evaluation. In the twenties, perhaps the most severe reviews of League programs focused on twelve tone music, with criticism riddled with ridicule. But a veteran critic who sat through years of listening to contemporary music summed up his farewell column thus: "I believe that all music by living composers should receive an apostolic blessing."

I like to hyphenate the words composer-conductor, as an increasing number of composers have this dual role today. These men, necessarily aware of the problems of the creative artist, lend their support to presenting the works of their colleagues. Among the recent names which come to mind are: Luciano Berio, Leonard

Bernstein, Benjamin Britten, Pierre Boulez, Carlos Chavez, Aaron

Copland, Lukas Foss, Bruno Maderna, Darius Milhaud, Olivier Messiaen, Gunther Schuller, and Stanislaw Skrowaczewski.

A panoramic survey of music centers in this country would be difficult to assess justly because of the great activity today at many levels. New ground continues to be broken for buildings dedicated to the humanities; new concert affiliations add to the ongoing effective Community Concerts, Inc., in the United States and Canada. The ease of communication today would have been helpful in the twenties when the League encountered bitter antagonism from a group of composers in Chicago who felt that our New York group neglected creative music west of the Hudson River. Contact in those times was difficult. However, we felt less guilty of geographic neglect when a society of composers in Texas and another in South Africa quietly organized and called themselves branches of the League of Composers!

In the Southwest a recent group called The Chamber Music Society of Santa Fe repeated one of their programs at Window Rock, a Navajo community where the Indian has remained unmoved for centuries. The new ethnic experiment met with the success this pioneer group deserved. In the small town of Santa Fe, a beautiful modern opera house, built in the high mountains, offers annual festivals with remarkable artists and sensational stage decor; works by Berg, Britten, Stravinsky and other twentieth century composers as well as the standard works attract appreciative audiences from far and wide, and assure confidence that "the hinterlands" are an anachronism.

A noticeable change during these past several decades has been the lengthening of the musical season, with its marked influence on summer activities. No longer do the contemporary arts sleep through a few warm months. Air conditioning of old and new public buildings was a vital step which led to the increased flow of seasonal events in many countries. The quality of adaptability, characteristic of the American temperament, was a factor which made us return to greater use of parks in New York. Young audiences, sitting on the ground, were attracted to concerts and opera in the open air. In the winter season, some museums realized that they could attract people to concerts at low prices utilizing floor space instead of chairs. Encouraged by a series called "Prospective Encounters," led by Pierre Boulez in a small hall removed from the conventional concert district in New York City, young people have crowded every inch of floor space. A few chairs were reserved for critics! This experiment led the New York Philharmonic Society to develop a spring season called the "Rug Concerts," with the orchestra playing on the orchestra floor, and the platform and remaining orchestra floor space completely filled with young people sitting comfortably on twelve inch rugs. The low price of tickets and informality of dangling legs over the edge of the platform (sometimes dangerously close to the double bass strings), added a new experience to this venerable orchestra! The programs, especially works by Copland, Ives, Stravinsky, and Webern, caused thunderous applause and cheers. Wise heads on some young shoulders believe that programs should include music of all ages and countries; if the new generation could be represented at an occasional confer- ence on programming with conductors and management, their opinions might bring balm to their composer colleagues.

In reviewing past and present directions and deviations in contem- porary music, I have referred to a few recent events which come to the forefront, and have compared them with facets of the League's long record. James Reston, The New York Times' keen observer of current events, recently summed up a quality of life in America: "This country has changed faster perhaps than any other nation in the world. But the physical world, which has been changed by America, is now changing faster than we can change ourselves." If there is a need to adapt to the rhythm of a faster world, America and its music will surely keep pace.

Claire R. Reis

New York City

February 1974

Postscript: The initial encouragement for this reprint of *Composers Conductors and Critics* is due to Dean Harry Goddard Owen, to whom I owe my very sincere appreciation.

COMPOSERS

CONDUCTORS

AND CRITICS

Jocasta, a puppet designed by
Robert Edmond Jones for Igor
Stravinsky's *Oedipus Rex*, directed by Leopold Stokowski
with the Philadelphia Orchestra.

# COMPOSERS

## CONDUCTORS

### AND CRITICS

*Claire R. Reis*

New York · OXFORD UNIVERSITY PRESS · 1955

*Printed in the United States of America*

# Contents

# Illustrations

*Oedipus Rex*, by Igor Stravinsky, with twelve-foot puppets designed by Robert Edmond Jones and executed by Remo Bufano
    Harvard Glee Club and soloists
    Tiresias

*The Devil and Daniel Webster* by Douglas Moore and Stephen Vincent Benét.

*Pas d'Acier*, by Serge Prokofieff, designed by Lee Simonson.

# Foreword

I HAVE KNOWN Claire R. Reis for more than thirty years. In that time I have appreciated her friendship, always devoted and faithful; her love for music, particularly contemporary music; her readiness to help the composer of today in his many problems; and her indefatigable activity in promoting contemporary music through the League of Composers, which she founded.

In this book you will enjoy the memoirs of Mrs. Reis, from the glimpses of her student days in Berlin to those of the innumerable contacts she has had with personalities in music, not only all the composers of our time and of every country, but also all the people interested in music, from performers to listeners. This is told in a lively manner with amusing anecdotes, avoiding technical considerations, which she leaves to the 'musicographers' or 'musicologists.'

In her telling about all the activities of the League of Composers, which she directed for such a long time, you will find the history of the past thirty years in contemporary music in America. What an amazing amount of first auditions, concerts, stage works, commissions, publications, and revelations of masterpieces, as well as youthful works of unknown composers!

On the very human side of this book, you will learn about 'The Composer' — his problems, his struggles, his fights to im-

pose his own way of expression, his difficulties with musical organizations, publishers — and about the public.

The book of Claire R. Reis is *a necessary one*, because all the
problems faced by the composers of today and the developments
foreseen in the future are evoked with an irresistible sympathy,
to the warmth of which no one who loves music can remain
indifferent.

DARIUS MILHAUD

Aspen, Colorado

# Introduction

IN THE NINETEEN-TWENTIES and 'thirties contemporary music in the United States entered an era of many changes. Through the League of Composers, which I helped to found, serving as executive chairman for twenty-five years, it became my good fortune to see at first hand the composer coming into a new and significant place in the pattern of our culture.

The League evolved into a form of Composers' Guild. Its history is a kaleidoscopic record of the times in contemporary music. Although the programs often aroused critics to acidly humorous protests, in time they settled back to dignified consideration of serious values in new music. At the same time, a new public awakened to novel concerts, opera, and ballet, and these became important in musical history.

Many of the great personalities in music and theater, in close sympathy with the League's aims, gave unstinted support and enthusiasm for new ideas in allied arts. Among them were Serge Koussevitzky, Leopold Stokowski, Fritz Reiner, Robert Edmond Jones, and others.

Providentially for educational institutions here, many renowned European composers who were exiled from their homelands by World War II have, through teaching positions, contributed their vast experience. The League of Composers was quick to welcome and honor these guests of our country; Schoenberg, Stravinsky, Milhaud, Prokofieff, Hindemith, Bartók, Weill, Krenek, and many others became in varying degrees part of an excitingly important era; some have made the United States their permanent home.

A major purpose of the League has been to bring out unknown composers, deserving of a first hearing. As urgent spiritual and economic needs of the composer were perceived and understood, a project to commission works developed into an important aspect of the crusading era of the 'twenties, and it continues today.

In the best sense of 'One World' our reciprocal participation in the international scene became rewarding. Our prewar contacts with composers in Japan and Russia have had quiescent periods; affiliations with men of music in South America, Canada, and many European countries gained in strength. The League of Composers' periodical *Modern Music* reached every continent, every library, every university, with its timely reviews and analytical contributions.

Special wartime problems of composers, their desire to share in sustaining cultural values in disturbed times; their need of protection for royalties; their struggle to secure a foothold in new developments with music and electricity, with motion pictures, with records, radio, and television — the past twenty-five years have seen these become real issues and also, happily, some progress in meeting them.

Having been privileged to know many of the composers and interpretive artists, both in their musical stature and as human beings, I have written this personal account of my association with the mature and experienced, the young and the growing, in the changing scene, for the reader who, out of feeling for the traditions of our culture, may like to follow this picture of the advent of contemporary music in America.

CLAIRE R. REIS

New York City
May 1955

# Acknowledgments

I AM GREATLY INDEBTED to Dr. Sidney V. Haas for his encouragement and faith in the undertaking of this book. I am also appreciative of his suggestion, made years ago, that the habit of taking notes might in time prove not only useful but also indispensable.

I want to express my sincere gratitude to A. Walter Kramer for his painstaking care in reading the completed text, and for giving me the benefit of his remarkable memory of past events.

I owe my thanks to Miss Janet Mabie for her editorial advice, and to Miss Vera Scriabine, Mrs. Claire S. Degener, and Miss Gladys Chamberlain for their assistance in research.

One can never enumerate, as one would wish, the friends who have been generous with time and helpful details. In my case they have been many, and I remember them with great appreciation.

# COMPOSERS

## CONDUCTORS

### AND CRITICS

# 1

## New Directions

AT THE KLAW THEATER in New York that December evening in 1922, a crowd filled the auditorium. There was an electric anticipation in the air. This was the uptown debut of the group known as the International Composers' Guild. Hitherto this organization had modestly presented concerts of contemporary music in Greenwich Village, far downtown. The move to the theater district was strategic, made in the hope of overcoming the apathy of critics who were reluctant to take time to travel below Times Square.

The Klaw was sold out. As usual, rumors were abundant of an *ultra* program, attracting the serious listeners, the musical *intelligentsia*, and, inevitably, members of cafe society and other sensation seekers ever on the lookout not just for the new but for the newest.

Neither the audience, the composers, nor I could realize that evening that the series just opening would turn out to be the precursor of a new organization — the League of Composers.

My part in it all had begun a few months earlier.

At Cooper Union I had initiated a series of concerts that gave composers the opportunity to perform their own works. Among

3

others, Louis Gruenberg played his series called *Polychromes*. Louis and I had been friends since student days in Germany.

He and Edgar Varèse were two of the struggling composers in the International Composers' Guild. One day Louis telephoned that he and Varèse, bearing in mind the experimental programs at Cooper Union, would like to ask my advice about some of their composer-problems.

Paul Rosenfeld once described Varèse's arrival in a room, likening it to 'a locomotive, with blazing headlight and trailing plumy smoke.' I could see what he meant! Clearly this handsome, rugged, shaggy-haired, dynamic individual seethed with a zest for life; every gesture, every movement expressed driving force.

Rushing into my living room he came right to the point, exclaiming 'We need your help!' From Gruenberg he had learned about the work at Cooper Union. 'I hope now that you'll help us too. I'm tired of all the difficulties we encounter in giving chamber music concerts down there in that little place in Greenwich Village. We might as well expect the critics to travel to the moon, evidently, as down to a theater below Washington Square. Our audiences are, also, too small to fill even that little hall. And what can we do to persuade more artists to be interested in learning the new music?' He flung up his hands in a gesture of exasperation. 'If you'd help us to reorganize the International Composers' Guild — our society to advance contemporary composers and their music — there may still be some hope for what we're trying to accomplish.'

It was certainly not difficult for these two men to convince me that the cause of the living composer needed help. Sporadic attempts had been made at giving concerts of contemporary music but they did not answer the need of presenting the new music and stimulating sympathetic interest in the many and varied problems of the composers. It seemed to me that this group, led by Varèse, might well be made into a true guild of composers, and I agreed to devote my energies to it.

This concert at the Klaw Theater was our first move.

We had announced that the program would be one composed entirely of *premières* — 'first performance,' 'first performance in America,' 'first public performance in America' — and the public looked for a sensational event.

I think no one was disappointed. With 'Angels,' from Ruggles' symphonic suite for six muted trumpets, *Men and Angels*, the sensation was visual as well as musical, as six prodigiously fat gentlemen walked out on the stage and placed their trumpets in playing position. Barnum and Bailey could not boast more poundage with their fat men! Alas, from the standpoint of the composer, the visual effect overwhelmed the musical. Disregarding the serious importance of the suite, of which 'Angels' was the second movement, the house burst into such a prolonged roar of laughter that the performance was over before the audience could compose itself, with the result that the composer never really had his chance to be adequately heard.

Madame Georgette Leblanc, former wife of the great Maurice Maeterlinck, fared better. She interpreted several Paul Verlaine poems set to music by Maurice Gaillard, and also a song by Arthur Lourié. Although no longer a young woman, Madame Leblanc made a picture of great glamour with her spectacularly white make-up, blonde hair, and slinky black gown, creating somewhat the effect of a Toulouse-Lautrec poster. She exerted all the art of the truly great *diseuse*; her personality, which she well knew how to project over the footlights, made up for what her voice lacked for great singing.

Although it certainly did not affect the quality of the concert, in this first important move to capture the interest of a public which we were convinced existed for contemporary music, the printed program was unwittingly marred by small mistakes. Opposite his sonata, the first name of one of our most important contemporary composers was cut to one initial, A. *Honegger!* Had it been forgotten by the program committee? Carl Ruggles and Arthur Lourié received better identification and Maurice François Gaillard was allowed the splendor of his full three names. I felt a bit disturbed over the misprints, but I was learning that there were many ins and outs in what I had undertaken, and decided the mistakes could be charged up to the profit and loss of a changing situation.

In general, the opening concert gave off a flavor of contentment. Varèse and a number of his colleagues seemed satisfied. Our being in the Klaw Theater had resulted from what seemed to me the first and important step of reorganization, the attempt to build a new and larger audience for contemporary music. The Klaw family had recently built the theater on West 45th Street. They were personal friends of mine and had consented to let me have the theater Sunday nights for a very modest rental. As it was in the center of town, I reasoned that the critics would no longer have the excuse of distance for staying away from our concerts.

The manager of the theater, sizing up the box-office receipts for this first concert, frankly predicted a big season for us, and forthwith he constituted himself as a sort of guardian over us. Perhaps we were a refreshing change from routine theater managing; certainly concert routine was lacking, as later events often proved.

In advance of this first concert we had worked hard, particularly circularizing anyone to whom we could appeal for subscriptions to the reorganized Guild. We could not afford to hire clerical help so we pressed into service the wives of board members; among them, Varèse's wife Louise, and Salzedo's wife Mimi, joined around my long dining room table to address envelopes and stuff circulars. For a while some of the musicians helped, too. Louis Gruenberg was the first to rebel against licking any more stamps. 'Claire!' he cried finally, 'I'll do any amount of musical work you need but, please, no more of this!' Having put in some hours myself at licking stamps and sealing envelopes, I could not really blame him.

We plunged into a thoroughgoing reorganization of the International Composers' Guild. The frequent board meetings were usually at my home — hours of discussion around the dining room table ending with beer and cheese. Varèse and Salzedo, being gregarious like many musicians, often brought along a few guests, who liked what went on and turned up more or less regularly thereafter. Occasionally I had qualms about parliamentary rules. Everyone was so highly articulate, plunging without hesitation into any and all internal matters, that sometimes I wondered nervously who, among those that voted with gusto, were actually entitled to vote.

Varèse's particular province was to search for new music. In all matters of programming, his best friend, Carlos Salzedo, was next in power to him. Salzedo was what would be called in football a triple-threat man. His extraordinary musicianship, combined with an indefatigable energy, quickly made him indispensable. He would be pianist in one concert, conductor in another, harpist in a third; in all roles he was truly a great artist. So intense was his enthusiasm for the Guild concerts that on one occasion, when the program offered no place for any of his talents, either as harpist, accompanist, or conductor, he hurried into the box office, buoyantly relieved the box-office manager of his duties, and sold tickets with exactly the same enthusiasm and confidence he displayed on the concert stage.

Whenever the affairs of the Guild appeared to be on the upgrade, another member of Varèse's composers' committee, Carl Ruggles, became the delightful iconoclast. A report of good attendance at a concert was his cue to thunder that the reason for it was probably that we were not upholding our ideals. One evening he announced ominously, 'I would prefer to see only six people at our concerts! If you had a full house last Sunday it only goes to show you've descended to catering to your public!' This remarkable opinion touched off a discussion of such violence that Varèse was quite unable to control things, and the meeting broke up in shrill disorder.

Varèse and Gruenberg, with several of their colleagues, put in long hours calling on all the music publishers. In the early 'twenties comparatively little contemporary music other than

in manuscript was to be found. Occasionally a score of some
European ensemble work would be available, but to procure
the parts necessitated renting them from an overseas publishing
house. Finding American compositions was not much easier.
Only a few names of contemporary composers were generally
known, such names as Henry Hadley, Edgar Stillman-Kelley,
Charles Loeffler, Rubin Goldmark.

With the hope of discovering unheralded American composers, we hit on the plan of advertising in the newspapers, appealing to aspiring American composers to make contact with
the International Composers' Guild. In retrospect, of course,
it looks ridiculously naïve. Then, because the Guild was not
widely known, we hoped that the advertisements would bring
us to the notice of at least a few good composers, who would
communicate with us.

In less time than it takes to tell it, the office was inundated
with packaged manuscripts of all sizes and shapes bearing some
of the strangest titles ever placed over musical notation. I remember a piece that, while plainly marked 'The Minnesota
American Legion March,' was accompanied by a note reading,
'I prefer *not* in march time.' Another composer, who evidently
was having a very difficult time indeed, sent in two songs, 'A
March of Death' and 'The Last Dance of the Corpse,' also accompanied by a note saying, 'If you like these pieces please
keep them as I might throw them away, for they are my last
composition; how I wish I could keep on, but I refuse to starve.'
The sad mood of a waltz song by another frustrated composer
was called to our special attention by a little scribbled explanation, 'It's a quaint little, sad little, do-re-mi.'

We looked carefully at everything that came in, but long before we finished, we knew that placing advertisements in the
newspapers was not the method to unearth compositions worthy
of hearing.

There were several instances of American composers hearing
of our plight while they were in the midst of work on new
compositions. After rushing feverishly to finish the opus, and

hurrying it to us 'hot off the griddle' so to speak, the composer would see it sped to the program committee and, if acceptable, on to the rehearsal hall.

On one occasion that great innovator among composers, the ingenious Varèse himself, had just completed a work for chamber orchestra called 'Hyperprism.' As he was conducting a rehearsal in his studio a sound that was new to his ears came from the street, the siren of a fire engine dashing past his house. Rushing to the window, he leaned out and listened intently. Then, turning back to the musicians, he announced, 'The rehearsal is over; I'll call you soon.' Without waiting for them to pack up their instruments and leave, he clapped on his hat and coat, and dashed out the door and off through the streets to the nearest fire station. There he announced flatly to an astonished fireman, 'You must lend me one of your sirens for a concert!' He was advised to wait until the district chief returned. It had been customary for people to drop in at the firehouse to demand one of the Dalmatian mascot's pups, but this was the first time anyone had come around to try and get one of the sirens.

The chief was intrigued by the request, but sirens had only lately been replacing bells on fire engines, and it seemed unlikely that any would be let out. 'Why'n't you go ask the Mayor?' hazarded the chief, using as good a way as any of getting out of the situation.

But after carrying the sound of the siren around in his head for several days, Varèse had a better idea. He raced up to the Department of Acoustics in the School of Science at Columbia University. To his delight it turned out that they had such a siren. Sympathetic to his desire to experiment musically with it, they lent it to him. He then called the men back into rehearsal on 'Hyperprism.'

In this connection, the siren was introduced by Varèse again years later, this time in a composition titled 'Ionization.' Unexpectedly it became a subject of controversy. The work was programmed for a concert in the American Festival, over New York's municipal radio station, WNYC. It happened that simultaneously a Civil Defense program was being developed, involving sirens as air raid warning signals. Even the Fire Department was forbidden to use sirens. The director of WNYC, Seymour N. Siegel, and Herman Newman of the Music staff had no choice but to rule the siren out of Varèse's performance. Varèse was appalled and made no effort to hide it. In the way that he wished to use it, in his opinion, the siren could not possibly be confused with any other city noise. 'I didn't compose for the siren to evoke a city noise!' he protested stubbornly. 'I use it because I need the pitched curves of its parabolic sound!' Incredible, that the civic authorities could not comprehend this simple aesthetic necessity!

I was so taken up with the idea of inveigling the music press into attending all our concerts that I did not foresee some possible results. In the first year, the Monday morning reviews of the critics chiefly poked fun. To our dismay this often served more to bring sensation-loving crowds, curious to hear and see the fun, than serious listeners, moved by genuine musical interest. To be sure, it materially increased the number of our subscribers. Yet as I look back on some of the critiques — for example, a reference by the New York *Evening Post*'s celebrated H. T. Finck to Schoenberg's *Pierrot Lunaire* as 'musical tomfoolery' — I wonder that some of the composers, at least the twelve-toners, did not then and there organize some sort of terrorist society to deal for all time with this type of critic. Happily, however, we were in time to experience other, very different, reactions from critics than their early, frivolous efforts at mere comicality.

In the early 'twenties *Pierrot Lunaire* was being played in many of the capitals of Europe, creating endless argument among critics and considerable dissension among audiences. In Italy the *Corporazione del nuove Musica* had given it ten performances. Alfredo Casella, the Italian composer who conducted the work, spoke of it as 'a Bolshevik composition,' meaning 'revolutionary.' It seemed altogether fitting that the International Composers' Guild should be the first group to prepare the American *première* of this unique music.

Charles Henry Meltzer, then music critic of the New York *Herald*, offered to provide us with a freely adapted translation into English of *Moon-struck Pierrot*. We knew that some aid would be needed and were delighted to have something that would guide the audience to better understanding of Schoenberg's ideas. Mr. Meltzer also contributed a page headed 'A few words about *Pierrot*,' setting forth that sometimes Pierrot was humorous, sometimes pathetic, occasionally dramatic, tragic, and even sinister; but that above all 'Pierrot is whimsical, Pierrot is half human, half visionary.' Mr. Meltzer further compared the character of Pierrot to Harlequin, to Peter Pan, and to Punchinello.

Louis Gruenberg had studied *Pierrot Lunaire* very carefully and accordingly was selected to conduct the work, with Greta Torpadie as soloist. Both musicians were prepared to pour great interest and endless time into making this first American performance a memorable success.

It happened that the studio in our home was well adapted for rehearsals. Gruenberg planned the ensemble of five solo instruments, arranging for the musicians to meet with him and Greta Torpadie. We agreed on fifteen rehearsals. But as we neared the fifteenth, three more were decided upon. Not only was the work difficult, but also the instrumentalists, even though they had been very carefully chosen for their musicianship, had not yet become accustomed to playing Schoenberg's music.

At the eighteenth rehearsal Gruenberg informed me suddenly that there would have to be two more rehearsals. At the twentieth rehearsal he announced calmly, 'Claire, this work will not be performed on this Sunday night.' I was aghast. Announcements of this important American *première* of a work celebrated all over Europe had gone out far and wide. Utterly confused I said, 'But the Klaw Theater is completely sold out!' This was only one of many disturbing thoughts; but, as I well might have known, it carried no weight with Louis.

'No,' he said flatly. 'It may take as much as two more weeks of rehearsals before I'll be sure that the musicians thoroughly understand the work so that we can perform it.' Naturally it was Louis' desire to give as perfect a performance as possible. He was a young, untried conductor; he felt the serious responsibility of this occasion; he was also inclined to pessimism; and he was unable at this point to envision the likelihood of a successful performance.

As I began to recover my poise and judgment I said firmly, 'Louis, we have two days left before the scheduled performance of *Pierrot Lunaire*. We can add two more rehearsals. But then, after twenty-two rehearsals, the work will simply have to be given according to our agreement with the public.'

For the next two hours Louis and I walked up and down my living room, arguing contrapuntally about conducting the work on schedule — why he would not conduct it until in his opinion it was ready, and why we were obligated to go through with our plans on a certain date. It was as strange and turbulent a walk as I have ever taken in my life.

'I will not do it,' Louis said over and over again.

I did not know anyone equipped to replace him and I said, 'It is essential that you do it. Two more rehearsals will fully prepare you. I am confident of that.'

'The work is not ready for performance,' he said obstinately.

Over and over I said, 'At this late date no other work can be substituted. This *première* must be given.'

Every now and again Louis would halt, peering at me blankly, as though nothing we said made the slightest sense. Did he finally simply grow weary of marching up and down? To this day I do not know what reason brought him round, unless it was my stubborn repetition that his best attempt with this work at its present state probably would be as good, and very likely better, than an attempt by anyone else.

And so, at the twenty-two rehearsal mark, the American *première* of *Pierrot Lunaire* was finally achieved before a distinguished audience which packed the Klaw Theater. There was a snowstorm of compliments for the conductor, for the soloist, for the very intelligent interpretation by the instrumentalists. As I listened to the performance my thoughts traveled back to the abundance of rehearsals. How few people in the audience even suspected the difficulties fought out in the preparation! I vowed then that in any future plans I would never let musical problems — or temperaments — overwhelm me, no matter how many pairs of shoes had to be worn out in pacing.

In the spring, at the final directors' meeting for the 1922 season, in an unexpected moment of excitement and temper, the whole organization of the International Composers' Guild as it existed seemed to disintegrate. A storm of bitter dissension blew up, with disgruntled composers ranged on one side, and highhanded program-makers on the other. The argument that brought on the explosion was Schoenberg's *Pierrot Lunaire*, which had been conducted with such success by Gruenberg.

The sensational reviews of the work — notwithstanding the dislike for it of many critics — and the avalanche of fan mail seemed to call for an early repeating in New York of this composition already so famed in Europe. On the other hand, the Guild's charter, which, by an unfortunate oversight, I had not previously read, specifically stated, 'This Society will give *first performances only.*'

At the outbreak of the quarrel, my role being simply executive director, I tried to remain on the sidelines. I saw, however, that the point had been reached where what was regarded as Varèse's domination of the Guild was no longer acceptable to some of his colleagues. I did think that because he was European and rather new as a leader among colleagues of equal artistic and intellectual stature, his attitudes might stem from a misunderstanding of the democratic method expected of the chairman of an organization in this country.

During the weeks of discord that ensued, Salzedo, Varèse's close friend, explained anxiously to me, 'This is Varèse's society; it must belong to him.' Since I had succeeded in having full houses for the Guild all season, which, in turn, had enabled it to pay up all past debts and have some surplus for the future, I could see that Salzedo was in hopes of making an ally of me.

'But in this country,' I countered, 'no society belongs to an individual.'

'But,' wailed Salzedo, 'without Varèse what would happen to this Guild?' He hesitated a moment, then added with sly humor, 'Just like the harp, for example. To most people the harp means only Salzedo!' Notwithstanding the rather unusual *après moi le déluge* implication, Salzedo was indisputably one of the greatest harpists in the world.

A major policy that Varèse had put in operation, and with which he would not compromise, was, as the charter stipulated, that this society for contemporary music must give only *premières*. The idea that *Pierrot Lunaire* should be repeated was in line with the feeling of the dissenters that many works were or would be deserving of a second hearing.

True, it had seemed important in the early days to stress the 'first' performance. As we all know, 'It's a first' was to become part of the American idiom. Perhaps the time will come when we may say, with equal effect, 'It's a second.' In fact, a musical society has recently arrived on the scene whose purpose is to present *only* second performances. Nevertheless a definite vogue does remain for the *première*, and it is still difficult to achieve the second performance of a contemporary work.

I was in complete disagreement with the policy of only first performances. I could no longer remain neutral in this situation; I threw in my lot with the seceding group, which immediately began talking about a whole new organization, with an entirely different policy from that of the International Composers' Guild.

The result was that within a few weeks the League of Composers, Incorporated, was launched. There was an exchange of letters between attorneys for the two groups — no more, no less acrimonious than a routine divorce of two parties. Aaron Copland pointed out, in *Our New Music*, 'The important thing for us to note is that this schism profited public and composers alike, for where there had been one forward-looking group, now there were two.' [1]

This and other developments led me to see that I was becoming more and more deeply involved in the composer's many problems. Taking on the new and greater responsibilities of the newly founded League, my sympathies were directed to the really great need for someone, or some group, to take hold and seriously promote the cause of composers and their careers. I found myself with a profound enthusiasm for trying to build a solid and true guild of composers. Suddenly, in relation to a definite purpose, my background and training seemed to fall into place. I had a sense of great challenge.

1. McGraw-Hill Book Company, New York, 1941.

# 2

## *Music for the People*

I REALIZE today from experience how fortunate I am to have been an American student in Europe in the early 1900's, with the opportunities of the cultural life of that artistically vigorous period. At the time, though, I rebelled strenuously against being uprooted from a pleasant school life and from friendships at home.

My father had chosen as a very young man to exchange New York for the sandy wilds of Texas, in order to make his way in the mercantile and banking worlds.

On a business trip abroad he met my mother at a party in Edinburgh and returned a year later to marry her, bringing her home to a border town on the Rio Grande. She came of a long line of French ancestry, and the family traditions, remaining true to France, had been little affected by the settling in Scotland; but the transplanting to Texas meant a drastic change in every convention and habit of my mother's early life. Even the climate familiar to her — the misty, chilly vales of Scotland — was exchanged for the other extreme — the heat and droughts characteristic of Brownsville, Texas. She made their acquaintance abruptly in the two-day trip by stagecoach from the railroad terminus, a little town fancifully named Alice.

When the time came for my schooling, and that of my brother and sister, our parents were worried because there was only one school in Brownsville, a very mediocre one where the educational methods left a great deal to be desired.

My class teacher, old Miss Butler, clung to an unique way of disciplining inattentive pupils. She wore a stout leather belt to keep her shirtwaist and skirt in place. She would take it off when occasion demanded, roll it into a tight coil, and — aiming over the heads of the class — fling it with unerring accuracy so that it would land with stinging force on the culprit, bringing him — or her — back to the subject of the moment. It was an unwritten rule that the hapless pupil would then pick up the weapon and return it to Miss Butler. She always seemed to me an improbable figure to be so skilled at this unusual type of marksmanship.

We lived in an environment that called not only for frontier hardihood but also for preparedness for a possible and special kind of terror. This was impressed upon me one day when Mr. Cummings, the school principal, came into our classroom to make the anxious announcement that we would be kept in an extra half hour and, when we did leave, should go straight home by way of certain streets. 'Something serious has happened in the jail,' he said nervously and hurried out. By the next day we all understood what he had meant. A Mexican had been lynched. Then and there the word *lynch* made an impression on me which I would never forget. The awareness of a kind of unleashed savagery was a shock to the child mind.

Father died. It made a radical change in our family life.

Mother, a widow at forty-four — still handsome — with her only friendships in this country in Brownsville, resolutely closed the books on her personal life, deciding thenceforth to pursue it through the lives of her children. Her first step was to move us north from this remote region to New York, where she felt we would be afforded more of the educational advantages she craved for us.

With single-minded determination and energy she established

our home in the city of New York. Her brother and his wife, already acquainted with New York, came down from their home in Montreal to help us find a suitable place to live near good schools.

Among other things, I remember with mingled amusement and gratitude my aunt's dogged way of familiarizing us with the city transportation system. Daily she drilled us, compelling us to recite all the crosstown trolley-car lines. In sing-song, as though doing our multiplication tables aloud, we chanted 86th Street, 79th Street, 72nd, 59th, 42nd, 34th, 23rd, 14th. For some reason it seemed unlikely to Aunt Maud that we would ever have need of going below 14th Street, and our memorization halted there. She drilled us also in the avenues but again our training was restricted to those from Fifth to Lexington. Eventually we were 'graduated,' and were allowed to go shopping and to school alone.

It was natural that mother's plans for us were colored by her European background. After a winter in New York we were taken out of school to spend two years in France. Besides learning the language, our education included a weekly visit to the opera, no doubt to placate us for the drudgery of piano practice.

The decision to take us subsequently to Germany grew out of the conviction that our musical talent necessitated the study of music and language in Berlin. My brother Angus succeeded in escaping this, arguing that it was necessary for him to return to Columbia University to continue his studies.

Berlin was a brilliant center for the arts. In her role of Juliet at the Royal Opera House, Geraldine Farrar's beauty and youthful voice captivated the Hohenzollern family as well as her Romeo. Isadora Duncan was drawing immense crowds to the famed Kroll Theater, shocking her public by dancing in bare feet and revealing draperies. Richard Strauss had just written *Salome,* and was anxious to complete *Elektra* and *Die Rosenkavalier.* He was obsessed by his need to devote his entire time to composition, but the Kaiser was refusing imperiously to free him from his contract as a staff conductor at the Opera House. Strauss thereupon devised a curious reprisal, a veritable sit-down strike. He would raise his baton for the opening bars of the overture, then, maddeningly, he would simply cease conducting, thus publicly dramatizing his resistance to his sovereign's wishes.

Felix Weingartner was the great conductor of the Berlin Philharmonic Orchestra. An orchestra seat for his concerts was rarely available except by inheritance; bequeathing one's season tickets was as serious a part of making a will as choosing an executor. We soon learned, however, about an 'underground system' of buying balcony tickets. The neighborhood grocer boys could be cajoled by a substantial *pourboire* to stand in line from 5 a.m. until the box office opened. Only the boys who arrived in the queue early were successful in this matinal quest. Somehow, ours were always lucky, and Dr. Weingartner's programs became a great experience in my musical education.

The music season catered continually to the student, with a wealth of concerts beginning conveniently at 7:30 in the evening. Night after night we crowded into the recital halls, no matter how hard we had to study the next day to make up our regular school studies, German language, and practice hours.

At first I protested vehemently against the long hours of piano practice. Yet soon I found myself caught up in the attitudes of my fellow students. All seemed to have a profession in view, whether as concert artist or as teacher, and since the atmosphere was contagious, I began to practice willingly four or five hours a day. My teachers did their best to encourage me in a career as pianist, but somehow I felt that it would not be my choice for a profession. At the same time the extraordinary artistic atmosphere of the life in Berlin made a deep impression on me and it became more or less inevitable that in one way or another my adult life would be connected with music.

We varied music with the theater. Max Reinhardt was currently the *ne plus ultra* and the public flocked to his performances. For Sophocles' *Antigone* he transformed the whole interior of the theater into a Greek stadium; this epochal achievement was a landmark in theatrical production.

Throughout a long winter we lived in a 'Damenheim,' or Ladies' Home, on Viktoria Luise Platz. This excellent *pension* occupied an entire apartment house, wherein a number of elderly ladies — predominantly widows with small titles and even smaller, and rapidly diminishing, fortunes — could live graciously in their own apartments. In the dining room, where we all met in common, it was fun for the young to observe the small pretentious foibles of the establishment and the determined aristocracy of dowagers who were quick to scold the maid for serving my mother first — 'Imagine, an American, with no title!'

Among the seasonal residents were several young music students from Holland and Czechoslovakia, sent by their parents with the confident knowledge that they would be well chaperoned by Frau von Hesse, hostess of the 'Damenheim.' She was an aristocratically imperious old lady with a built-in disapproval of American and Dutch girls, and it taxed our ingenuity to elude her watchfulness when young men came to call on us.

Lessons, concerts, opera, and dance recitals kept us in a whirl of activity. The vast number of music students in the city's residential sections made imperative regulations governing the hours when one might practice. Permissions varied with the neighborhood. Before my mother was allowed to take a lease for our 'Damenheim' apartment she had to sign a declaration regarding the number of hours my sister Alice and I would practice.

One day I became absorbed and unwittingly exceeded my allotment, whereupon a maid whisked in with a letter from the apartment overhead. It was in German script, which I could not read. Guiltily, fearing a complaint, I left the piano immediately. But I need not have been alarmed. When my German teacher translated the letter we found it addressed 'To the lady who is playing so beautifully.' It contained a request: 'Will you kindly tell me the name of the piece you are playing, as I enjoy it so much?' With the aid of Fraulein Lenz, I wrote back that it was a Brahms Rhapsody. After that I had no apprehension if I ran over my practice time.

In the fall I returned to school in New York for my senior year. The winter abroad convinced me that I should keep up my interests in the arts and also find a wider circle of enlightened friends. I went through the motions of rejoining the group I had known before going to Europe, and I resolved to take an active part in the school life, including the senior magazine and various other activities. At parties when everyone wanted to sing current popular songs I let myself be drafted as pianist. But I found myself craving new sympathies and associations and felt that I was moving toward an entirely different kind of life.

I spent the next two years at the Institute of Musical Art, then at Fifth Avenue and Twelfth Street. I was devoted to a wonderful piano teacher, Mrs. Bertha Feiring Tapper, but the teaching methods used by Dr. Percy Goetschius in Theory and Harmony courses were both trying and stultifying to me. Although I had no illusions about developing into a composer, I wished that his discouraging manner of teaching would give way to newer ideas, lending greater incentive to creative study.

Leaving the Institute I concentrated on a study of chamber-music literature. Besides professional ensemble lessons in the classics, one evening a week I read sonatas and trios with A. Walter Kramer, a young composer and violinist, who was also a music critic. Waldo Frank, then a budding author, was our cellist. Since many of the works we read were by composers whose names were unknown in this country at the time, together we made up an *avant-garde*, exploring a new world in the universe of music.

The only 'outsider' allowed to listen to our trio-evenings was the late Paul Rosenfeld, a sensitive young student of music just graduated from Yale, who had recently become my friend.

While we played, Paul would lie folded up on the sofa. Once he said, 'I feel like some royal personage, with a private trio playing just for me.' As we chatted in the late evening over our beer and sandwiches, Paul would make discriminating remarks about such American composers as Horatio Parker and Charles Ives, about whom in those days we knew very little. It was James Huneker who soon recognized Paul's passionate drive as a youthful explorer in the arts and made the prediction, 'Young man, you are starting where I left off!' Paul often told me later that, as an audience of one, 'those evenings marked the beginning of my interest in becoming a music critic.'

My circle of friends was beginning to include a number of earnest-minded young people, who like myself were adventuring to find a new channel of life in progressive pursuits. Walter Lippmann and I attended the same dancing class in our early teens. I was always one of his interested audience when, instead of dancing, Walter held forth in a corner about the seriousness of life and the social injustices of the world. It did not matter to him whether or not he learned the waltz; it did matter that he could expound some of his precocious theories on socialism to a group of adolescent sixteen-year-olds. A few years later Walter, then a brilliant student at Harvard, though still a shy, insecure youth, was an intellectual leader of our circle, guiding us in and out of our reading and thinking. I remember his urging particularly that we should seek our individual niches within a framework of social causes, and I must admit he took his own advice. Soon after graduation he became secretary to Mayor Lunn, the first Socialist mayor of Schenectady.

My own first venture took me to an East Side settlement house where I organized a group of young pianists for the purpose of teaching children to play the piano. It turned out rather unsatisfactorily. In addition to their lack of any wish to be taught — perhaps their perpetually sticky fingers were their psychological resistance — we realized tardily that there were no pianos in their homes on which to practice, even if they would.

My interest moved quickly to more promising activity among

some serious young violin students, prodigies in need of a professional accompanist in order to develop their careers. One of these was Max Rosen, aged ten, a blonde, blue-eyed, pink-cheeked boy whose talent carried on a running war with his love of chocolate cake. His practice room was behind the curtains in his father's lower East Side barber shop. Too often I brought him goodies from home. 'I don't think I'll play my best today,' he would groan; 'I've eaten too much of your chocolate cake.'

Shortly after I began working with him we played for that great music patron, André De Coppet, founder of the Flonzaley Quartet. Forthwith De Coppet invited a number of eminent violinists to hear Max, among them Fritz Kreisler, Albert Spaulding, Jacques Thibaud, and Edwin Grasse. Unanimously they predicted a great future for Max, and thus De Coppet became his original patron.

To find additional friends and money to help Max go abroad for study with the great Leopold Auer, we gave one concert at the MacDowell Club and another at Cooper Union, the latter before an audience of newly arrived European *émigrés*. In 1909 our ports were open without restriction to foreigners. The need of music was as great in their lives as their need to find a new life in America, for they had come from homelands where even the smallest village supported ensemble groups or band concerts in the public squares.

Until that evening at Cooper Union I had never seen such a large gathering of people hungry for music. In New York in wintertime there were few free concerts. The various settlements occasionally presented concerts, as did also the Metropolitan Museum of Art. But few free concert tickets were distributed to music lovers of the foreign population. For days after the Cooper Union program the memory of that audience troubled me. It proved to be the means of bringing a new and preoccupying experience into my life.

It was encouraging to notice that new ideas to be developed in public-school education were discussed at the People's Institute in the 1900's. It seemed the logical place for presenting an idea of mine, namely a project to give good music — free — to the large numbers of foreign-born living in New York City.

I was acquainted with several trustees of the Institute and, one of them referred me to the director, Dr. Frederick C. Howe. I went down to 70 Fifth Avenue to explore the idea with him.

'I understand the need and your ideas completely,' said Dr. Howe. 'I have had wide experience through my work with immigration and have often wished more was being done culturally for these newly arrived people.'

I explained that I had not recognized the problem until the evening at Cooper Union but hoped now to plan some concerts in the public schools, especially in those districts where there were the largest number of newcomers. 'Would your People's Institute help me to organize a People's Music League?' I asked. The title had popped into my head on the way downtown.

'It certainly would,' said Dr. Howe enthusiastically. Encouraged by him and by the prospect of using the school auditoriums as well as Cooper Union, I became chairman of the new project, gathering together a small committee of musicians to help me. There was an immediate response to our request for talent among young professional artists who were glad to have the opportunity to play before large audiences. The artists received $5.00, or at most $10.00, for an evening performance. I recall many soloists who earned their first 'fiver' in this way, and I have the impression that the pleasure they derived from playing before our appreciative audiences was as important to them as the fee.

Often the size of the audiences exceeded the seating capacity of the school auditorium, and people perched on deep windowsills or corridor stairs. To avoid turning the crowds away, in desperation we often persuaded the janitor of the building to open up a smaller assembly room or several adjoining classrooms. Inviting the overflow to wait there, we would then appeal to the artists, who were always ready to repeat their share of the program in another part of the building. If the improvised concert hall was too far away from the main auditorium for the music to carry, we would run the two programs on a sort of conveyor-belt system so that by ten o'clock, the end of the concert period, the audiences would go away satisfied.

Soon there were 600 People's Music League concerts in Greater New York in one season alone! They continued for ten years, presenting mainly classical music, occasionally interspersed at Cooper Union with a folk-music series.

At about this time my friend Margaret Naumburg, who had been in Italy studying with Dr. Maria Montessori, interested me in her new methods of teaching young children. I felt that Dr. Montessori's pedagogical principles could well be adapted to the teaching of music. Margaret and I planned to meet abroad in the summer to investigate further new methods of teaching music and dancing, including the eurythmic classes of Jaques-Dalcroze. In London I joined some of the Yorke-Trotter pedagogical classes at the London Conservatory of Music.

On our return we organized an experimental Montessori class at the Henry Street Settlement, with young children for whom the public schools did not have room. As it was one of the first Montessori groups in this country it attracted many educators, who came to see these progressive ideas in action. Among them were Miss Curtis, who was director of the New York Public Schools kindergarten department, and Miss Farrell who was in charge of the ungraded classes. They insisted that we should establish a group in a public school to try out our new approach to teaching young children. Margaret's license as a kindergarten teacher was quickly approved by Miss Curtis.

Since I required an examination as a music teacher I came up before Dr. Frank Rix, then head of music in the public-school system. Although I had had many more years of intensive musical training than was required of kindergarten teachers, it was apparent to him that I was interested in something other than the conventional method of teaching. 'You play exceedingly well,' he said, 'but your theories are not legitimate.'

I tried to explain a few of the Montessori principles, particularly the method of developing individuality and initiative through creative efforts. But Dr. Rix only shook his head, saying sternly, 'It is not legitimate.'

Our advocates, Miss Curtis and Miss Farrell, were furious. 'He is an old man who is soon to retire,' they cried, and hurried off to seek the advice of the assistant director, Dr. George H. Gartlan. When he heard me he exclaimed, 'Why, Miss Raphael, you know a great deal more about music than we ever require for our kindergarten teachers. You are an excellent pianist, too.' Whereupon he issued my music license on his own responsibility.

Red tape creates problems in any public-school system. For many weeks we traveled to a public school at 182nd Street but we were without a promised piano and of course many of the needed Montessori materials. By late spring, Margaret and I were convinced that our real need was to establish our own private school, and we therefore closed our public-school classes. I was pleased to have 'Excellent' written across the record of my work and wondered wryly if Dr. Rix still regarded me as an 'illegitimate' teacher. To Dr. Gartlan, whenever our paths crossed in the ensuing years, I was always 'Dear Claire.'

We opened the Children's School at 17 East 60th Street in the fall of 1914. My real struggles at home date from that time. My mother's ambition to make me a good pianist was primarily for 'home consumption' or at most to 'do good' by playing at charity affairs. Happily I often satisfied her hopes in this direction. I remember being somewhat surprised when I was able to hold the attention of even the so-called 'bad boys' at a reform school when I entertained them with a classical program. My new project, a children's school, was, however, a complete negation of my mother's strongest ideas about my life. I always believed, nevertheless, that when young people showed real determination to live their own lives, the older generation would fall in line. Gradually my home problems did subside. Eventually the Children's School changed its name to the Walden School, now celebrating its fortieth year. One of my most cherished souvenirs of that pioneer period is a notebook of melodies created by my young pupils, aged three to six years; another is the memory of the delightful free dancing, based on ideas originated by the children as I played for them. There was a large measure of satisfaction for me in sharing in their creative music.

Three years after the school opened I married Arthur M. Reis and was soon busy bringing up a family. Although I withdrew from full-time daily work with other people's children, I did conduct a small Montessori class in my home for our children and those of a few neighbors. My husband understood my temperament and drive and approved of all my interests — the violin prodigies, the concerts in the public schools, and, subsequently, the League of Composers. We agreed that, as his business day ended at a specified time, so my life outside the home would also cease at five o'clock or at least no later than six. Then we withdrew to private life with our children and friends, leaving for the next day the problems of musicians and manufacturers. The waking and working hours of businessman and artist are on opposite sides of the clock, and I found I had to train many composers never to call me in the late afternoon, which, in effect, was their morning. Sometimes I found it necessary to exercise a bit of bribery; if they wouldn't call me after hours, I wouldn't wake them with early-morning telephone calls!

More and more music was being played and enjoyed by men and women workers in shops and factories. The Cloakmakers' Orchestra changed its name to the Schubert Society, for prestige and also out of jealousy of the Mozart and the Beethoven Orchestras that were giving some public concerts in their neighborhood. Volunteer conductors rehearsed these ensemble groups and choral societies in the public schools at night. Singing groups, often comprising three or four hundred people, and programs given at Ellis Island to welcome immigrants were added to the many other professional concerts (at Cooper Union and in the public schools), developing in the ten years from 1912 under the sponsorship of the People's Music League.

In 1916 Ernest Bloch and his family arrived in New York from Switzerland. I met him shortly after he settled down in a crowded apartment on East 74th Street. He made an immediate impression on me and I felt sorry to find him bogged down by a heavy teaching schedule, in order to earn a living for his family.

He too was irked by the treadmill, as he called it, of trying to teach pupils with little talent. One day in his home we chatted about choral music and I described the enthusiastic 'sings' going on in some of the neighborhoods.

Bloch became quite excited. 'I do wish I could lead some for a while!' he exclaimed, jumping up to show me some of the music he had brought with him from Europe. 'Just look at these scores! If the enthusiasm you speak of is profoundly in these people, I feel sure I could easily teach them to sing some of this great choral music, by Josquin des Prés, for instance, or by Orlando Lasso. This music has never been excelled in craft or in power. If those choral groups of yours can read parts, they can sing Palestrina just as easily as 'My Old Kentucky Home.'

We called the group 'Palestrina on Twenty-second Street.' All through the spring it met every Monday night at the Manhattan Trade School. Whether the results were due to the contagious enthusiasm of Ernest Bloch as leader, or to the sixteenth- and seventeenth-century music — which in a certain sense seemed more akin to our times than the music of the eighteenth century — they were amazing, even at the first rehearsal. 'The singing was crude, the voices uncertain, but the art of music was functioning. . . . After the unreality and sterility of the past season of concert-giving in New York, music has been heard again. . . .' Thus Paul Rosenfeld wrote in the *New Republic*.

The infusion of a creative spirit into a difficult community project had greatly stirred me. Since we were approaching the

tenth anniversary of the People's Music League, I had been
casting about for some new way to celebrate it. Having made
friends with a few composers, I thought perhaps they might
present their own works in a concert.

I went to Dr. Howe, and said, 'For a special event at Cooper
Union — as a gala evening — I think some composers I know
could be persuaded to play their own works.'

'Why not?' cried Dr. Howe. 'Didn't Mozart play his own
works? I'm sure the Cooper Union constituency will enjoy hearing some living composers.'

Thus we launched a new era in program-making at Cooper
Union, in February 1922. Rebecca Clark, Louis Gruenberg, the
late Frederick Jacobi, A. Walter Kramer, Lazare Saminsky, and
Deems Taylor all took part, playing one or more of their own
compositions. The audience received the program with enormous enthusiasm and the press recognized it as a real innovation.
One critic wrote that he 'doubted whether so promising an array
of our present composers has ever before appeared together.' In
*Musical America*, the writer of a column headed 'Mephisto's
Musings' noted that the People's Music League, having done
excellent work in giving the best music for audiences of modest
means, had decided 'to go a step further and encourage the
American composer, of whose very existence there is some doubt
in the minds of certain of our leading critics.' He added, 'Now I
would suggest, in order to make the affair memorable, that the
People's Music League engage a barker from Coney Island, who
could appeal to the audience.'

> Here we are, ladies an' gemmen! All alive and kicking, the
> American composers! This great aggregation collected at vast
> expense for one night only! Come in an' see 'em! They have
> not been exhibited before! They have not appeared before the
> crowned heads of Europe! Come an' see the great American
> Composers an' hear 'em perform. All alive! All alive! Yes
> ma'am, we feed 'em at 6:30, concert's at 8:30! No, miss, they
> will not appear in tights. That feller over there is Louis Gruen-
> berg, who won the thousand dollar Flagler prize for the best
> symphonic poem, produced by Walter Damrosch and titled

'The Hill of Dreams.' This, ladies an' gemmen, is Fred Jacobi,
an American from Frisco, once an assistant conductor at the
Met. And this, ladies an' gemmen, is Deems Taylor, who was
discovered and lassoed by Reinald Werrenrath, the great
singer, when Taylor was editor of an electrical paper. Taylor
is now the renowned music critic of the New York
World! . . .

A short time after that concert I went to see Dr. Eugene Noble, first president of the newly organized Juilliard Foundation
for Music. Thanks to a wonderful patron, Mr. John W. Froth-
ingham, the People's Music League was not in need of money, for
he had generously met every deficit all through those ten years.
What I sought from Dr. Noble was advice, as I had heard that
he was making a music survey in preparation for the Juilliard
Foundation's program.

I explained to him that I was puzzled because some of our
audiences at the concerts in the public schools had been leaving in the middle of the programs. 'Do you think our idea of
free concerts has worn thin?' I asked him. I mentioned that in
certain sections of the city some of the foreign-born were evidently making money, that poverty seemed somewhat dimin-
ished. 'Is it possible that free music is no longer the necessity it
was to these people when they were newly arrived?' I wanted
to know.

'Mrs. Reis,' he said, 'it may interest you to know that for
some time I have not only been watching your work with the
People's Music League but the reactions of the audiences as
well. In fact, some of these people have been observed after they
left your concerts. Do you know where we found they were
going? It may be a shock to you, but they were going straight
to the movie houses which, as you know, have been opening
up in their neighborhoods. Now, Mrs. Reis, they pay admission
to the movies! So, if you ask me what is happening, I will say
that I think people often lose interest in something they get
for nothing. If you were to begin charging a small admission
to the concerts I believe you would be sure of one thing, namely

getting an audience which came because it really wanted to hear the programs and would therefore remain throughout.'

After leaving Dr. Noble I did some serious thinking about changes that had taken place in the city during the past decade. Reviewing the recent experiment at Cooper Union, with the concert of living composers' works, I surmised that perhaps the need now was for more of these programs.

The phrase 'dissonant music' was heard now and then, and it was vaguely associated with concerts being given in Vienna by a man named Arnold Schoenberg. To the average concertgoer Debussy was still the arch-modernist. On the whole, however, symphonic programs and recitals rarely included contemporary compositions. True, in New York City, the president of the somewhat precious 'Friends of Music' Society, Mrs. Harriet Lanier, was gradually becoming a champion of Ernest Bloch; and at the Society's concerts on Sundays at three o'clock at the Ritz-Carlton, a contemporary work was being sandwiched in between some of the rarely heard classics. In making this innovation Mrs. Lanier had been influenced by Dr. Artur Bodanzky. The atmosphere of the ballroom in the aristocratic old Ritz-Carlton might well have been part of the attraction for subscribers to the 'Friends,' and I wondered whether the velvet softness of its well-stuffed chairs was not more conducive to sleeping than to enjoyment of the rare selections of modern music.

I felt compelled to find new and better ways to help with the development of contemporary music. Something told me that now my activities of the last ten years had served the purpose, but had reached their logical end. It is my belief when it comes time to shut the door on anything there should be no vacillation. It should be shut quickly. With this in mind, I turned to the new interest I had taken in helping living composers.

## Building a League of Composers

AT THE END of our first concert that November evening in 1923
I wanted to thank some guardian angel that the new League of
Composers had been launched without any real catastrophe. We
had announced that we would bring before the public the entire
range of modern tendencies in music, including the most experimental, and we were on our mettle to prove our claims as
champions of contemporary music. At the end of this first evening it seemed to me that our audience had been receptive from
the very opening number, the world *première* of Ernest Bloch's
Piano Quintet, accepting it as an omen of musical solidarity.
It had been presented brilliantly by that great master of the
piano, Harold Bauer, who, with the Lenox Quartet, had volunteered to help our new society to make its debut. This capped
the cordial reception of this important contemporary work.

A young British composer Arthur Bliss — now Master of the
Queen's Music — had arrived in the United States just in time
to add international prestige to our first board of directors. We
had invited him to conduct several of his own compositions on
this opening program. At a directors' meeting several days before the concert, Bliss brought up the subject of encores, urging
us to rule that they should be omitted from any program. We
agreed to this unanimously.

When he appeared on the platform he was greeted with thunderous applause. He finished conducting the chamber orchestra in 'The Women of Yueh' and 'Rout' whereupon the audience gave him a tremendous acclaim. It took him so by surprise that it drove from his mind the ruling on which he had insisted; he whirled around to his orchestra, picked up his baton, and did an encore with 'Rout.'

'What else could I do after such a reception of the work?' he exclaimed with a laugh, when a few of us clustered around to congratulate him. The incident warned me that I was in charge of a society of artists which would probably often afford me surprises. Over the years I was to find that few of these unexpected moments would contain any unpleasantness. On the whole our disappointments were to be accepted without serious rancor, and our struggles were to be resolved with a modicum of good spirit.

Our first announcement of the League's purposes stated that 'the creative artist needs contact with the public, and we believe the public is willing to give him a hearing.' Although 'first performances' were to be a feature of our concerts, modern works that the board considered of sufficient importance to have a rehearing would not be excluded. To effect co-operation between composers of all nationalities was a further aim. Thus, it was made known that the *raison d'être* for establishing our new group was *the composer*. I was completely convinced that this was to be a real composers' guild.

On the top floor of our house on 68th Street was a room that had been used chiefly for toy trains and ping-pong when our children were little. As it was no longer needed by them I turned it into an office for the League, thereby saving rent and telephone bills. Miss May Gober presided faithfully over the office for twenty years as Secretary for the League; and for twenty years she never allowed her instinctively calm nature to be upset by even the most trying temperament.

The ping-pong table became the repository for circulars and programs as they arrived from the printer. Music manuscripts were kept in the closet, and sometimes they remained unclaimed for years. Many a night I awakened worrying about fire hazards and irreplaceable unpublished music.

Among the secessionists from the Guild who became original directors of the League were Louis Gruenberg, who was developing into a forceful leader in contemporary music circles, and Lazare Saminsky, who was a dynamic young composer recently arrived from Russia and whom I nicknamed 'The Ambassador' because of his travels in so many musical circles and countries. Another director during the League's early years was the late Alma Morgenthau who became a most generous patroness.

For many years Dr. Thaddeus H. Ames, a psychoanalyst, was our treasurer. Because music was Dr. Ames's hobby, he volunteered to do the treasurer's work, and, in order that the books might be kept to the letter, he took instruction from a certified public accountant. Once or twice there was mild protest from one of the board that his ability to psychoanalyze might be inadvertently employed with the composers. 'I know I have kinks,' said one, 'and I want to keep them!' Nevertheless for twenty-five years Dr. Ames performed ably and unselfishly as treasurer, never introducing his knowledge of 'kinks' at meetings.

Minna Lederman, who had had professional newspaper and magazine experience writing chiefly on the subjects of music and the dance, volunteered to help us with publicity, and it would be almost impossible to estimate the value of her contribution. Her job evolved from necessity. One successful result was the development of our magazine, *Modern Music.*

Among others who became League members were Stephan Bourgeois, an art connoisseur; Emerson Whithorne, a composer and publisher; and Leo Ornstein, in those days often referred to as 'the futurist composer.' In 1914 Ornstein's compositions had startled New York, London, and Paris. Gustav Mahler had to quell a riot in London because of the furor of disapproval occurring in the concert hall when Ornstein played his 'Wild Man's Dance.' In New York, A. Walter Kramer, then a young critic on *Musical America*, was one of the few who defended Ornstein's compositions; the result was that, more or less seriously, several of Ornstein's severest critics occasionally questioned Mr. Kramer's sanity.

Leo Ornstein had toured all over Europe and the United States as a concert pianist. He preferred playing the little known music of Béla Bartók, Maurice Ravel, Darius Milhaud, and Isaac Albeniz, but his concert manager insisted, on the contrary, that Chopin and Liszt were better for the box office and would show off his extraordinary pianistic talent.

Stubbornly Leo rebelled. 'I am not a virtuoso,' he objected, 'I am a maker of music; these moderns are my comrades in the new adventure. Let me help my new friends by helping the public to know them.' I was most happy to renew my friendship with Ornstein in this new League of Composers, because we had earlier been fellow-students at the Institute of Musical Art. His dynamic personality and fiery enthusiasm as an artist made him very attractive.

One evening at our home while discussing Ornstein's difficulties with both managers and programs, my husband offered him our studio for a series of contemporary programs, on the understanding that Ornstein would choose what he should play, and have the chance also to talk to his audience about these new comrades-in-music.

I recall that at one gathering of the so-called 'inner group' Leo was asked to describe how he wrote a 'new' composition.

'It comes into my mind full-fledged, complete as far as it goes,' he explained thoughtfully. 'When I hear it in my head I make frantic haste to get it down on paper, lest I lose a note. This is difficult because the rhythms are so often intricate, and I must preserve them and the harmonies. When I have written them down I say to myself, "Ornstein, how could you write like that!" I then tear up what I have written. It is gone, passed into oblivion!'

After hearing Ornstein play some of his works, James Huneker wrote, 'I never thought I should live to hear Arnold Schoenberg

sound tame; yet tame he sounds — almost timid and halting —
after Ornstein who is, most emphatically, the only true-blue,
genuine Futurist composer alive.'

The 'twenties proved to be crusading days indeed. Many circles were forming in the arts, and rivalry ran high, especially in
the musical world. For instance, in addition to the League of
Composers and the International Composers' Guild, there were
Pro Musica, the American Music Guild, and the United States
section of the International Society for Contemporary Music;
organizations coming on the scene subsequently were the
Copland-Sessions Concerts and the Composers' Forum.

As a result of the functioning of the several societies, a very
competitive market developed, which proved both a good thing
and a bad. Besides the fact that the composer could be heard,
it developed that once his work was presented on the program
of one society he was doomed not to be heard again by any
rival organization during that season. One might say the composer tossed a coin and hoped that his hearing would be before
the largest audience. Moreover, if he should happen to be singled
out for election as a committee member of one society, he had
a good chance of being ostracized at once by the other societies.

Crusading became a contagion. Many adventurous spirits were
stirring in the theater, too. The Neighborhood Playhouse on
Henry Street drew crowds away from Broadway to see rare and
beautiful productions of plays new to New York, plays of serious
implication and significance. The Provincetown Playhouse was
introducing Eugene O'Neill as *the* great American playwright;
contributing to this same theater, the late Robert Edmond
Jones was pioneering a new era in stage design and lighting.

At the Garrick Theater the Theatre Guild was giving American *premières* to plays by famous Europeans. As Lawrence
Langner, one of the original directors of the Theatre Guild
points out in his book *The Magic Curtain,*

> . . . during the first few years of the Theatre Guild's career
> there were no playwrights in America of the stature of Chekov,
> Shaw, Galsworthy and Granville Barker with the sole excep-

tion of Eugene O'Neill who was connected with the Province-town Theatre. . . . It was my feeling that we should produce the important plays of European authors to set a standard for American writers and we did, *force majeure*, until our own native dramatists entered the field, and then we began to produce their plays.[1]

The lack, in the early days of the League, of a group of American composers of stature equal to the European composers was similar to the lack felt by the Theatre Guild in the mid-'twenties.

In 1931 the Group Theater entered the lists, not only with a new plan for dramatic productions, but also with a specific philosophy for the Group's activities.

At this time the League of Composers had been active for eight years, but at no time had our directors discussed any theory or policy for the group as an entity, or for the individual relations within the League. Our meetings together grew out of belief in a cause for which we wanted to work; social relations were neither accepted nor denied as essential.

The Group Theater, on the contrary, had, according to Harold Clurman, '. . . the desire for a center around which one might build a complete life which was basic.' As he saw it 'almost all the people in and around the Group clamored for it even more insistently.' Unlike the Group, we in the League gave no thought to the development of 'an artistic organism.'

Among our directors there arose sometimes a seeming lack of loyalty to the organization, and frequently criticism from without was met with passive acceptance within. I found this difficult to understand, especially in the early years; it seemed to me that if the existence of the organization was worth while, it was worth defending. I even tried to argue for a sense of loyalty, on the ground that we were all equally responsible for the League.

One day at a meeting I presented the gist of various criticisms which I felt some of the composer-directors should answer. 'Why is it,' I asked, 'that some of us agree with composers — those,

1. E. P. Dutton and Company, New York, 1951.

by the way, not on our board — when they say that we constitute a "clique"?'

For a moment the composers remained silent. Then our one European member inquired, 'What is a clique?'

The editor of our magazine was not only highly articulate but also always quick if argument loomed, and she replied, ' "clique" applies to a snobbish or narrow coterie.'

I added, 'Inasmuch as our concerts present contemporary music of all trends, how then can we be cliquish and narrow?' My hope was that ways would suggest themselves to our composer-directors whereby the organization could be protected in future from attacks.

As no one seemed inclined to reply, I went farther; 'As a matter of fact the more conservative groups in music today think of us as radicals, quite wild. The extreme modernists, on the contrary, already charge our programs with a growing and fatal conservatism. As for snobbery, doesn't anyone outside a group inevitably suspect those on the inside of some sort of snobbery?'

Several of the composers laughed at this, yet I could not pin down any one of them to agreeing that, because they were directors, they must naturally defend their own organization.

I often compared our experience with activity in other fields. Would not directors of any enterprise defend their product? We were being confronted by an important point: plainly, our work thus far did not stand for a unifying philosophy to which we all felt impelled to adhere.

Fortunately, this lack did not affect the League's fundamental activities. The trouble was that, aesthetically, our composer-members' views were so individualistic that the idea of bothering their minds about each other's beliefs simply was not real to them.

Much more to the point was the frequent cry from one of the twelve-tone disciples, who threw down the gauntlet, demanding to know, 'Why must we continue each year to play one or more Stravinsky compositions?' Often it seemed to me that Stravinsky and Schoenberg were becoming the guidons of two separate and distinct camps; and yet the year that we combined in our program Schoenberg's *Die Glückliche Hand* and Stravinsky's *Le Sacre du Printemps*, the Schoenberg faction cast no oblique glances at the Stravinsky wing, or vice versa.

In my own mind there was no doubt that the heterogeneous qualities and the personality differences among the directors on our board added something to the vitality of the group. Naturally, temperament often got the better of meetings during the early years, and misunderstandings were frequent. Dinner meetings usually were held in some convenient — and economical — French *bistro*, and often flaring tempers and strident voices shortened them, one composer storming out of the place after angry outbursts at another. 'I'll never come to another meeting with that mad musician!' was a frequent last, heated word. Since we were forced to adjourn, some of us could not help wondering which was the maddest. Other patrons, and the waiters, would look at us with disapproval. We would feel abashed, like badly behaved children, and would know we had to find another restaurant for our next meeting. Only when we reached a climax in name-calling, bringing actual blushes to the cheeks of even our most sophisticated members — when a group of composers heard themselves assailed as 'a bunch of eunuchs, the way you accept the ideas suggested by two women!' — did we decide that our meetings henceforth had best be held in a private house whose walls had no ears!

We were not too different in such matters from other artistic groups. In the 1880's, the Café Guerbois in Paris became famous as a haven where artists joined each other casually after threatened duels. Parisians remembered for years afterward the incident of Edouard Manet and Louis Duranty, with Émile Zola offering his services as Manet's second. After such crises everybody would gather around a table, offering toasts impartially to artists, critics, art collectors — in fact to any and everyone to whom art was something worth fighting for. Evidently the crusading spirit is nourished alike by war and peace.

I was reminded recently of these intensities between composers by a postscript to a letter from one of our charter members: 'I met H—— again for the first time in some fifteen-odd years, in fact since the League meetings; he still behaved as though he expected me to bite him, or perhaps attempt to borrow money.'

In a mood of appeasement, one spring day one of our most quarrelsome composers startled us by suggesting that we should all plan on going away together into the country that summer for a few weeks to talk over our mutual interests. 'We might get to know each other better,' he said, 'and understand how to get along more peacefully during next season.'

His idea met with stony indifference but he persisted. 'Other groups have done this, why shouldn't we? Our League affairs take so much of our spare time that we never get to know each other intimately; I'm sure there would be fewer hurt feelings if we could just become better friends and take the time to talk over our ideas.'

'But,' cried one of our habitually frank members, 'we don't *want* to know each other better!' There was dead silence for a minute. When it began to be embarrassing, I said, 'Judging from early experiments of literary groups in New England, and some more recent experiences of theater groups, a retreat in which to explore the collective soul isn't guaranteed to work much benefit.'

No, apparently we wanted no part in personality problems. This formula did not seem to be our answer for a more smoothly functioning organization and better understanding among creative artists. The League of Composers,[2] at the present in its thirty-second year, has existed so much longer than most artist groups, that I believe now, as I did then, that the purpose which brought it into existence was sufficiently important cause without the addition of a hard-and-fast ideology. The bonds of friendship which did develop within the group were not the result of by-laws.

---

2. Recently merged with the United States Section of the International Society for Contemporary Music. See Appendix, 253.

Fortunately there were periodic changes in the board of directors, bringing in new blood and allowing dissenting members to pass out of office without too great detriment to the society itself. Sometimes wishful thinking would convince a resigning member that the League was dying anyway, that the next season — if any — would see the closing of its doors. However, when we knew a resignee was harboring hurt feelings, we usually managed to soothe him with an invitation to join the large National Committee of Composers which, though it had little voting power, appeared as a distinguished list on our stationery. Only one former director ever refused to be included on this list. Having been forced to resign for cruelly overstepping critical bounds with reference to a colleague, he wrote loftily, 'I am sorry that I do not find it possible to continue serving The League of Composers in any capacity, still less to figure in its mausoleum of composers.'

In discussions of methods for strengthening our varied activities, one of our more severely critical directors would often harp on the slogan, 'The League has no profile; it must be given a face.' Sometimes, however, the fact — if it was a fact — of not having a face seemed rather to be a virtue, inasmuch as our programs — indeed all our projects, including our magazine, and the commissions — constantly proclaimed our allegiance to all trends of music, and to all nationalities. I remembered the words of Stravinsky's condemnation of Alexandre Scriabin, in which he described Scriabin as being 'devoid of all national character; he has not even a passport, and one *must* have a passport!'

Our 'face' or passport was our internationality, for composers from eighteen countries were on our programs. In the early years one of our markedly chauvinistic members complained bitterly that we neglected American compositions. Yet in the second decade of our concerts, in a complete turnabout, he complained with equal vehemence that we were neglecting European composers! There was a reason for this. When in 1923 we began giving programs, the stature of the American composer by no means equaled that of the European. Because American music grew in quality, as American composers grew in numbers, we felt it incumbent upon us to encourage American music, particularly through first performances and commissioned works.

The schism, separating us from the International Composers' Guild, spurred us to set a record of achievement quickly, and, although our first year had been well occupied with making up concert programs and developing a new public for the League, we were very ambitious, eager to develop a variety of projects that would improve the composers' lot both artistically and financially.

A most important addition to the concerts had come about a few months after our first programs. This was our magazine, later known as *Modern Music*.

One day Stephan Bourgeois, a man with a scholarly knowledge of music, was discussing the League's public relations with Minna Lederman. 'I think,' he said, 'that we ought to publish some kind of bulletin or "review."' Minna agreed with him, realizing it would be a new way to bring the realities of contemporary music before the public. 'You know,' she commented to me, 'how cavalierly we are often treated by the press, how our releases are overlooked. Besides being a good thing to give our subscribers a publication, it will help our public relations right along the line.'

Bourgeois was inclined to think that a serious publication might well modify existing frivolous reactions to our programs, and Minna agreed with him on this, too. Bourgeois suggested, 'I feel sure that through my contacts with modern painters and illustrators I could get many artists to give us illustrations for a periodical devoted to contemporary music.' His art gallery on 57th Street was a popular rendezvous for artists and art lovers of the modern schools.

Within a few weeks (February 1924) the League of Composers magazine was launched; we plunged into the project with the same impulsiveness that characterized many of our later ventures. Bourgeois delivered on his promise. The first issue carried full-page drawings by Pablo Picasso of three composers: Manuel de Falla, Erik Satie, and Igor Stravinsky. There were articles on music from England, France, Germany, and Italy. We felt that it was an impressive beginning.

Perhaps this is the place to say that, as my home was used as an office for the League, for twenty-one of the magazine's twenty-three years, through their generous sympathy with our aims, it was published in the apartment of Minna Lederman's parents, with the aid — large and small — of several individuals never even known to the League's board and at no small expenditure in time, comfort, and money by Mr. and Mrs. Lederman. Only because they were ill was the magazine finally forced out of the home of Minna's parents in 1944, and into an office of its own; perforce, expenses sky-rocketed.

I am indebted to Minna for giving me in retrospect some details of her efforts to establish the publication. 'Everyone in the first two years gave everything "for free," ' she recalls, 'time, energy, contacts. Too, as you remember, a long internecine struggle began at once to make and keep the magazine a house organ. The fact that it became quite early and definitely something different, detached from the League's other activities — in a word, a general music magazine of opinion, with exacting technical and literary standards — was due, I suppose to the fact of fighting so hard to make it that way, incurring many enmities in the process. I don't regret that struggle, and take pride in the outcome. When the magazine ceased publication, the estimate offered by the press and the character of mail received from friend and former foe alike supported the judgment that this had been the best kind of publication for the League.

'Financial difficulties were great. The economics of *Modern Music* were always misunderstood outside the inner circle and often inside it. The League had to meet *Modern Music*'s annual deficit of about $1500 until greatly increased costs became an insuperable obstacle to survival. But the fact that the magazine could live and grow at all was incredible, because the total overall budget including subsidy and earnings was so small.'

Minna had taken on a colossal job. She guided composers who had never written a line of prose, in expressing themselves on burning issues in the contemporary musical scene; also she edited their appraisals. It was a magazine of opinion with standards of which we all could be really proud. To Virgil Thomson's mind 'this quarterly magazine of modernist opinion is the most vigorous forum of its kind in the world; it is the indispensable journal of our tonal times.'

Its cessation was forced in 1947–8 by the rise in printing costs and the real need for a paid staff. When it closed down Irving Kolodin said, 'Where now are we to turn for the latest information on what composer thinks of composer? Minna Lederman succeeded in creating and maintaining for nearly a quarter of a century . . . the only first class journal of musical opinion in this country.'

In an effort to give every member a chance to express his individual aesthetic values as well as to divide the bulk of work actually to be done, the League board often allocated to a particular composer the responsibility for making up a concert program. Sometimes the results met with strong disapproval from the majority of directors.

On occasion individuals proved prophetic. One example followed a program which had met with great criticism. With full expectation that as soon as the meeting could be called to order there would be a general outcry, Lazare Saminsky, who had planned the unfortunate program, rushed into the meeting and, before anyone had a chance to utter a word, he burst forth with, 'How could you *let me* put on such a bad program.'

Years later Aaron Copland was the impresario *pro tem* to arrange an evening in honor of Heitor Villa-Lobos, the renowned Brazilian composer, who was here for a short visit. The program was disappointing because Villa-Lobos had brought with him very little chamber music and because so few of his works were available in New York City.

Copland had always been a just but severe critic on any

occasion when he felt our standards were being let down, but here was a program that had been completely in his hands and which, and through no fault of his own, had turned out badly. At the end of the evening he said to me over and over, 'To think that *I* put on such a poor program!'

Though we knew perfectly well that the outcome was due to no fault of his, the experience gave us a greater understanding of some of the problems which had confronted several of our colleagues on past occasions, especially during the 'twenties when new music was scarce, or artists able to interpret the new compositions were few.

Inevitably, repeating some of the sensational works heard in the 'twenties has tended to bring with it an historical coloration, a dated overtone dimming the spontaneous atmosphere of the original event. Works that have survived, to be heard occasionally today, must in consequence state their own case. Today's young composers long to experience with their *premières* some of that excitement belonging to the early days of modern music societies.

In 1949 we planned a program which was in memory of the eminent critic Paul Rosenfeld. Included in it were works by Ornstein, Harris, Sessions, and Varèse, who were among the composers whom Rosenfeld had recognized. It was said of Rosenfeld that, being a great friend of artists as well as a critic, he often discovered people before they discovered themselves.

In the 'twenties there was an atmosphere of adventure in the reception of this music; somehow in 1949 the mood could not be recaptured. Perhaps it was because audiences — even the attitudes of critics — had changed, affecting the atmosphere in the concert hall.

The curiosity of the younger generation today, regarding the Klaw Theater concerts, the productions of the Provincetown Playhouse, the Washington Square and the Group players, the literature of the so-called 'Lost Generation,' is really not far different from that experienced with respect to some of the anti-Victorian customs of the Gay Nineties.

Composers may look wistfully to the past, because now their compositions seem not to cause the furor in concert halls as when the League was young. But does it not simply indicate that it is their task to represent this generation by seeking a new path? Today young musicians have the advantage of having grown up from childhood with an established modernist idiom; this, in itself, constitutes a long step forward.

In its very nature, no matter what form it seeks, the adventure of experimenting belongs to the young. Inevitably each era develops its own form of experimentation; not to attempt something new only deprives us of the joys of discovery. Stefan Zweig pointed to this in his book *The World of Yesterday*, when he wrote, 'Whenever an experiment was attempted . . . everywhere we were in the vanguard, the shock troops of every sort of new art, *merely because it was new*, merely because it changed and widened the world for us, whose turn had now come to live our lives . . . But it was something else that interested and fascinated us so boundlessly in this new art; it was almost exclusively the art of young people.' [3]

---

3. The Viking Press, New York, 1943.

# 4

## *Artists and Audiences*

THEORIES ABOUT jazz rhythms vary. Paul Rosenfeld defined jazz as 'an entertainment form . . . which temporarily removes people from contact with the realities. . . . An extraordinarily popular, drug-like use of the materials of sound . . . just another means of escape . . .' [1]

In the early 'twenties some musicians declared that there were only two kinds of music, the classic and the popular, and that they were at opposite poles. Composers of the stature of Stravinsky, Milhaud, and Weill among Europeans, and Carpenter, Copland, and Gruenberg among Americans experimented with jazz in their compositions during the 'twenties and 'thirties, but many musicians felt that the Americans caught the spirit of jazz in a way never quite achieved by the Europeans.

In 1924 it was wholly fitting that, in its serious efforts to explore every phase of contemporary music, the League of Composers should devote an afternoon of music and discussion to the subject of jazz. In the so-called 'jazz age' it had indeed become a music with many faces. On the one hand, it was condemned as an expression of neurotic modern life and, on the

---

1. Paul Rosenfeld, *An Hour with American Music*, J. B. Lippincott Company, New York, 1929.

other, extolled as the original source of American rhythm, therefore a true representation of American music.

Serious consideration was being given by Professor Edward Burlingame Hill, then head of the Department of Music at Harvard University, to the question of whether or not jazz was merely a sophisticated form of light music. He regarded the study to be of such importance that he accepted our invitation to take part in a Sunday afternoon program at the Anderson Galleries to discuss 'Jazz in the Music of Today.'

Gilbert Seldes, then editor of the *Dial*, a magazine, took the position of 'innocent bystander.' We also persuaded Vincent Lopez to come with some members of his jazz orchestra to demonstrate the musical material. In their theatrical coats and caps, Lopez and his men were indeed a new type of ensemble for a League program, yet they did not impair the atmosphere of purpose and dignity in the auditorium.

Professor Hill and Mr. Seldes treated the occasion with the greatest respect. The band, choosing from classical and popular music to illustrate the discussion, played jazzed excerpts from *Carmen*, *H.M.S. Pinafore*, and such tunes of the day as 'My Sweetie Went Away,' and 'Mama Loves Papa.'

Before the program commenced, I had noticed a young Negro elevator boy, employed to set up chairs for the orchestra. At every possible moment he hung around the fringes, staring wistfully at the musicians. Finally he disappeared, but at intervals I heard a rhythmic tapping sound, somewhere outside. My curiosity got the better of me and I went out to look around. There in the anteroom was the elevator boy, dancing away to his heart's content to the Lopez rhythms. It was rather a conclusive answer to any doubts I had harbored about the functionality of jazz; jazz was speaking to this boy, and he was responding.

The days seem long ago when we stopped to ask ourselves whether it was properly within our sphere to go into the subject of jazz, and yet, research on this subject still goes on. For instance, recently an Institute of Jazz Studies was established 'to foster an understanding and appreciation of the nature and significance of Jazz in our society.' Under its announced plans complete recorded archives of jazz literature will be made available to the student, a series of jazz courses at the college level will be available, and participation in annual round table discussions will be part of the Institute curriculum. Publication of books on jazz will also be encouraged.

Within the circle of the League, jazz was to attract a wide variety of champions over the years, including serious concert artists and leading music critics. Eva Gauthier, a singer who for many years lavished her great musicianship and brave spirit on liberal causes, believed strongly that song literature must not be restricted — as a majority of programs would have us believe — to the conventional. In the 'twenties she was one of those who were determined that jazz should have a place on their classical programs. Why not, when it was receiving scholarly consideration by serious composers, even by musicologists?

Accordingly, she introduced George Gershwin in one of her recitals, in Aeolian Hall, then on 42nd Street. The young composer accompanied her in her closing group of songs by Irving Berlin, Jerome Kern, and himself. The program ended with 'Alexander's Ragtime Band' and this pioneering combination of Gauthier, Gershwin, and popular song brought down the house.

Although we had few doubts about the audience's enjoyment, serious doubts were expressed the next day by the music critics. Many of the critics severely reproved the artist for presuming to introduce into a concert of classical songs the type of music which, they pointed out, 'simply did not belong.' Disciplinary action followed: the next week Gauthier was booked to give a repeat program in Boston and it was canceled. 'The Hub' let Gauthier know that it would have none of her frivolous ideas; the place for jazz was Broadway, not the concert hall.

At the time Deems Taylor was a young critic, one of the few who understood Gauthier's courage and her valuable contribution. For the New York *World* he wrote a column and a half, defending 'the right of jazz to hold up its head in the company of the classics, and to take its place as the American rhythm. If a Metropolitan Opera artist could sing an Italian jazz tune such as "Donna e Mobile" and be solemnly appraised by the critics, why shouldn't someone sing "Carolina in the Morning" which is just as sincere, as good, as profound?' Taylor headed his article 'Respectabilizing Jazz.'

The majority of critics, however, would not accept this break in the tradition of serious concert music, holding that in the Aeolian *concert* Hall, jazz was an intruder. It is interesting to notice in this connection that, more than twenty years later, the Campion Society — devoted to stimulating interest in lesser known phases of song literature — was to recognize Mme Gauthier's outstanding service with a 'Campion citation.' This was made on the recommendation of a committee of nationally prominent musicians and critics. Besides celebrating her contributions to the study, performance, and teaching of the best in song literature, it credited her with being 'a pioneer in emphasizing the importance of jazz as a serious artistic experience.'

One day, following his first tour as soloist with Paul Whiteman and his Orchestra, George Gershwin talked with me about the effect of their orchestral concerts, playing jazz through the West. 'Whiteman and I didn't feel,' he said anxiously, 'that this new type of orchestra is yet understood everywhere.'

'Which were the places where you felt that audiences did respond well?' I asked.

'That's an interesting thing; in the cities which support regular symphony programs, we found people enthusiastic about this new kind of music. But in small towns, where symphonic concerts are heard only infrequently, if at all, they were noticeably unresponsive.'

It left a question in my mind, did not jazz as performed by Whiteman's orchestra with Gershwin call for a rather sophisticated ear?

From the beginning the League's concerts in New York were patronized by cosmopolitan audiences with a rather high leaven

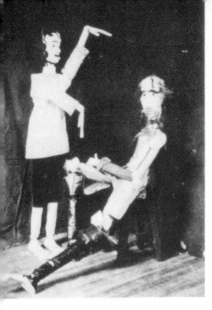

Sancho Panza and Don Quixote, man-size puppets, designed by Remo fano for *El Retablo de Maese Pedro* Manuel de Falla.

The Devil designed by Donald Oenslager for *L'Histoire du Soldat* by Igor Stravinsky.

The Chimera designed by Robert Edmond Jones for *Die Glückliche Hand* by Arnold Schoenberg.

*Le Sacre du Printemps,* by Igor Stravinsky, designed by Nicholas
Roerich: *above,* Martha Graham; *below, The Corps de Ballet.*

*Oedipus Rex*, by Igor Stravinsky, with twelve-foot puppets designed by Robert Edmond Jones and executed by Remo Bufano: *above*, Harvard Glee Club and soloists (Vandamm Studio); *below*, Tiresias (Maurice Goldberg).

*The Devil and Daniel Webster* by Douglas Moore and
Stephen Vincent Benét (Will Rapport).

*Pas d'Acier*, by Serge Prokofieff, designed by Lee Simonson
(Vandamm Studio).

of the 'musical intelligentsia.' Nevertheless there were times when audience reactions were disturbing, obviously stemming from lack of familiarity with some of the new trends in composition. For example, whenever a work was particularly difficult to follow, the audience quickly grew restless, tittering as understanding fell out of step. Too, there was a temptation to be on the *qui vive* for some sensational effect to laugh at, as happened, for instance, when percussion instruments for Honegger's 'La Mer' included tapping tumblers filled with water.

Bartók's works were little known in this country in 1926, when we programed the world *première* of his Second Sonata for Piano and Violin. We invited a Hungarian compatriot — a fine pianist — to play with Albert Stoessel, a serious violinist-composer and great admirer of Bartók. The sonata was difficult for the audience to grasp and soon a mood of restlessness spread through the hall. Sensing a wavering interest with the increasing dissonances because people fidgeted about, the pianist, giggling nervously, turned her head away from the keyboard to smile along with the audience. Mr. Stoessel, meanwhile, continued performing his part with real dedication and reverence for the composer.

Seemingly encouraged by one of the artist's grasp of their reactions, the audience continued its smiling and whispering. When the sonata was finished and the artists stood to take their bows, the pianist suddenly went over to the side of the audience, frankly breaking out into laughter. Whereupon the audience, which had hitherto demonstrated only slightly, now laughed aloud, openly ridiculing the work. It forced the directors to the conclusion that at a first public hearing the work was altogether too difficult at that time to be understood.

It was not the first or the last time that nerve-ends seemed to be exposed under the impact of musical innovations; more than one program ended on an explosive note. For instance, when Varèse's 'Hyperprism' was performed, loud hisses and disapproving 'Bah-s' mingled with shouts of 'Bravo! Bravo!' In

an instant Salzedo bounded onto the stage, calling out in his
high-pitched, far-reaching voice, 'Those of you who don't like
it should go home, but we are going to repeat "Hyperprism"!'
A roar of fresh objection greeted this broad hint of dismissal,
only adding to the excitement. Half of the audience then settled back to listen quietly; those who took Salzedo seriously
about leaving, made a point of talking loudly and with extreme
disapproval as they clattered out of the hall.

In *The Fervent Years*, Harold Clurman has described these
events in the 'twenties as

> a time of boisterous individualism . . . No matter who you
> were or what you did, you were thought of in terms that be-
> longed properly to the realm of gangsterdom. I dwell on the
> Luna Park rather than the more sober aspects of the period
> because the former were actually more dominant. Everything
> seemed to be affected by them. There were the League of
> Composers concerts. No matter what they played, how much
> in earnest the partisans of the new music were, or how out-
> raged its detractors, the atmosphere of the concerts had some-
> thing giddy about it. They were a sort of aesthete's prom.[2]

Critics continued having their fun over modern music, too,
perversely treating audience reactions humorously. The New
York *Sun*'s music critic, W. J. Henderson, did a sort of 'profile'
for *The New Yorker*, which he entitled 'The Modern Music
Jag.' Forsaking his usually astringent protests against contemporary music, he launched into what amounted to an exaggerated
burlesque about what he called 'the new game.' His parody ran
this way:

> 'My dear,' said one charming creature to another, 'the music
> at these concerts is positively thrilling. You never in your life
> heard such strange sounds. They actually make your ears
> jump, even ache. When I first heard some of the music I
> wanted to scream; then suddenly I found myself laughing.
> I thought I was having the most beautiful evening of the
> winter. Did you ever try the pipe, dear? If you did then you
> know what I mean! After you get the habit it is simply won-

2. Alfred A. Knopf, Inc., New York, 1945.

derful. You don't have hysterics any more, you just get such peculiar sensations — quick little spasms and irritations — sometimes actual pains shooting up and down your spine — You wonder if you ought to go to the osteopath — It's wonderful!'

We in the League did not consider our programs habit-forming in the narcotic sense. We felt sure that in time our audiences would patronize the concerts for more serious reasons than just to be shocked. Moreover, we felt that the critics would eventually tire of such exaggerations as, 'The League contrived to assemble an audience of almost psychopathic distinction.'

Very likely some of the music played at League concerts did cause some hearers to have disagreeable reactions. Because our 'inner group' was somewhat inclined to be fanatic in the cause of modern music, we did not always sympathize quickly with those who did seem actually to suffer.

On one occasion, Walter W. Naumburg, one of our faithful patrons, came to hear the American *première* of a most difficult twelve-tone quintet for wind instruments by Schoenberg, at Town Hall. Mr. Naumburg, who had established the Walter W. Naumburg Music Foundation for the express purpose of helping music and musicians, is by nature a classicist, and it was not to be expected that twelve-toners would be among his favorite composers.

The instant the Quintet was finished, he dashed to the door, gasping to me 'for fresh air,' as he exclaimed bitterly, 'Claire, this is the first time in my life that music has nauseated me!' In my zeal to uphold modern music at all costs, perhaps I reacted a little spitefully, for I replied, 'Well I'm glad at least to hear you admit that contemporary music has so much effect on you!' As soon as the fresh air of West 43rd Street had done its work, he regained his normal good humor and laughed with me.

At the time I had not read Paul Hindemith's book *A Composer's World*, in which he takes occasion to discuss pain, as caused by certain obscure tonal effects. I am sure I would have

been more sympathetic with Walter's discomfort had I been
aware that Hindemith had said, 'I do not see why we should
use music to produce "spatial dizziness" . . . or the effect of
sea-sickness, which can be provided more convincingly by other
branches of our amusement industry.' [3]

It is only natural that over a period of years an organization
will meet with a few calamities. The League was to have its share
and certainly on some occasions the blame for unexpected situations was rightly ours.

For example, who could possibly have foreseen that a platform would come apart in the middle of a concert and that one
leg of a piano would vanish in the chasm? It had certainly not
entered my head that it was necessary for someone to get down
on hands and knees before the concert to make certain that
the platform was sufficiently sturdy to last through the evening.
This was our experience at the Town Hall Club when the
League gave an evening to honor Florent Schmitt, in those
days a great musical personality. His compositions received such
world-wide recognition that frequent Schmitt Festivals were
given in Europe. It befitted our New York occasion that M.
Paul Claudel, the French Ambassador, should be invited as
guest of honor, and Dr. John Erskine should be on hand to introduce the renowned composer to the distinguished audience.

After acknowledging the greeting of a great burst of applause,
Mr. Schmitt took his place at the piano to play a work with
Alfred Wallenstein, formerly a cellist. Everything — an audience of representative personalities in the music world, the generous comments of the press, the presence of the Ambassador,
the references of Mr. Erskine to Franco-American amity —
presaged an evening of rich musical interest.

About halfway through the finale of Schmitt's opening number, a nervous movement suddenly ran through the hall, breaking the spell of absorption. A sea of heads turned this way

---

3. Harvard University Press, Cambridge, Massachusetts, 1952.

and that, trying to gauge something so strange that it seemed hardly possible it could be real. Was the piano tilting at a crazy angle, or was it an optical illusion? Was one of the front legs actually sinking through the platform? But how could that be possible?

The position of Mr. Schmitt only too clearly confirmed the evidence of the eye. With determination he continued playing, but by now his right hand was a good six inches lower in space than his left. Moreover Alexander Smallens, who had been turning the pages for him, seemed now to be practically sitting on the floor. At the same time he was trying with might and main to stay the fast-tilting piano and hold up the fast-disappearing piano leg. Schmitt was like a gallant foot-runner who is determined to finish the race in the face of fatal handicaps. Rushing to finish out the composition he peered nervously from music to pedals, and tried to grasp what was happening to the instrument under his hands. No piano had ever given him trouble before! How could this one lose its equilibrium without warning, assuming the angle of the leaning tower of Pisa?

Meantime, Wallenstein, in his seat near the front of the piano, continued calmly with his cello part in the performance, seemingly unaware of anything so inconceivably preposterous.

By now the audience, convinced that its eyes were telling the truth, was beginning to laugh. Mr. Smallens remained at his post, trying valiantly to prevent the chasm from growing any wider or deeper. After finishing the last note, Mr. Schmitt jumped up from the bench his face red with rage and stalked off the stage. Later he told me that he had wondered during the last minutes of the performance if he were having a bad dream, or if he might be experiencing a delayed reaction from his rough crossing from Europe.

'Whose fault,' he demanded to be told, 'was this? A platform splitting in two, a piano sinking out of reach while being played.'

How could I answer such a question! I could only stammer that in ten years of concert experience I had never been confronted by such a calamity, nor did I know anyone who had. I piled apology on apology, but I certainly could not blame him for being too angry to take them in.

Meantime the house carpenter was busy with hammer and spikes, mending the brace that usually held the platform sections together. I explained this to Mr. Schmitt. At first he was skeptical and I had to admit he had reason for being afraid to go back on the platform. But, then the artist in him asserted itself. As he walked out once more the audience gave him a tremendous ovation. Later he must have forgiven me for on his return to France he sent me a signed photograph and a warm letter of appreciation for the evening in his honor.

Inevitably, concerts of new works by young American or European composers were to be a major part of the League's mission. In fact, looking back, statistics show that out of over 1200 works performed 75 per cent were 'firsts' and/or world *premières*. Our archives laudably chronicle the first performances of works whose composers are better known today in many countries by reason of their presentation by the League. As time went on we were fortunate that the constituency of the League should include an increasing number of interpretive artists who, in addition to an interest in hearing new compositions, often placed their talents at the League's disposal in performing them.

Before one of our Sunday-afternoons, a program of unknown young American composers to be heard at the New York Public Library, we were assailed by a combination of adverse factors. A blizzard had been raging since Saturday morning. Trains into New York were late and in many cases stalled altogether. Also during the previous week, an influenza epidemic had swept the city and outlying sections. All Sunday morning, we received wires and telephone calls from one artist after another. Several were ill with influenza. Others were marooned in the suburbs or farther away; they did not dare try driving cars and the trains were uncertain.

The program was scheduled for three o'clock. Ironically, by

two-thirty, an audience which had braved the elements filled the hall practically to capacity — and not one artist listed on the program had been able to reach the auditorium!

Marion Bauer, one of the directors, who was in charge of the concert, eyed the door in the hope that at least one advertised artist would materialize; it was not going to be a pleasant chore to dismiss an audience after it had demonstrated such unconcern for the weather.

Suddenly she noticed a man about to take his seat. 'Mr. Kirkpatrick,' she said, 'could I speak to you alone for a moment?' She explained our predicament to him. 'Would you do us an enormous favor and repeat the Charles Ives piano sonata which I heard you play so brilliantly last week at Town Hall?'

John Kirkpatrick looked thoroughly startled. But then he grinned, 'Yes, I'll help out.'

At that moment Marion overheard someone in a rear row say, 'If they don't get going pretty soon we'll miss our recording date.' She hurried over to the group. 'Did I hear you say you are recording today?' She prayed frantically that they might be going to do some contemporary work.

'Yes, we're doing Copland's *Sextet* for Columbia Recording.'

Like lightning she explained our difficulty, and also that John Kirkpatrick had agreed to perform. Holding her breath, she said, 'Could you have an extra rehearsal, so to speak, by playing the *Sextet* for us here?' Without a moment's hesitation, the six instrumentalists rose, went to the Green Room, and began tuning up. Owing to a spontaneity that grew out of the emergency, the concert turned out to be even better than the one planned.

The enjoyment of an interpreter in performing contemporary music is usually due either to genuine personal interest in the music of today or to a sympathetic feeling for an individual composer. Also, I think he may have some mystical sense of relationship with an era, an urge to share emotionally in experiences relating to his own generation.

Although, today there is a wide choice of artists upon whom

the composer may call for performances of contemporary music, the composer often has preconceived ideas about the soloists or conductors who are acceptable to him, in which case difficulties may arise.

Nicholas Nabokov, in his book, *Old Friends and New Music*, speaks of his instinctive reticence about becoming friendly with either interpretive artists or renowned conductors:

> When I meet a famous performing artist I always have the feeling that he knows I want something from him, that I have wares to offer and consequently that at some point I am going to pounce on him, asking 'Would you like to look at my latest?' Embarrassed . . . he will say that he has already refused over a thousand new scores . . . or that his manager will not allow him to play more than four new pieces a year, or that his programs for the next season are already made.[4]

An artist, on the other hand, is not reluctant and is often eager to have the opportunity to create a new interpretation — especially in a world *première* — because it is by no means unusual to discover fresh interpretive capacity through a new medium.

This was our experience when Dr. Koussevitzky decided to conduct the world *première* of Gruenberg's 'The Creation.' He asked me to look for a fine baritone, able to sing the part of the Negro preacher. The text had been written by the great Negro poet, James Weldon Johnson. Gruenberg's composition, a very stirring work for chamber orchestra, combined a vocal part in the form of a Negro sermon.

At the time Jules Bledsoe, the Negro baritone, was having a great success in *Showboat* on Broadway. Although he had never sung any classical music — certainly never sung in Town Hall — he was touched and flattered when we invited him to sing under the baton of Dr. Koussevitzky.

On first looking at the score, some of his fears were allayed when Gruenberg, himself, promised to coach him. Because his career had been with lighter music only, he naturally found this

---

4. Little, Brown and Company, Boston, 1951.

new music 'very different, very difficult.' This reaction continued throughout the rehearsals.

But Bledsoe was as conscientious in studying 'The Creation' as Gruenberg was patient in helping to prepare him. The final rehearsal at Town Hall pleased all three, composer, conductor, and soloist. After the grueling hours of coaching, it was a triumphal success.

As the rehearsal ended, Dr. Koussevitzky suddenly realized that Jules Bledsoe had never gone out to take a bow on a concert stage; actually Bledsoe did not know how! Thereupon, Dr. Koussevitzky, taking Bledsoe gently by the arm, marched him from the wings to center stage, from center stage back to the wings, each time showing him how to bow gracefully, poking him now and then to make him bend from the waist, and gradually instilling in the singer the concert-artist manner, in movement as well as in voice.

The great Yvette Guilbert held a deep conviction about the need for training young artists to be great interpreters. As Guilbert grew older and appeared less often on the stage, she longed to pass on her vast experience to the younger generation. For this reason she attempted to create a school of the theater. Unfortunately she had insufficient financial backing. Also, although greatly admired as an artist, she lacked the organizational ability needed to give a firm foundation to the school.

Once she invited me to one of the school's *Soirées instructives et passionnées*. She wrote, 'Our school has no other goal than to create artists to interpret Art conscientiously. Our only pride consists in creating magnificent workers. It is up to the others to employ them, to use them.' Today, it seems to me an artistic calamity that her great talent was not securely harnessed to some group with teachers in allied arts. She possessed a unique genius which could have contributed greatly to the interpreter of song, to the *diseuse*, to the actor and actress.

In contrast to Mme Guilbert's wish to train great interpreters, Schoenberg's desire was to develop better audiences. His view was that 'listeners must work for the true enjoyment of music.'

We cannot teach everyone to be a creative artist, but we can teach many people to be receptive listeners.'

In his early days in Vienna, on occasion, Schoenberg deliberately included several poor examples of composition in the programs of the society that he had organized; he did so believing this to be a means of training audiences to listen to new music with more intelligence and discrimination.

It is not always easy to acquire a new ear when one has been trained to listen only to the classics. The average concertgoer today recognizes that learning as well as listening is fundamental in the appreciation of unfamiliar music. Today, recordings, tape recorders, radio, and to some extent television make it possible to hear works more than once. Consequently, there is much more reason for the interested listener to feel himself among the 'initiated.'

Roger Sessions writes in his book, *The Musical Experience of Composer, Performer, Listener,* about four phases in the listener's development. He says in part

> Listeners are like composers, variously endowed . . . and differ in experience. FIRST, he must hear . . . without preconceived ideas and without strained effort. The SECOND stage is that of enjoyment. The THIRD stage is what we call 'musical understanding' . . . what the layman needs is not to acquire facts but to cultivate senses: the sense of rhythm, of articulation, of contrast, of accent . . . the key to understanding of contemporary music lies in repeated hearings . . . the FOURTH stage is that of discrimination. It is important that it should be the final stage since real discrimination is possible only with understanding; and both snobbery and immaturity at times foster prejudices which certainly differ from discrimination in any real sense. Actually it is impossible not to discriminate if we persist in and deepen our musical experience . . . in other words, WE will become critics.[5]

There are three R's to guide the convert to new music: Relaxation, Repetition, and Rehearsals. Relaxation breaks down the

---

5. Princeton University Press, Princeton, New Jersey, 1950.

tensions created by resistance to new ideas; repetitions (recordings or one's own playing) make possible the review of a work many times, as one might review any new subject of interest. Rehearsals afford opportunities to hear a work in its development for performance and to hear difficult sections repeated until they become familiar.

It must be admitted, however, that few concertgoers really want to add an educational pursuit to their conventional pattern of pure enjoyment of music! How few really want to undergo the labor of becoming converts to any new idiom!

The late Mayor La Guardia was a lover of Italian music of the classical and semi-popular schools. In an unexpected way I believe I converted him to the cause of contemporary music. From my first meeting with him he teased me about modern music. He, with Newbold Morris, then President of the New York City Council, invited me, and a small group, to form the charter board of directors for the New York City Center of Music and Drama, a project begun by Mr. Morris.

The warmth of Mr. La Guardia's manner made me feel as though I had known him a long time. He seemed well informed about my interest in contemporary arts and invariably opened conversations with me by saying quizzically, 'Tell me, Mrs. Reis, who *is* your favorite composer?'

One day I received a call from the Mayor's secretary. Would I do the Mayor a favor by bringing down to City Hall a group of singers who had recently given an audition of 'Troubled Island' at our home? The secretary went on to explain that the Mayor was entertaining a convention of Negro newspaper and magazine editors from all over the country. He had heard that Stokowski wanted to conduct this opera by William Grant Still. Since it had been written by a Negro, the Mayor thought it would be a nice gesture to make it possible for the editors to hear excerpts from it.

I rounded up the necessary group. Something told me to inquire if we should send a piano. 'No,' said the Mayor, answering my call himself, 'I always have a piano here; it'll be in my office.'

On the appointed day, when we were ushered into the handsome and historic room, I looked immediately for the piano but none was in sight. I wondered whether it was camouflaged in some piece of furniture because the Mayor certainly had said, 'I *always* have a piano here.'

At that instant, a door opened and in came a tiny piano on wheels; while two men shoved the instrument, four men followed, doing nothing. Tom Thumb could have moved this piano with three fingers. Presumably the Mayor was honoring the union's 4- to 6-man rule about moving pianos!

All rose to greet the Mayor as he entered. Inviting the fifty or so editors to seat themselves, he stood before them and gave a brief synopsis of the opera which they were about to hear in part. 'The story is about Jean Dessaline in Haiti,' he explained. 'It is about a man who rises to power and forgets the wife who helped him in his early struggles, all because he took a mistress who, in turn, took too much power to herself.' The Mayor grinned. 'You've all known men like that. But this Dessaline should have realized that a mistress must be treated like a politician — never let a politician get the breaks — ' The roar of laughter shook the room.

The Mayor turned then to discussing the music. 'I'm told,' he said, 'that this music is modern but not, like some contemporary music, noisy. Personally I think we have enough noise in the world. What we need is melodies, like the melodies in the Italian operas.' He glanced across the room adding, 'Mrs. Reis may not agree with me on that; however, she has told me that I may like this music.'

The program was well received by the editors. Before leaving I had a chance to ask the Mayor if he had liked the music. 'Yes, I found it very pleasant,' he said, 'it has quite a Puccini flavor!' He was not going to let me forget his allegiance to the classical and Italian music; but I did infer that some of his prejudices were beginning to melt.

'Then you agree with Stokowski's theory?' I said, not wanting to let any missionary work go undone.

'What's the theory?' asked the Mayor cautiously.

'That there is good music and bad music, not old music or modern music.'

'Yes, I'd agree with that,' said La Guardia. 'Stokowski's right, quite right.'

I decided that the Mayor had shown a sign that day of becoming a convert to modern music. If he wanted to discover a Puccini flavor, it was his privilege.

5

## Koussevitzky Encourages Commissions

AT HIS BOSTON home one spring afternoon in 1925 the late Serge Koussevitzky said enthusiastically to me, 'In Paris there has been living a young American, very talented; you should know about him.'

It was my first meeting with this great conductor. His elegance of manner and formality of dress suggested a gentleman of the Old World rather than a warring champion of a modern cause. I had gone to him on a mission for the League of Composers in the faint hope that we might persuade him to conduct a concert of contemporary music. It was exciting to watch his mind busily at work on what could be done. 'I could make up a very interesting program of new works, by Serge Prokofieff, Arthur Honegger, and Alexandre Tansman,' he said eagerly; 'a Russian, a Swiss, and a Polish composer — all good men — friends of mine. And I would like also to include this talented young American, Aaron Copland. He has been a pupil in Paris with Nadia Boulanger. He recently returned to this country. I would like him to write a work for us.' The difficulties Koussevitzky was still having with English words and syntax were small and eventually vanished, but at that time they only added a certain charm to his conversation.

'Then you will be interested in conducting a chamber orchestra in Town Hall?' I ventured timidly, hardly daring to count on such good fortune. I had wondered if he would expect nothing less than Carnegie Hall; alas, the League could not as yet afford Carnegie, with full orchestra.

'Yes, yes!' he cried excitedly. I was to learn that it always excited him to discuss new compositions. 'We can make up a beautiful program with chamber orchestra. Perhaps I'd bring one or two soloists with me to New York. But first you must receive permission from the Trustees of the Boston Symphony for the orchestra members to give this program.' He had become the Boston Symphony Orchestra conductor the season before.

When I rose to leave he urged me to write at once to Copland and to be sure to tell him that Dr. Koussevitzky personally wanted a new work from him for the following season.

Thus it came about that in 1925 the League of Composers commissioned the first work in its long history of awards. It may have been a good omen for Aaron Copland for it was the first assignment he received in what was to become a long list of honors.

This particular work was called *Music for the Theatre* and was completed in time for Dr. Koussevitzky to conduct its world *première* at Town Hall in November 1925. It has remained one of the very popular compositions in contemporary literature.

The following spring I talked with Dr. Koussevitzky again, about conducting a second program for the League. He was on the point of leaving for Europe. By letter and telephone he had given me little encouragement about the prospect of his conducting another concert with chamber orchestra, so I had come down to the dock at Hoboken to speak of it face-to-face, and to bid him *bon voyage*.

When he suddenly launched forth on the subject of commissioning new works from composers, I had no further doubt that he would again be conducting in Town Hall for us the next season.

The instant I arrived to see him, he exclaimed, 'Let's ask some more composers to write new works for chamber orchestra!' Then when the ship's whistle emitted the 'All Ashore!' blast he laid a detaining hand on my arm, insisting, 'Write to Béla Bartók — you can find his address in Budapest — ask him to send us a new work for chamber orchestra.' It was an inspired idea. I wanted to discuss it, but the final whistle blew and, after all, I could afford to be content with this much! With an affectionate farewell to him, I dashed home, feeling overjoyed.

In response to the letter sent, immediately Bartók wrote 'Village Scenes' for chamber orchestra and vocal quartet.

This concert, whose make-up had been settled so impulsively at a Hoboken dock, was conducted by Koussevitzky in November of 1926. The program of American *premières* was one of rare beauty: Bartók's work, Anton Webern's Five Pieces for Chamber Orchestra, and Louis Gruenberg's 'The Creation,' based on the poem in *God's Trombones* by the great Negro poet, James Weldon Johnson.

Bartók's name was already well known, though few of his compositions had actually been played in this country. Webern's composition probably was the first work of his played here.

At the end of the program, Dr. Koussevitzky repeated the Bartók and Webern compositions, and a majority of the audience seemed extremely pleased by his desire to give a second hearing, for the better understanding of these new works. A tiny minority in the audience, less adventurous and somewhat less ambitious for contemporary music, left the hall.

The success of these first commissioned works by Copland, and Bartók, opened up a new horizon for our efforts to help the living composer. In those early days the prestige of being selected to write a new work, and of being promised a major performance, was sufficient incentive, even if the composer could be paid little or nothing for his labor.

Gradually, some of the conductors of the major symphony orchestras began looking to us to find world *premières* by American composers for them. If they happened to be sympathetic to the composer in question they would even promise to play a work not yet written. Naturally we pursued these opportunities as diligently as possible, with the result that the first season produced *premières* of eight new works, the second season six, all receiving performance by renowned conductors and major orchestras.

Notwithstanding, we constantly felt great anxiety about the financial plight of the composers, even if the League's charter did limit the scope of our organization to the aesthetic and the educational. Occasionally we received a letter applauding our efforts to commission works even though there was no monetary reward. We felt however that the practice raised a serious question.

In one instance we asked Robert Russell Bennett to write a short symphonic work; a leading conductor had already accepted the work on faith. Bennett was in Hollywood at the time, very much occupied with the film world. Finally he wrote us, 'I deeply appreciate the honor of a commission from the League. I shall try to do a work worthy of the occasion. I feel very noble, as I count the Hollywood gold I have to give up in order to devote the time needed to the effort. This at least should leave no doubt as to the respect and esteem I have for the League's place in modern music.'

The resulting work, entitled *Hollywood*, has been played by many of the major symphony orchestras.

From the late Nicolai Berezowsky, I received the following comment:

> Perhaps some of us have felt a certain diffidence about the little money for a commission; but I want you to know that I personally am satisfied and feel grateful. This, I might add, is over and above the more important fact that the commission has given me a pretext for writing a new work for a new combination of instruments, and includes the distinction of a performance without delay and under the finest auspices. All in all, a very happy combination of circumstances.

These letters, of which there were many at that time, caused
me to realize how important our campaign to increase commissions was growing to be, not only to the composer, in showing our confidence by choosing him, but also to the conductors
who encouraged *premières*, especially of works by American
composers.

We were delighted to receive letters also from the conductors,
who congratulated us on our 'splendid enterprise, in enlisting
the support of American orchestras in behalf of American composers' and praised the League for 'commissioning works by
native composers, which excites the admiration of all who want
to encourage progressive tendencies.'

In the 'twenties and early 'thirties there were a few competitions, and occasional prizes for composers. Mrs. Elizabeth
Sprague Coolidge seemed to be the only music patron who,
through her innate wisdom and fortunate financial position,
furthered the cause of contemporary music to an extraordinary
degree. At the time we felt that Mrs. Coolidge was our only
real ally in the crusade upon which we were embarked, to establish more commissions in place of competitions. To us it was
obvious that competitions often represented a great waste of
time for men of talent, when only one or two composers could
receive recognition. Others who had to give a great deal of their
time in order to enter the competition found themselves without either honor or compensation for such expenditures of time
and labor. For this very reason many composers of real stature
would not enter some of the competitions. If a man was worthy
of consideration, we believed he should be chosen — as in the
time of Mozart and Haydn.

I decided that I must take up the cudgels whenever the opportunity presented itself to debate the importance of competitions versus commissions.

Arthur Judson, the manager of the New York Philharmonic
Symphony Orchestra, had announced through the press that
he was arranging a competition for American composers. The

awards were two large purses plus performance by the Philharmonic Symphony.

I went to see him; in no time we were in heated debate. In my effort to dissuade him from his plan I gave him all our reasons against the method of competitions. Even if the awards were large, I pointed out, the contest remained a gamble, too often, between inferior artists. We, on the other hand, had experienced progressive success with our commissions.

At this point, meeting with absolutely no reaction from him, I gathered my forces for the next argument. 'You know, Mr. Judson,' I said, 'a pretty important list of conductors has performed the works commissioned by us. Koussevitzky and the Boston Symphony, Frederick Stock and the Chicago Orchestra, Artur Rodzinski and the Cleveland Orchestra, Eugene Goossens and the Cincinnati Orchestra, Vladimir Golschmann and the St. Louis Orchestra, Frank Black and the National Broadcasting Company Symphony; in addition, the Harvard and Princeton Glee Clubs, the Adesdi Chorus, the Westminster Choir, and others.'

With his next question Mr. Judson took a very positive line. 'But Mrs. Reis,' he said, 'have any of these works which were premiered ever been played a second time.' Actually he made a statement rather than posing a question; in his position Mr. Judson was seemingly not much interested in raising questions.

With the feeling that he would not allow time to answer, I said hurriedly, 'So far our all-time high has been forty repetitions of Roy Harris' 'Song of Occupations' with the Westminster Choir, on a European tour.' As his expression darkened, I rushed on, 'and I would like you to look at this letter that I received this morning.' It was from Randall Thompson, then on the faculty of Princeton University.[1] It read:

> Dear Claire: Knowing how interested you are in what happens to commissioned works, I want to let you know that last

---

1. Randall Thompson is now Chairman of the Music Department at Harvard University.

year 762 copies of the score of *Peaceable Kingdom* [2] were sold,
and 669 copies of the individual choruses from it. I give you
this information, not in boasting, but in acknowledgment of
what that particular commission has meant to me.

For a moment Mr. Judson's expression remained unread-
able. Then he said firmly and coldly, 'This is my party. I have
raised $1500 for this competition, so now we shall see what
the American composer can do.' From the granite in his voice
I could tell that there was nothing more to be said on the subject that day. In his own mind, at least, the American composer
was more or less on trial to show what he could do. The following year Judson made one more attempt to give one of these
'parties,' as he described the competitions; after that there were
no more.

It is true that some of the competitions have occasionally
had praiseworthy results, as in the case of the George Gershwin
Memorial contests. Nevertheless one year an announcement appeared in the newspapers to the effect that 'For the George
Gershwin Memorial Contest, although fifty-one orchestral works
were submitted, not one was considered worthy of performance
by the Philharmonic Symphony Orchestra, and awards were not
made.' Consider the waste of time and effort by fifty-one composers! How much more fruitful it would have been to choose
wisely one composer, commissioning a work which in all prob-
ability would have lived to have not only its *première* but also
possibly a series of performances!

As I sat one day with the Music Committee of Town Hall
and listened to the account of the Artists' Awards that had been
given, I realized that here was another opportunity to crusade
further for composers' commissions. So I raised the question,
'Why should Town Hall give awards for interpretive artists
only, and not for composers?'

Olga Samaroff, sitting opposite, gave a quick, approving nod

2. *Peaceable Kingdom* was commissioned by the League for the Harvard
Glee Club and the Radcliffe Choral Society.

and this seemed to encourage others on the committee to take up my suggestion. 'After all,' said one member, 'composition does come before performance.'

Walter W. Naumburg, chairman of the committee, and president also of the Walter W. Naumburg Music Foundation, then asked to whom a commission should be given. Because a main purpose in establishing Artists' Awards had been to encourage young artists, I suggested William Schuman, a young composer of twenty-eight who was at the time teaching composition at Sarah Lawrence College.

No one on the committee seemed to know his work; but then, with the exception of Olga and myself, presumably none of the other members present followed the contemporary music scene closely. I described Schuman's ability at length, and a few of the performances of his work that had been given, including a symphonic work conducted by Koussevitzky.

'What would we do?' interjected our chairman, 'if the commissioned work turned out to be poor?'

Another committee member put in quickly, 'Shelve it after the first performance, as was done with many Beethoven and Mozart works!' In this afterthought there was a note of glee.

As the meeting broke up Walter took me aside and said, 'Well, Claire, now the responsibility is on your shoulders. It is due to your confidence in this young Schuman that we have been won over.'

The next season William Schuman's Third Quartet was played in Town Hall by the Coolidge Quartet. The Town Hall committee, as well as the general group of critics, seemed very pleased that this young man had been selected for the award.

A few years later Schuman was in the forefront of musical activities, not only as a composer whose works were being widely played but also because of the fact that he was Director of Publications of G. Schirmer and President of the Juilliard School of Music. I have never needed to explain since, who William Schuman is!

However, we still had not found a solution to one problem

of the commissions situation. The prestige of a performance had been a great morale builder, but it remained insufficient. The League's efforts in the early years to pay composers for commissioned works had brought in only an occasional money contribution. We were more and more aware of the real need for establishing a specific fund for commissions.

Meanwhile the League had strengthened its position in the musical history of this country by its sensational productions for music and stage, conducted by Leopold Stokowski, Pierre Monteux, Artur Rodzinski, Tullio Serafin, and others, and by bringing a public to New York from all parts of the country. Our quarterly magazine, *Modern Music*, through its articles which included critical analyses by eminent writers from many countries, had helped to establish a wide international prestige.

The spectacular American stage *premières* of works already renowned in European capitals, with a roster of great conductors and artists volunteering their services, had encouraged the so-called 'international set' of patrons and patronesses to sponsor a series of the League's galas at the Metropolitan Opera House. The list of 'names' was formidable — Aldrich, Alexandre, De Bravan, Crane, Gould, Harriman, Jennings, Kahn, Mesta, Pratt, Roosevelt, Taylor, Wilson, and many others, including a sprinkling of princesses and countesses led by Countess Marie Mercati. No wonder we concluded that the Metropolitan's Diamond Horseshoe was really interested in contemporary music! Would it not afford the opportunity to interest musical patrons in the economic plight of composers?

For these gala performances there was a festival program. We included in it a page headed 'The Composers' Fund.' It read in part,

> . . . to improve the situation of the composer, *the forgotten man of music*. The League of Composers has devised a plan for his benefit, the chief feature of which is the commissioning of new American works. At the same time it calls on other musical organizations throughout the United States to follow its example. For almost everyone working in the domain of

music there is more adequate recompense than for the composer. Therefore the League proposes to raise a fund with which to commission the works of composers. It also promises to have the commissioned works performed. Thus it can best serve the cause of the artist to which the League is dedicated — the composer of today.

We were keenly disappointed when not a single response came from any of the hundred-odd 'pillars of art,' although they had gladly spent $250 for a box from which to see and be seen for one evening. While Stokowski conducted a work by a living composer whose profession did not provide adequately for his needs, they seemed little aware of the composer as a fellow human being.

Many years later when we were planning the League's twenty-fifth anniversary observance, and again seeking a means of raising money to commission more works, I remembered the rueful comment which Walter Damrosch once made, *à propos* a music theme for the World's Fair in 1939.

A small group of us, serving on the World's Fair Music Committee, were asked to consider some music written by the late George Gershwin, since a few bars of music were needed for the opening of the exposition.

The price set by the Gershwin estate for eight or ten bars of music was $3000. The committee approved the music, but Dr. Damrosch shook his head when he heard the price, saying sadly, 'Beethoven never received any such money for any of his symphonic themes. How much easier it is for a composer of popular music to make money!' Many times that remark by Dr. Damrosch crossed my mind.

A few years later in an effort to find commissions for some anniversary works, I decided to write to Irving Berlin and Richard Rodgers. 'Will you commission a composer to do a work for our twenty-fifth anniversary celebration in 1948?' I asked, briefly outlining the problem which of course they well knew, namely the economic struggle of the composer writing for the concert hall.

Both accepted the suggestion and jointly commissioned Samuel Barber's Piano Sonata which Vladimir Horowitz has played repeatedly all over the world.

Since then Richard Rodgers and Oscar Hammerstein have given an annual commission through the League. Leon Kirschner (whose work was premiered by Dmitri Mitropoulos), Irving Fine, Aaron Copland, Henry Cowell, and Stefan Wolpe have been recipients of these commissions.

In all circumstances the League has always insisted that the composer should have full ownership of his work. This has been in contrast to a tempting proposition made by one organization, offering a large award for a new symphonic work, with the proviso that the composer then give up forever his right to the work!

In all fairness some of the League of Composers members advised their colleagues to 'beware of injustices'; in this way the group of composers, in a sense functioning as a protective guild or union, forced at least one unwise contest to be discontinued.

We have sometimes allocated the sole rights for a limited time to a specific artist or an ensemble. Such was the case when the Westminster Choir toured Europe and performed Harris' 'Song of Occupations.' For two years Ellabelle Davis had sole rights to Lukas Foss's 'Song of Songs' — which we commissioned through Louise Crane's co-operation — Ellabelle Davis sang this work with Koussevitzky and the Boston Symphony ten times in one season, also with European conductors and on broadcasts. In this case the work gained performance by a special kind of promotion.

Today the word 'commisson' brings to our minds a new development. For example, due to efforts of a former Mayor of Louisville, Kentucky, the Hon. Charles Farnsley, the sum of $800,000 was guaranteed — half of it pledged by a business committee, the other half donated by the Rockefeller Foundation — for the purpose of commissioning composers to write works for first performance by the Louisville Orchestra.

My belief has always been that commissioning works is a major form of benefit to composers. Unquestionably, excessive commissioning can, under certain conditions, have an unfortunate effect. Possibly the large number of Louisville commissions has produced more new works within a short space of time than could be absorbed by that orchestra's audience. One composer, a man of musical stature, who had just returned from hearing his *première* at Louisville, reported that only seventy-five people were in the concert hall. It left him with the impression that the subscribers of the Louisville Orchestra were suffering from musical indigestion, from hearing far too many new works in too short a time.

On the other hand, the commissioned works are being repeated three and four times by this orchestra; hence, even though the audiences may be small, a certain proportion may really study the works. In addition the works will become known through recordings and broadcasts. All in all, results are definitely 'plus,' with all honor to the former great Mayor of Louisville.

It will be unfortunate if, because of the 'first performance' vogue, more conductors do not avail themselves of 'second performance' opportunities from among these new symphonic works. A real need exists to support The Society for Second Performances, to constructively break down the 'world *première*' convention still stressed by too many. Various embryonic societies have attempted to help along little-known contemporary music — such as The Society for the Friendly Enemies of Music, and The Society of Unplayed Works — by taking their turn at trying to cause a stir in contemporary music circles. Even Walter Damrosch once organized 'Evenings of Pleasant and Unpleasant Music.' When he called on the audience to vote between pleasant and unpleasant, the procedure itself turned out to be decidedly unpleasant!

An ingenious idea was tried out recently by a society called The Creative Concerts Guild, in Boston. As a means of commissioning composers they set aside a portion of the price of each concert ticket, to create thereby a fund for new works. The theory of this group is that the average composer who is not renowned receives such small royalties, if any, for performance fees, that they do not even cover the average cost of his copying expenses. Therefore, if a fund will allow a certain percentage from box-office receipts for commissioning works, the public will know that the composer receives the same consideration as the performer on the program, the manager, and even the printer! This experiment may set an example for other musical organizations.

Another approach may be made with the co-operation of a group of conductors. I have recently written to ask five leading orchestra conductors, interested in contemporary music, if they would jointly commission one work, to be premiered in five cities during the same season; thus we might avoid that one world *première*, which so frequently prevents a second or third performance for a long period of time.

It is heartening to review some of the commissions, in addition to those of the League, that have been awarded in the past decade. Today there is a long list of commissions from the Koussevitzky Music Foundation. Others have come from the Alice M. Ditson Fund, Dumbarton Oaks (through Mr. and Mrs. Robert Woods Bliss), Lado, Inc., Samuel R. Rosenbaum, the National Federation of Music Clubs, the Paul Fromm Foundation, the Elizabeth Sprague Coolidge Foundation of the Library of Congress, the Edwin Franko Goldman Band, and the very generous Rockefeller Foundation with its grants both to the Louisville Orchestra and to the New York City Center of Music and Drama.

In its crusade the League has commissioned 110 works. In almost every case, we believe, they have been successful; first, in the creation of the work; second, in the performance, which has been by renowned artists. I recall only one instance that might be regarded as 'suspended animation.' A now renowned composer accepted a commission for an orchestral work. As he was in need of money at the time, he asked for payment in advance. This was not our usual procedure but I felt that we must make an exception in his case.

Some years passed and no composition was forthcoming.

One day recently I renewed my acquaintance with him on his return to New York after a long absence. In the course of conversation he remarked, a little timidly, 'I have not forgotten that I owe the League a work.'

'That,' I said, smiling, 'is rather an old situation now, isn't it?'

'Yes, it is,' he replied, 'but I do intend to write it. And,' he added cheerfully, 'I am going to dedicate it to you, Claire, for I have not forgotten the circumstances at all [although only he and I really remember this].'

'I shall feel greatly honored, naturally,' I said, for of course I appreciated the gesture of a composer who is now really distinguished. I hope — and I wonder — whether the work will be written in my lifetime!

Though many new avenues have opened up in the last two decades, particularly in the educational field, whereby the composer may gain a livelihood, even the renowned composer of concert music — as distinguished from popular music — can rarely make a good living if he must depend entirely upon royalties from performances of his work. Nevertheless the prestige of a commissioned work is an important tribute to the composer.

# 6

## Stravinsky and Schoenberg with Stokowski

WHEN LAZARE SAMINSKY, who was one of our directors, persuaded the League's board to allow him to stage his new one-act opera, *Gagliarda of a Merry Plague*, his eager suggestion was accepted only after long, embarrassing argument. At that time we were not geared to present works for the stage. On the other hand, except for seasonal presentations of *Pagliacci* and *Cavalleria Rusticana*, there were very few short operas in any repertory company in the United States. To add to opera literature a short contemporary work was a worthy ambition for any composer.

We had considered the possibility of staging Igor Stravinsky's *Histoire du Soldat* which we had presented in concert form. We could be sure that neither the Metropolitan nor the San Carlo Opera companies would be at all interested in collaborating on a Stravinsky opera, and in the 'twenties there were no opera workshops upon which to call for assistance. All in all, the problems of a stage work seemed far beyond the general resources of the League and the capabilities of the board.

Mr. Saminsky, a man of unbounded energy, however, finally won us over, or wore us down, with arguments that he would assume the complete responsibility of a production of *Gagliarda*.

78

We decided to include with it two important concert pieces for chamber orchestra.

Saminsky moved into an impressive 'high,' constituting himself a one-man producer, stage manager, director, property man, and general helper. He chose his cast, coached the singers, taught them how to act. One minute he would be coaching singers on stage, the next moment he had jumped into the pit and was conducting the orchestra. More than once as he executed the flying transition he lost his eyeglasses. At one rehearsal he demonstrated with an old pewter loving cup how an actress was to raise it; leaping back into the orchestra pit, in lieu of a baton, he conducted with it. He had persuaded a patroness of the League to lend him items from her collection of antique pewter and some Italian furniture from her drawing room. As a subtle means of beguiling singers and orchestra to work overtime — unions notwithstanding — this fairy godmother even brought hampers of sandwiches to rehearsals.

The best quip of that musical season resulted from a new percussion effect invented by Saminsky. At a foundry he purchased some heavy iron chains which the percussionist rattled in the opening bars of the overture. At the first rehearsal a violinist inquired in astonishment what the chains were for, because while taking his seat he had stumbled over them.

'They're to keep the music from skidding!' laughed a colleague, as the chains began to clang.

*Gagliarda* came off without any real mishaps, although the critics' acclaim and the public approval went chiefly to the two concert pieces: Louis Gruenberg's *Daniel Jazz,* and the second performance in the United States of Schoenberg's *Pierrot Lunaire.*

When the last pewter mug and the last piece of Italian furniture had been safely returned to the courageous patroness, we resolved firmly that we would not attempt any more stage presentations until we could achieve professional standards equal to those in our regular concerts. We put our little operatic experience behind us — but not, it turned out, for long.

A year later we launched another experiment with a stage production. This time the results were to bring us rewarding acclaim, both theatrically and musically. News had come from France of the world *première* of Manuel de Falla's marionette opera, *El Retablo de Maese Pedro,* which was presented in the private theater of the Princesse de Polignac in Paris. The work was dedicated to her.

The Princesse was the great friend of many of the contemporary composers in Europe, and a program in her home automatically gave great prestige since the musical elite always gathered there.

The beauty and originality of *El Retablo* invited repeat performances and they were given in many of the European capitals. We had read some of the ecstatic reviews and decided to give a concert version of the opera during our next season. As was soon to be proved, it was fortunate that I cabled to London to the publisher for the rights of performance.

It chanced that the great genius of the harpsichord, Wanda Landowska — of whom it is said that she plays the harpsichord better than anyone else plays anything — had asked me to come to see her. Mutual friends in Paris had suggested that she look me up.

In her apartment in a West 44th Street hotel, we chatted first about Paris, and what she referred to as 'a beautiful past.' She talked graphically about her recent dreadful experiences, when the Germans had absconded with her famous harpsichords and her great library of music. During the early days of Hitler's regime, emissaries had been sent to the musical afternoons at her home in St. Leu le Forêt; during the very concerts, the Germans made careful notes about the valuable treasures in her home. Then, one day when she was touring, they arrived with a truck, forced their way into the house, and made off with her instruments and books. Naturally, the little maid left in charge had been powerless to stop them.

Nevertheless, Landowska showed great resolution in her desire to forget past experiences and almost an impatience to immerse herself in a new life. 'I want to help the League of Composers,' she said firmly, 'so let's talk about de Falla's puppet opera which he gave in Paris last season. Can you get the material from Europe?'

I told her that I had an affirmation from the London publishers and that we expected to give a concert-version soon.

'You must do it with the puppets!' she cried; 'I'll help you.' Her confidence was contagious. 'I'll get a *big* conductor to do the opera with us,' she added, knowing well her own influence in the circle of great artists. And so at that moment Landowska became godmother for the American *première* of *El Retablo*. Without her I doubt if we could have found the endurance to work through the myriad difficulties that cropped up during the preparation.

The *big* conductor she first consulted was Leopold Stokowski, then director of the Philadelphia Orchestra. When he told her that he was very eager about this composition she sent me to see him, to work out plans in more detail.

My first talk with him led to an incidental impasse, but it also opened the way to many subsequent years of pleasant and successful collaboration.

We had made an appointment to meet at the home of a music patron, where he was staying temporarily. As I waited for him in a charming Victorian drawing-room, I amused myself by deciphering the scrawled autographs on photographs of the famed musicians which decorated the patron's piano. One got the impression that some conductors waved the autographing pen as though it were a baton.

At a slight sound I turned to find that Stokowski had entered the room so silently that I barely heard him. He made quite a picture, dressed in a magnificent Japanese kimono of deep blue, his bare feet thrust into native sandals. I had certainly not expected to meet him at four o'clock in the afternoon in such exotic attire. Actually it helped to put me at ease, forgetting for the moment the usual superbly tailored and dramatic figure of the podium whom I had always looked at with awe.

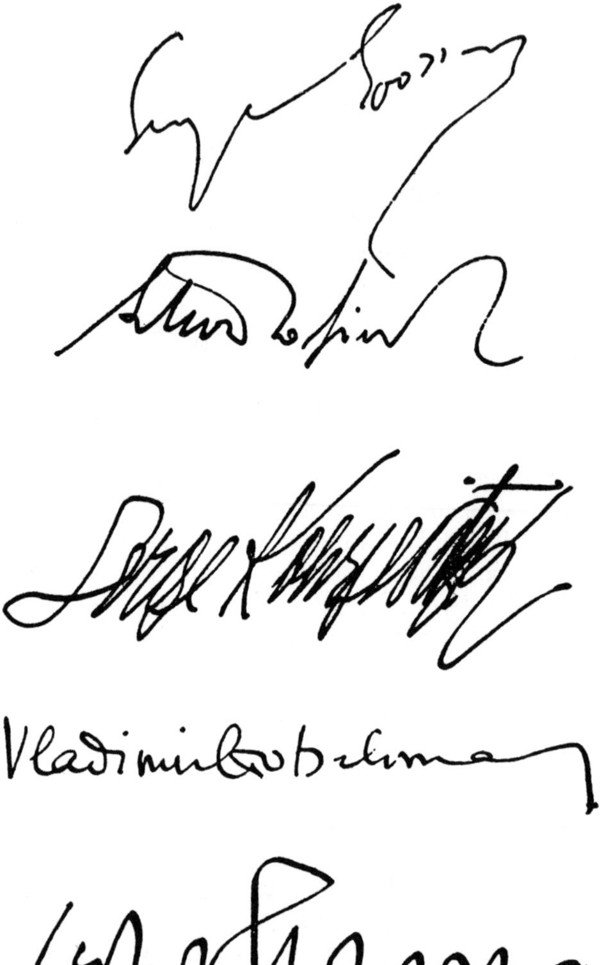

We plunged into a discussion of de Falla's opera. 'Have you secured performance rights from the publisher?' Stokowski demanded, for on such fundamentals he is completely the businessman.

'Yes I have,' I replied. 'I cabled London and have received their confirmation.'

'Will you then relinquish the rights and let me perform it with my friend Varèse's society, the International Composers' Guild?' he then said, to my utter amazement. At that time, in 1925, we were at the very height of rivalry between the League and the Guild, the two most active societies in New York for promoting contemporary music. For a moment I felt uncertain how to answer him.

'Madame Landowska has already begun helping the League to prepare the opera,' I said. 'I understand that she has talked to you about conducting it with us.'

'But I promised Varèse that I would do it with the Guild! Do let me have the rights to it!' Stokowski's tone was assured, almost a command.

Not at all, I thought obstinately. We had the performing rights; we had Landowska.

Yet this was the League's first contact with the great conductor. Our chances of co-operation with him hung in the balance. Could the immediate moment be waived for some larger future?

Involuntarily, I held my ground. Why should we concede, I asked myself. In our position, would Stokowski concede? I rose to go, saying pleasantly but noncommittally, 'Madame Landowska will call you.'

Landowska was furious at the outcome of this meeting. She made one more effort to win Stokowski over to our side. Then she approached Willem Mengelberg, the popular conductor of the New York Philharmonic Orchestra. He gladly accepted her invitation to direct the League's production of *El Retablo*, the following December, in Town Hall.

Although our problem regarding a conductor was ended, at

least for the time being, from that moment we headed toward all kinds of unpredictable problems.

The late Remo Bufano, a great artist and puppeteer, had agreed to carry out some of the ideas suggested by Landowska. She had played some of the music for him, and discussed the libretto while he made notes and drew sketches of the principal characters. The opera called for a theater within a theater, with some small marionettes of the usual size and four of the life-size to mime the vocal parts being sung by a group sitting in the orchestra pit. Bufano's life-size puppets were probably the first of their kind ever seen in the United States. Don Quixote, hero of the opera, was a dramatic looking figure seven feet tall, dressed in magnificent medieval costume. He and his companion, Sancho Panza, have since that time been exhibited in several museums.

Although the making of these large figures was not beyond Bufano's great skill and artistry, he little realized how difficult it would be to rehearse them. A studio was needed with sufficient height to allow for the necessary manipulation by the puppeteers working from a high bridge. None of us — not even Bufano — thought this problem through until the actual string-pulling of puppets began.

We kept moving the puppets from one studio to another, hopefully. At last we were offered an empty loft eighteen-feet high, in an old building on lower Fifth Avenue. It was six flights up. There was no elevator. The piano had to be hoisted up through a window.

We dragged Don Quixote and his co-actors up the stairs in sections, arms, legs, heads, bodies. I thought we must look like a troupe of medical students involved in a dissection, or maybe a cannibal gathering, on the way to a feast with their spoils.

Reassembled, the medieval hero, Quixote, Sancho Panza, Master Peter, and The Boy were rehearsed by puppeteers, who stood for hours at a time on ladders and dangerous temporary scaffolding while the pianist taught them the rhythms for the movements of the puppets.

One day Minna Lederman called me excitedly. 'I wish you

would get someone else to do this publicity-advisory job,' she cried; 'I can't go on letting Bufano call me at all hours of the night — and be blamed for a possible divorce!'

I'm afraid I laughed. That very morning I had had a similar frantic call from him, blaming me because his wife had moved out bag and baggage until the show was over. Poor Bufano! His nerves were frayed from the long difficult hours of rehearsal and from his determination to do a really masterful job with this difficult assignment.

Minna and I decided between us to keep out of Bufano's way until after the performance. His wife, too — a marvelous puppeteer and actually a tremendous help to him — saw that it was the better part of wisdom to just leave him alone during his trials with this brave marionette experiment.

With Mengelberg, Landowska, and several excellent singers, the opera was a delightful success. The musical achievement was overshadowed, however, by the sensational stage production. For the Town Hall stage, Bufano had designed a simple bridge, with side stairs; black-dominoed puppeteers, standing on the bridge to manipulate the life-size marionettes, were in full view of the audience. The stark primitive effect produced a form of puppet-opera startlingly new to patrons accustomed to the traditional Punch and Judy school. The interest in seeing the puppeteers in action intensified the dramatic experience for a majority in the audience. The great stage designer Robert Edmond Jones called it 'a landmark in stage production,' and said it was one of the most important experiments he had witnessed in the theater in this country. In the League we were so elated over the outcome of this unique venture that we decided to repeat *El Retablo* as soon as possible.

This time the renowned conductor, Pierre Monteux, then with the Boston Symphony Orchestra, volunteered to conduct, also asking us to include Stravinsky's *Histoire du Soldat* with stage.

We rented the Jolson — now the Century — Theatre. Here the puppeteers could be on a real theater bridge, above the eye-line of the audience. It was a more conventional arrangement, and a little easier for the puppeteers than the fragile make-shift in Town Hall.

In *Histoire du Soldat*, the role of The Reader called for an actor with good diction. Tom Powers, at that time a great favorite in the theatrical world, accepted our invitation to take part. Donald Oenslager, a young designer, imaginative and talented, volunteered to design the sets and costumes.

Mr. Powers had never been in any theatrical production in which a great conductor was the chief concern in all the preparations. Rehearsal arrangements were always planned to suit Pierre Monteux, and this finally put Mr. Powers' nose out of joint. Just before the dress rehearsal he decided to withdraw. After a lot of cajoling, in which Oenslager helped me, we convinced him that his beautiful diction was indispensable to the success of the work, even if the conductor did seem to be our first consideration. He stayed and added immeasurably to the evening's triumph.

We began to receive requests from other cities to send our productions out on the road. We felt excited to have set a new mark in the history of contemporary opera, but traveling with a show was very expensive. In consequence the most we could do was to loan the costumes in several cities where they gave *Histoire* with local groups. There were many demands for Bufano to present *El Retablo*, also; but again that was too costly to consider for it would have been necessary to travel with a group of trained puppeteers.

Stokowski did not forget our first talk in a patron's home, but evidently he carried no ill feeling. He wanted to conduct Stravinsky's *Les Noces* in a stage production, and was now ready to work with the League of Composers. The offers from Mengelberg, Monteux, and now Stokowski created great excitement at board meetings. The responsibility seemed to be chiefly on my shoulders for I owed it to these important symphony conductors to have all the 'wheels within wheels' rolling smoothly, especially in a theatrical production where each wheel contained many spokes. They were offering their precious time out of a personal belief in contemporary music, and the least I could do was to please them.

In anticipation of these stage performances, I had introduced to the conductors some of my young friends who were active in the theater, in the hope that they would prove acceptable as collaborators in our stimulating new ventures. All in all it was necessary for me to assume the self-confidence of a real impresario.

'I know all the musical geniuses,' Stokowski laughed, 'but I never have met the theater people.' Those days pre-dated his interest in Hollywood's pictures with music.

I began by introducing him to my most intimate friend in the world of the theater, who became the dean of stage design, Robert Edmond Jones. Bobby, as he was always called, found an immediate rapport with the impressive Stokowski.

'I'd love to do something with him,' said Bobby after their first meeting. 'We could do some beautiful things, have some wonderful times.' At the moment little did either of them dream how soon the 'beautiful things' would come into being.

Stokowski's wish to present, with stage, the great choreographic scenes of *Les Noces* was a fresh challenge to me. I was little prepared, however, for his next idea: to hire the Metropolitan Opera House!

'Nothing ventured, nothing gained!' I telephoned to Mrs. Otto H. Kahn, the vice-chairman of the League's auxiliary committee. We habitually distinguished this group by referring to them as 'The Ladies,' in contradistinction to 'The Women,' a name given to Minna Lederman and myself, two hard-working directors! I had won Mrs. Kahn's confidence by being able after our *première* of the de Falla opera to return the full one hundred per cent of underwriting raised by her and her circle of friends. This was in addition to the payment sent to the composer de Falla, which was twice the amount of royalties asked by his publisher.

Inasmuch as Otto H. Kahn was chairman of the board of the Metropolitan Opera, we were given the house at the minimum rent and the privilege of extra house-rehearsals. Mrs. Kahn even insisted that Edward Ziegler, assistant to Gatti-Casazza, the Metropolitan's famous director, let her oversee every one of our bills in that institution, from ticket printing to overtime for any union. Mrs. Kahn's profound love of art and music did not stand in the way of her being a keen business woman.

Thus we launched into a large-scale production, with Stokowski both conducting and directing *Les Noces*, which called for dancing, pantomime, singing, and a small ensemble of percussion instruments and four pianos.

Before the rehearsals began, each phase of the work was discussed and agreed upon by Stokowski and me, with the soloists and various departments.

Serge Soudeikine, who had recently achieved a great success with the décor for Stravinsky's ballet *Petrouchka*, was delighted to design the sets and costumes for this production. Sending me the drawings, he noted,

> The colors I have used are typical of the Slavic Russian peasant life, the colors of wood, wheat, clay, and flax, of beer and honey. There is also a feeling of the old Russian icons of Novgorod in abstract dynamic interpretation. My whole model is the type of wood sculpture that the Russian peasant can do with an axe; it is thus that I understand Stravinsky's music of *Les Noces*, which is based on the ancient Russian wedding ceremonies of the peasants.

Concealed in the pit with the orchestra were the soloists and a mixed chorus, whose vocal parts were interpreted on the stage by the dancers. Since the score called for four pianists, Stokowski was delighted when I told him that we had four composer-pianists who had volunteered to play. He felt that they would be particularly helpful in rehearsals. 'They will surely understand Stravinsky's music!' he said, with a meaning smile. Aaron Copland, Marc Blitzstein, Louis Gruenberg, and the late Frederick Jacobi were the four distinguished young composers; they attended every rehearsal faithfully, enjoying the new experience of being part of an orchestra under a great conductor.

Finding a place where we could have adequate rehearsals became a source of worry with every one of our productions. We needed a large space, we needed to rehearse for two months, and we could afford only a very modest rent. Our requirements now were even more difficult than when we had to find a loft to rehearse the marionettes. We could not hope to come easily by floor space for four grand pianos, instrumentalists, a chorus, soloists and fifty dancers. We had found our loft by laying our troubles on any shoulder that might be sympathetic, and we decided to do the same now. Signs of fanaticism within a group sometimes cause an infectious sympathy. Soon we had a small army of friends looking up real estate advertisements for us and scouting empty dance halls.

We were rescued through a friend, a trustee of the Young Men's Christian Association, who suddenly remembered that their Harlem branch, on 135th Street, could offer us space, free except for the cost of light and janitor service.

Mr. Stokowski came over from Philadelphia for the first rehearsal, and I decided to call for him at Pennsylvania Station. As I drove him up to 135th Street, I deliberately made a little speech of apology for taking him such a distance, but he was absorbed with our many rehearsal plans and little concerned about distances. This was his first experience with music and stage and every detail excited him. He kept up a running flurry of questions, too fast for me to answer. 'Have you seen the designs for the costumes? Do you think we have got a good group of dancers? Did you receive my sketch about the placing of the pianos?' Quickly I put in the answer to the last one, 'Yes, I gave your floor plan for the four pianos to the janitor, with instructions that he *must* follow it.'

As we entered the rehearsal room, Stokowski took one look at the pianos and cried, 'This is not what I sketched! I particularly don't want the pianists facing one another.' My heart sank. I had been especially anxious that everything about the first rehearsal should run smoothly. I realized that I must have expected too much of the janitor. Why should he know the difference between two ends of a piano?

I started for the door to find a strong man to help us move pianos. But Stokowski was ahead of me. He had stripped off his overcoat and jacket, and, in his characteristic Stokowski-blue shirtsleeves, was already rolling the pianos around the room in accordance with his own ideas.

That small incident augured well for the way we were going to work together, and it proved so. In all our stage ventures there was never a moment when he would hesitate to share in the labor that a stage production inevitably demanded; nothing was too much for him to do.

In those days, Stokowski was one of the few conductors who felt that an artistic production demanded a true synthesis of music and light. At the very first rehearsal, in the Metropolitan Opera House, a tug of war began between Soudeikine and Stokowski. 'We must co-ordinate our lighting with the development of the music,' Stokowski announced as he prepared to conduct the rehearsal.

With a wry smile, Soudeikine said firmly, 'I like my work to show off my sets and their costumes to the best advantage.' He was an old hand in the theater, but he did not realize that Stokowski had been giving thought to every stage detail, especially the synchronization of light with the music. Stokowski had been one of the few symphonic conductors who had been interested in some earlier concert experiments with a light organ — the Wilfrid — and music; it was natural to him to use light now as a factor in his musical interpretation of *Les Noces*.

'You know I don't agree with you about how we are to light this show,' Soudeikine blurted out in a sulky tone at the end of that first rehearsal. 'Unless we bring in some extra electrical equipment neither of us is going to be satisfied; the old-fashioned stuff that is here is absolutely insufficient.'

Consequently we had to put in additional and costly lighting material. Presumably it should have pleased both stage designer and conductor. Actually Stokowski and Soudeikine never did reach a happy rapport. The Metropolitan's stage electrician, accustomed only to the most conventional standards for 'spots on' and 'spots off' was visibly annoyed and quite unable to understand what all the argument was about. 'These big artists' ideas!' he kept muttering, shaking his head.

'Will you keep a record of all our problems?' Stokowski asked me one day, soon after that rehearsal. 'That way we will remember all the things we must improve in the future.' I agreed but, in fact, his memory for meticulous detail was better than any filing system. A year later, for our second production at the Metropolitan, he had the forethought to put his associate conductor, Alexander Smallens, into the booth with the house electrician. Smallens kept the score in his hand and directed the electrician, following the schedule of lighting which, this time, Robert Edmond Jones and Stokowski had carefully synchronized for the music and stage action.

Stokowski's ingenious idea for controlling a stage electrician should have become a tradition for lighting rehearsals; it would have saved many hours in ensuing years. Recently a famous Metropolitan Opera singer told me that, in a rehearsal of *Otello* he had been obliged to repeat a bar eighteen times, because the electrician (very likely tone-deaf) failed to throw the spotlight on him at the important moment of his high note.

As *Les Noces* would not fill an entire evening, we decided to contrast this work with a one-act opera by Claudio Monteverdi. *Il Combattimente di Tancredi e di Clorinda* had just been produced very successfully at Smith College under the direction of Werner Josten, a composer and professor of music at the college. This seventeenth-century opera, followed by a contemporary composition, afforded a happy contrast, dramatically and musically, and added great distinction to the evening.

For the Monteverdi production we were forced to omit a bit of stage realism, thereby avoiding a possible catastrophe. Since *Il Combattimente* called for a white horse on the stage, we hired one from a Seventh Avenue riding academy. At the rehearsal, as the horse was led in, he developed stage fright which took the form of mild blind staggers; he broke a piece of scenery and caused consternation to everyone on the stage and in the orchestra pit. It was all too evident that the horse lacked the training necessary for theatrical appearances.

We inquired of one of the opera staff about a certain well-behaved brown horse, recently seen in *Gotterdammerung* but were told that, with the close of the regular opera season, the horse had gone to pasture on Otto H. Kahn's Long Island estate. Notwithstanding Mrs. Kahn's keen interest in our work, we did not like to ask her to interrupt the vacation of Brunnhilde's horse. In consequence we omitted the equestrian scene in Monteverdi's opera.

Early in the fall of 1929 I went again to see Arthur Judson, to tell him that Stokowski wanted to co-operate with the League in another program. This time he expected to use the full Philadelphia Orchestra.

As I outlined the new plans for three performances in Philadelphia and two in New York City, I noticed Mr. Judson's expression growing tense and obstinate. In those days his genius as a manager was opposed to new music.

'And what works has Mr. Stokowski in mind to give us?' he asked in a decidedly irritated tone of voice. Resolved to get the agony over with as quickly as possible, I said enthusiastically, 'He wants to conduct Stravinsky's *Sacre du Printemps*' — then I added a real body blow — 'and Schoenberg's *Die Glückliche Hand.*'

'Why, Mrs. Reis,' Judson muttered, 'you cannot possibly think that you could fill the Metropolitan Opera House with that program!' His expression was growing more tense, more obstinate.

'Of course we can!' I replied, holding my ground. I, too, was feeling a rise in pulse. 'When we had so much success with *Les Noces* how much more can we have with *Le Sacre* and the full Philadelphia Orchestra and a Schoenberg opera. At any rate, the League is ready to take the responsibility for the complete stage décor, and present the two works to the Philadelphia Orchestra subscribers both in New York and Philadelphia. In return, the orchestra must play for the League on one of the New York evenings, so that we may run a benefit and repay the cost of these stage productions.'

'Well,' said Mr. Judson, putting his fist on his desk in a determined gesture, 'this Stokowski notion cannot be considered without special permission from the board of directors of the Philadelphia Orchestra Association.' I knew from his scowl and sharp tone that he was remembering frequent arguments in the past between the conductor and himself on the subject of contemporary music. I could see his mind wandering into the political realms of an orchestra meeting, so I rose to go. Stokowski and he would have to battle out the next round.

As we got to the door, Mr. Judson made one more attempt to deflect me from this reckless undertaking. 'Mrs. Reis,' he said, and his voice was more subdued, 'you will really have all my sympathy if you insist on carrying out this program.' I thanked him for his concern, replying, 'I personally find these difficult programs, with stage, a great challenge.' I relayed to Stokowski the gist of the interview with Mr. Judson. Within a week I had a message from Philadelphia, saying that the board of directors had agreed to co-operate with us in the new venture for the coming season.

We felt, as did Stokowski, that this double bill of stage *premières* by Stravinsky and Schoenberg made an exciting program. But for Mr. Judson the names of two of the greatest living composers held no magic; to him they were just two modern composers. Our League directors were convinced, even though we had already presented the *Histoire du Soldat* and *Les Noces* of Stravinsky, that his now-famed *Sacre du Printemps* evoked more interest in the United States at this time than operas or ballets by other eminent composers, and therefore it should be on our next stage bill.

In 1924 an unusually distinguished gathering of artists, musicians, painters, and writers filled Carnegie Hall, coming to hear the concert *première* in New York of the *Sacre*, with Pierre Monteux conducting. He had directed both the Paris and the London *premières*, where public and critics ranged between eloquent praise and tumultuous denunciation. Ten years had now passed since the European *premières*, and in Carnegie Hall an excited public waited with eagerness to hear a work that had a history of having caused not only many conflicting opinions but also actual public disturbances.

As Monteux put down his baton, the reception in Carnegie Hall was distinctly enthusiastic; applause was prolonged. As a concert piece the *Sacre* had made a profound impression, but one without the violent reactions which had made musical history in 1913.

Long after the concert was over, I noticed that the lobby remained crowded; people did not seem to want to go home, but stood around in small groups, discussing the concert and reviving stories about the Paris *première*. At the Théâtre des Champs Elysées opening, it had been virtually howled off the stage, a circumstance so upsetting to the genius of three men — composer, dancer, and producer, Stravinsky, Nijinsky, and Diaghilev — that they escaped in a carriage to the woods of the Bois where they drove around furiously all night to quiet their frayed nerves. Time has abundantly proven their faith. The well-known English musicologist, Cecil Gray, among many others has said, 'Whatever one's personal reactions may be to the *Sacre du Printemps* there is no denying the fact that it is one of the most conspicuous landmarks in the artistic life of our period.' [1]

The time seemed to be ripe in 1930 for Stokowski and the League to produce the ballet which had made history seventeen years earlier. It had been a serious problem to find a short work to precede the *Sacre*. After long consideration Stokowski agreed with us that Schoenberg's *Die Glückliche Hand* (called 'The Hand of Fate') was an appropriate choice for the curtain-raiser.

---

1. Cecil Gray, *Predicaments*, Oxford University Press, Inc., New York, 1936.

This opera called for a pantomime with mimes or dancers. The chorus sat in the orchestra pit, interpreting the admonitory chant and, by whisper, the story of three people and a chimera. Robert Edmond Jones designed a gigantic bat for the embodiment of the chimera; great shadows of his wings, magnified on the wall through Jones' expert lighting, produced a fantastic effect.

I had asked Rouben Mamoulian to be stage director. He had produced operas for the American Opera Company and had a great interest in music; his stage direction of Gershwin's *Porgy and Bess* added greatly to its initial success.

The difficult Schoenberg music became a challenge to Mamoulian and he spent hours of intensive work, planning the pantomime. After a succession of attempts he would change his ideas and begin all over again.

One day he called me on the telephone, 'Say, Claire, what is this thing you've given me?'

'Why Rouben, it's a Schoenberg opera,' I said; 'what did you think it was?' I felt somewhat on the defensive.

'Well, frankly I'm puzzled,' he replied. 'However, it's not going to beat me — or Bobby either — even if we have to work at it every night, all night. But I can tell you — it's not an opera, it's a whimsey!' He gave a roar of laughter and rang off. At least I knew they were taking their puzzling assignment cheerfully, and I felt that both would finally come through.

They did achieve a very 'eerie whimsey,' with Jones's angular sets and macabre lighting, added to Mamoulian's conception of mysterious, gliding movements, carefully mimed by Doris Humphrey, Charles Weidman, and Olin Howland. I have heard musicians say that Schoenberg considered this opera a musical idea of a spiritual experience 'materialized through the medium of the stage.' To all of us involved in the production, it remained, as Mamoulian had described it, a 'whimsey.'

The Stravinsky ballet called for a production on a much larger scale; some of the problems were even more difficult. Nicholas Roerich, to whom the ballet was dedicated, had created the original décor and costumes in Paris. Roerich was a painter, with an absorbing interest in the patriarchal and religious life of early Russia. It is generally believed that his mysticism gave Stravinsky the idea of 'reconstructing the mysterious past' in a ballet free of any traces of a European civilization for background.

Roerich had arrived in New York recently, after living in Tibet for many years. I went to see him to enlist his interest in our plans, as Stokowski had suggested that we ask him to re-create the décor for our production of the *Sacre*.

I found him at the Master Institute of Arts, where he had accepted a position in an advisory capacity. Professor Roerich (as he was introduced) sat behind a large bare desk in an enormous empty room. My immediate impression was that his face was more like a death mask than a living countenance. His domed skull, the waxen color of his skin, the slanting eyes and pointed beard, suggested a world very foreign to our Western hemisphere. I wondered why he had forsaken a mysterious life in the Himalayas to adapt himself to a desk position in a cosmopolitan whirlpool of institutional activities.

As the secretary ushered me in and introduced me to 'The Master,' I felt confused but challenged by this esoteric personality who seemed to have absorbed so many of the qualities of the East. (I later discovered that people used this second title in speaking about him.)

I unfolded the purpose of my visit, and as I talked about our plans to give *Sacre du Printemps* his expression seemed to lose a little of the faraway, forbidding quality that had disturbed me.

'Thank you for bringing me Mr. Stokowski's greetings,' were his opening words after a really long silence following my remarks. Then, weighing each word, he added, 'Yes, I will be glad to do the stage décor for this production, and particularly to work with Stokowski.' I left him feeling that to accomplish my purpose I had somehow traveled to a far country.

As Leonide Massine had been associated with the original Diaghilev productions, we asked him to join our group of artists and to undertake the choreography for this ballet which he knew so well. He was delighted and met with Stokowski, Roerich, and myself to discuss a dancer for the important role of The Chosen One, otherwise known as The Sacrificial Maiden. We decided that day to ask the courageous young dancer, Martha Graham, to take the part of the maiden who is sacrificed as a consecration to The Spring.

With the first rehearsal our tug of war began. It was only natural that Stokowski should intend the choreography to be correlated with his interpretation of the music. Although Nijinsky had created the original choreography, Massine told us *his* interpretation was subsequently used. He had assembled a group of dancers for us from the *corps de ballet* at the Roxy Theater, where he was carrying on some of the tradition of the great Russian school of the dance. Massine felt that the *Sacre* choreography belonged completely to his province. In this counterpoint of individual aspiration emerged an unexpected force, Martha Graham, the solo dancer. At this time she was little known; she had not yet taken part in any great ballet. Nevertheless she was already a great personality, with her own style of dancing and thinking. Even in this new role she felt the need of giving her own ideas.

The atmosphere of the early rehearsals became tense. Stokowski would walk over to the pianist and suggest slower tempi. Massine would then step before his dance groups and say, 'No, Mr. Stokowski, I must have the dancers move faster, like this,' and he would illustrate with his lithe body what he wanted. Martha Graham struggled meanwhile, not only with a new experience but also with the problem of submitting her will to that of another choreographer from a very different school. She felt strongly that, in her solo role, she must interpret her part as her individuality demanded.

Stokowski threw her an occasional encouraging remark, 'I like that part of your dance. It is true to Stravinsky's music.' Then he would walk back to the corner of the rehearsal hall where he and I often sat as observers and critics, and he would continue to discuss the point he had made, which, naturally, was always based on the musical interpretation as he felt it.

As rehearsals progressed the three individualistic artists frequently fought bitterly. Each had a particular message; each wanted to give his interpretation to a great work; yet the three were faced with the problem of finding some means of correlating their important contributions.

Martha's friend and colleague, Agnes de Mille, described a scene she witnessed at one of these rehearsals.

> I saw Martha Graham only once in one of her alerted moods . . . working under the direction of Massine in the *Sacre du Printemps* . . . they achieved a really splendid clashing of wills. He accused her of stubbornly refusing to do anything he asked; she claimed he asked her to do what was outside her technical abilities. . . . She had resigned twice before they got the curtain up.[2]

'You must dance for *me*,' Stokowski telephoned to Martha one day when she was suffering from a real hysteria after a Massine-Graham battle for supremacy. The intimate tone in Stokowski's voice calmed her. From then on, Massine turned his back on her at rehearsals, refusing to look at what she was doing in her solo dance.

As the work began to achieve a real unity the tensions subsided. Temperamental differences of three great individualists had been submerged; in their genuine pleasure in bringing out a great work, each had contributed to a truly harmonious interpretation. When it was all over Martha said to Agnes de Mille, 'I wouldn't have gotten out for anything in the world. I think Massine hoped I would. Of course I had to resign repeatedly. . . . Oh but I was angry! I strode up and down and lashed my tail!'[3]

In the *Sacre* — the pictures of pagan Russia — the costumes

2. Agnes de Mille, *Dance to The Piper*, Atlantic-Little, Brown and Company, Boston, 1952.
3. Ibid.

designed by Roerich emphasized motifs found among primitive peoples everywhere, from natives of Tibet to Indian pueblos in North America. He wanted to accentuate universal rather than narrowly Russian characteristics in his design, in keeping with the composer's idea regarding the abstract nature of the music. Roerich carried out Stravinsky's ideas for the set, retaining his theory that the rites of the consecration to The Spring were indefinite in point of time and place.

There was a last-minute uproar between Stokowski, with the dancers, and Massine. It came at the dress rehearsal and concerned the length of the women's skirts. No one had any historical data about 'universal' peasant skirts; to most of us they did look clumsy about the ankles. Fortunately, Roerich did not attend this rehearsal, so there was one less to join in the argument. As a result of the unvarying Stokowski technique for getting things done quickly, a carton of large safety pins suddenly arrived on the scene; all hands began pinning up the dancers' skirts. As leader of this bit of emergency restyling, even Stokowski did his share of pinning-up!

The five performances went off with great flair, both in Philadelphia and New York. In front of the curtain, no one would have suspected that there had been so many arguments, so many lacerated feelings in the preparation of this production. Thanks to the artists' all-important sense of 'face,' the ruffled feelings had been smoothed out: Massine's, Graham's, even the electrician's!

As the curtain fell on *Le Sacre du Printemps*, I hurried with my husband, Arthur Jr., and Hilda to see Stokowski. Invariably after his symphonic concerts, he rushed away in order to escape the 'green room dowagers'; on this occasion he was in no hurry, however, and we found him in the green room, excited and happy, glad to stay and chat with all comers.

My husband, Arthur, and Stokowski had fallen into a friendship which reminded me of what Jean Sibelius once said, when he was asked how he could enjoy spending so much time with businessmen. 'When I am with musicians,' he said, 'they only want to talk about their financial troubles. But when I chat with men in business they like to talk about the arts.'

I thanked Stokowski again, saying, 'There seemed to be something electric in the air tonight. It was a marvelous evening, better than all the rehearsals put together.'

'I knew it would be,' he said; 'I always know when a work is going to go well — I have a feeling about it ahead of time.'

The day before the *première* in Philadelphia (preceding the New York performance), I had talked with Bobby Jones about our struggles with obstacles which seemed to bedevil work in the theater. I wondered if the fact that so many artists were involved had made our productions particularly vulnerable. 'It has taken us so long to prepare,' I said, 'yet now, with the opening so near at hand, I have the most awful sinking moments.'

'Why should you?' said Bobby encouragingly. We had been close friends ever since his Harvard days; admiration for each other's capacities made a sympathetic bond in our work together.

'Has it occurred to you, Bobby, that only one of each of you is carrying out this Stravinsky-Schoenberg double bill — one Stokowski, one Graham, one Massine, one Bobby Jones, one Mamoulian — and each of you is absolutely vital to the production. What would happen if any of you fell by the wayside at this time. That's what I ask myself when I wake up worrying in the night! We can*not* have any last-minute substitutions!'

Bobby had lived through many a crisis in the theater. In his early days he had rescued a play by himself, sewing up the heroine's costume at the eleventh hour! He was such a kindly, assured person that even the stagehands had thanked me for the opportunity of working under him.

'In the theater,' he replied, in that deep tone he used when talking out of his vast technical experience, 'in our show business there is a fundamental belief that one may die a thousand deaths in the preparation of a production but that the night of the show, when the curtain goes up, everyone is right there, everyone is right on the job.'

A year later Stokowski, Jones, and I were talking over the forthcoming production of Prokofieff's ballet *Pas d'Acier* and Stravinsky's *Oedipus Rex*, another double bill by two of the important composers of this century. We had finished our various criticisms of recent rehearsals — a frank chat always was part of our work together — and were relaxing, sitting out cn the terrace of Stokowski's 88th Street apartment. For the new production we had another large roster of artists, each an individual of great stature. I recalled to Bobby the bit of theater philosophy he had imparted to me a year ago. Yet, personally I was beginning to worry again. 'Now we're embarked on another enormous undertaking,' I said,' and again there can be no substitutes, none for you, Leopold, nor for you, Bobby.'

'Let me tell you my theory about our theater,' Stokowski said with a slightly mystical air. 'I interpret our situation this way' — he spread his hands in a 'who knows?' gesture. 'You, and you,' he said, pointing to Bobby and me, 'and I, and all our artists are working together in these enormously difficult works because we want to do so. There is a collective will among us. It holds the work together. Therefore *no one* will fail in his *task*.' There was a great conclusiveness in his manner and his words.

Of course he was right. I came to see how right both he and Bobby had been. When the curtain rose every artist was *right there*.

# 7

## Opinions and Contradictions

ONE DAY as I sat in Olin Downes's West 57th Street house discussing with him the fortunes of the League of Composers, I said, 'You know, we feel that your generous Sunday articles in *The New York Times* about our various undertakings have greatly helped us, over the years.' I had with me a batch of reprints which I showed him, saying, 'Did you know we had made these? We've sent them all over the country.'

He leafed through them; there were such headings as *The Avant Garde; New Works Commissioned by League; Composers Group Plans Twentieth Year; League of Composers Plans To Help an American Lyric Theater.* 'Well, Claire,' he remarked with a grin, 'if all this which I wrote has helped the League to grow, I'm glad because I believe in it. But I must tell you now, I swore many a time after those early concerts that I'd never come to hear another such program of . . .' — he made a little grimace — 'I think what I called it was *unmitigated tonal asperity!*' We laughed together at what a critic had often found bitter medicine in doing his job.

'Even so, you did come again,' I said, smiling at him.

'Yes,' he replied frankly, 'somehow there always was something which drew me back one more time. I became convinced — slowly — of new and important music-in-the-making.'

'Admit it now, though, Olin, in the 'twenties you and a few other critics practically competed with each other to see who could write the most disparagingly humorous review for Monday's paper about those Sunday concerts at the Klaw Theater! All of you threw the word "cacophony" about. And I remember the music of one program being compared to "Broadway taxi-toots"!'

'Remember my using the phrase "sonorous acerbities" — or was it "acerbic sonorities"? However, this is today. Tell me, what do you want me to do now for the League?'

'Well, next week we're meeting at Mrs. Myron Taylor's house to talk about plans for the twentieth anniversary, this coming season. If you would just come and tell them why you have believed in the League all these years, even when others described it as "a queer little bubble on this planet, run by a futurist gang," I think it would lend weight to our plans.'

The gathering typified faith in important quarters in the cause of the living composer. Our own directors, and composer-members of the national committee, were joined by such loyal friends as Countess Mercati, Mrs. W. Murray Crane, Mrs. John Rogers, Jr., and Mrs. Kenneth Simpson. Like many, they had not always liked the music on our programs, but they had been staunch in supporting our objective to have it heard.

Olin complied with our request to speak. He said in part, 'When a comparatively small percentage of new ideas in music were at work in this city, no single organization did more to keep things going than the League of Composers, with its concerts and stage productions, its magazine and varied other activities. It upheld the most forward attitude, the most productive principles, of any of the established musical institutions here. No musical enterprise is more essential, more worthy of your sustained support.' He went on to say that, if critics treated the early concerts as though they were attending a circus, if a little later they grew irritable at hearing so many dissonances, eventually all of them had come around to giving the League's programs serious consideration. There was an outburst of laughter when he ended by saying, 'A famous critic I once knew in Berlin told me that when he had heard a new work by Schoenberg, he had said "if this is the music of the future, then I pray my Creator not to let me live to hear it again"; I confess that in the early days of the League I was tempted to give a similar prayer.'

Naturally, critics loomed very large in the life of the League; to a certain extent our very continuance depended on them. Some critics adopted the double function of reporter and analyst. We regard the reporter as being responsible solely for setting down what he sees without interpretation. The analyst functions in deeper waters. He may not be infallible by all standards, but he must be able to discern objectively the crossing of mind with mind, and conscientiously make his analysis not only critical but also constructive.

Virgil Thomson holds that 'a critic's review is itself a public performance; its aim is to instruct and to convince the whole body of its readers. . . the case of constructive versus destructive criticism is not (primarily) one either of aiding or injuring the artist in his career or in his knowledge of himself; it is one of aiding the public to digest music.'

Another critic, Alfred Frankenstein, believes that 'it is the function of criticism to close the gap between the accomplishment of the creative personality, and the willingness or ability of the contemporary public to accept his work. It is the function of criticism . . . to bring the artist and his audience closer and more quickly together.' Frankenstein adds that perhaps the critic should always be under forty years of age, as after that he loses 'the perennial curiosity which he needs in order to know what is going on!'

Perhaps the concertgoer must to some degree share the responsibility of premature — one might almost say undigested — reviews. The majority in any audience feels unsure of its own reactions and, seeking to be reassured or enlightened or both, wants without delay to read an authoritative opinion. By definition this puts the critic under pressure. Granting that he is not concerned with merely making the artist feel pleased (or, contrariwise, concerned with prodding the concert manager's ulcer!), then, in order to write an opinion on which the public may safely rely, he ought at least to have time for considered judgment and reflection. How else can the opinion crystallize which will serve all concerned: the composer, the interpretive artist, and the public?

An example of a critic who arbitrarily took time for study and reflection before rendering judgment was the leading critic of the New York *Tribune* in the 'twenties, Lawrence Gilman. Perhaps in a certain sense he was emulating the famous Hanslick. At any rate, before an important *première* Mr. Gilman liked to study new scores at home and would often ask us to send music to him. In the case of Hanslick, days often passed between the performance and the publishing of his criticism.

It is certainly true that the task of reviewing concerts, especially at the height of the music season, overcrowds the schedules of critics. On the other hand, when the League's twentieth anniversary was marked by a program of world *premières* at Town Hall, including works by Copland, Jacobi, Milhaud, and Piston, one first-string critic overlooked the event altogether. One wondered if 'perennial curiosity' had at last failed him.

Even though the public tends to want its mind made up overnight about a new work, should the critic be forced on the basis of only one brief performance to render what may then amount to a superficial judgment? Time frequently changes, modifies, or seasons opinions, even though meanwhile the artist may have died of overexposure to virulence!

Nicholas Slonimsky, in his *Lexicon of Musical Invectives*,[1] presents a bitterly amusing, certainly startling, index of 'Vituperative, Perjorative and Deprecatory Words and Phrases' employed by critics with reference to many works that today are recognized as classics. For example: in 1907, Schlemuller, a famous critic, wrote in a Berlin publication, 'Debussy's score of *Pelléas et Mélisande* resembles . . . a gallery of harmonized

---

1. Coleman-Ross Company, Inc., New York, 1953.

abortions.' In 1879, the Boston *Gazette* wrote of Bizet's *Carmen*
— 'Of melody, as the term is generally understood there is but
little.' As recently as 1932 a review in the *American Mercury*
of Ravel's 'Bolero' described it as 'a tune little removed from
the wail of an obstreperous back-alley cat.' These blunt asper-
sions lend some point to the late Percy Hammond's description
of the drama critic in which he said, 'I would define his criticism as venom from a contented rattlesnake.' On more than one
occasion, a critic and his venom have been brought into court.
Forty-eight members of a cast that performed *Rigoletto* in Vienna descended on the courts en masse to get a judge to say
whether the music critic had libeled them when he said that
their singing 'sounded like a bunch of miniature pinschers [a
species of small, sharp-voiced dog].'

The question is, does a critic really believe himself to be a
'do-gooder' when he waxes almost sadistic in describing a performance he has disliked? I once heard a critic say, with a wry
laugh, 'We have to stir up these conductors or else they get so
bored!' This was after a performance of which he wrote,

> The conductor did everything to the orchestra but conduct
> it. He whipped it up as if it were a cake, kneaded it like bread,
> shuffled and riffled an imaginary deck of cards, wound up a
> clock, shook a recalcitrant umbrella, rubbed something on a
> washboard, and wrung it out. There were very few moments
> when a film taken of the conductor alone, without sound,
> would have given any clue to the fact that he was directing a
> musical composition.

Roger Sessions says in *The Musical Experience of Composer,
Performer, Listener*,

> [There is danger of] producing a type of artistic culture in
> which the critic rather than the productive artist is the central
> figure. The danger . . . that we allow ourselves to cultivate
> . . . a predominantly critical attitude toward art in preced-
> ence over a *love* for it . . . that we make judgment an end
> in itself instead of the natural and full-grown by-product of a
> total artistic experience.

How well Rainer Maria Rilke, the Prague-born poet, summed up this attitude when he wrote 'Works of art are of an infinite loneliness . . . only love can grasp, and hold, and fairly judge them.'

A composer who has been subjected to omission of his name on a program or newspaper release considers this as disparaging as a severe criticism. For many years I watched the announcements and the reviews of dance programs. In some instances everyone taking part in the performance got his name in the newspaper, except the composer of the music! For example, reviewing a new ballet, a dance critic praised the dancer's talent, the choreographer's ingenuity, the dance group's co-ordination, the designer's costumes, even the expert lighting. All were mentioned, yet I looked in vain for the name of the composer who wrote the score!

I began a new crusade, a sort of game of 'Find the Composer!' The first time I tried it out was in connection with a work produced by Valerie Bettis, in which she danced with a company of actor-dancers. The title of it was *As I Lay Dying*. A critic wrote of it, 'It is a creation which uses dance movements, acting, speech, music and poetry-like composition.' The review even mentioned the title of the novel from which the ballet synopsis had been drawn. But the mystery remained; who was the composer? The implication was that nobody cared.

I continued my game. In a New York newspaper an announcement of Ballet Theater for March 1951 scheduled eight novelties. Each ballet had a given title, choreographer, company artists, and guest artists, all of whom were named. The only mention of music was 'A ballet, with Brahms Variations.' Aaron Copland's music for *Rodeo* was passed over as Agnes de Mille's *Rodeo!* Copland's name was not to be found.

I had to stop playing my game; my blood pressure protested. I could only hope that some day a composers' union, a real guild of composers, would rise to serve such issues.

Happily at the present time, dance critics are more conscien-

tious in their reviewing, rarely failing to acknowledge the work
of composers.

The wrong kind of publicity, however, can have as serious an
effect on a man's career as no publicity at all. A case in point is
the American *première* of George Antheil's *Ballet Mécanique*.

A book publisher, who had met Antheil in Paris, decided to
present this new ballet at Carnegie Hall; he would create a stir
in the musical world by being the patron of this novel composition.

I called on the publisher, to ask him to allow the League of
Composers to co-operate with him, perhaps bringing thereby a
certain musical distinction to the event, since he was quite unknown in musical circles.

'The League is not necessary,' the publisher replied curtly.
'This will be entirely my affair.'

What was planned was more a circus than a concert. Sensational advance publicity attracted a curious public. Claques
had been drilled to tie handkerchiefs on the end of walking
sticks and wave them in the air. As men wore hats in those days,
the claque practiced throwing their hats up to the ceiling,
boomerang-wise, catching them again if possible. When the performance ended the instructions were faithfully carried out.

The result was a musical fiasco. Antheil wrote me years later,

> It was one of the most dreadful disasters of my life when I
> made the error — for which I have paid most dearly and for
> twenty-seven years of my creative life — of choosing that
> dreadful publisher instead of the League of Composers for
> the first performance in New York in 1927 of my *Ballet
> Mécanique*. I was young and stupid; also, at that time, I had
> been living in Paris for some years, and did not know the
> situation too well, nor what I was walking into. I regret it
> with all my heart.

This music was played again in 1954, at the Composers'
Forum in the McMillin Theatre of Columbia University. Thirty
years earlier Ezra Pound had cried out in Paris, 'Silence, im-
beciles!' when there were mild riots by Parisians in the hall.

This time, in New York, there was a three-minute ovation for the composer.

For some time I had been troubled about the reviews of the stage productions directed by Stokowski for the League at the Metropolitan Opera House. As great artists of the theater worked with him — men like Robert Edmond Jones, Rouben Mamoulian, Lee Simonson, and Donald Oenslager, bringing out new décor, new lighting methods, new stage direction such as had never been seen on the Metropolitan stage — it seemed to me important that the productions be reviewed from the dramatic as well as musical standpoint. Indeed, drama critics were asking us to allow them to review the performances.

For many years Arthur Hays Sulzberger, president of *The New York Times*, had been a friend of ours. I knew him as a man of liberal mind and went to see him, to discuss the possibility of assigning two critics, from both Music and Drama departments, to cover our productions.

'I'm quite agreeable to your idea, Claire,' he said, 'so long as you can get the music and drama critics to divide the material between them.'

'That might not be so simple.' I asked him, 'How do you think I should go about it?'

'Well, since you know Downes well, why not talk it over with him? Then talk to the critics on the other papers, too. Perhaps they'll all take to the idea of dual reviews and agree on their own method; if they do, I don't believe their publishers will oppose the plan.'

I telephoned Olin who said, 'I have no objection if a drama critic publishes a review in the Sunday drama section. Nevertheless, the music critic must be free to give his all-round opinion — the stage part as well as the music — in the edition the morning following the performance.' He declined to be budged from that stand, even though I tried to convince him that — as the new stage effects represented dramatic values equally important to the music — the drama critic often would be more informed on that aspect.

As Sulzberger advised, I talked with several other critics. The only one who was receptive was the late Pitts Sanborn (then music critic on the *World-Telegram*), who agreed with me fully. As a critic he was peculiarly well fitted to discuss both dramatic and musical aspects. Not only was he in constant attendance at Metropolitan Opera performances, but also he had studied dramatic production. 'There are really few music critics who care much whether the stage is adequate, just so long as the music is what they consider satisfactory,' he pointed out one day over lunch as we wrestled with my problem.

'That may well be,' I said, 'but sometimes I find it very annoying to read some of the articles about our productions; for instance, so little understanding of Martha Graham, in the *Sacre*; moreover, not one word about Bobby Jones's wonderfully creative lighting or Mamoulian's clever stage direction for Schoenberg's opera.'

Sanborn smiled indulgently. 'Now why should you expect a music critic to know the dance, or for that matter any dramatic material, no matter how new or interesting?' To smooth my feathers he added, 'But I think that some day all this will change.'

Almost two decades had to pass before the change came.

After its *première*, 30 December 1949, *The Rape of Lucretia* by Benjamin Britten was reviewed both by the music critic, Virgil Thomson, and the drama critic, Howard Barnes, in the New York *Herald Tribune*. From the League's standpoint, the victory for my idea was rather empty. Virgil Thomson criticized the opera, finding that 'There isn't enough music to hold the ear . . . Certainly Britten has failed to offer a score of sufficient intrinsic interest to hold together a two-hour show.'

On the drama side Mr. Barnes concluded his criticism with the estimate that 'Music without a play is the best way to describe *The Rape of Lucretia*.'

Having waited patiently for two branches of critical judgment to be brought to bear on what we saw as an integrated production of music and stage, the result was disappointing.

Another question that long had disturbed me was a workable means of obtaining correction of errors of fact in a newspaper, when the music editor declined space for clarifying correspondence.

For instance, in a Sunday newspaper article, a music critic printed statistics which were totally incorrect, about League performances of American composers. In the most friendly spirit, I sent him a simple statement of fact, regarding the high percentage of American compositions presented in the period in question.

His reaction was brief and to the point — as he saw it! 'Thank you for your information,' he wrote, adding ominously, 'Some day I may give your organization a real blast!'

In 1945 the National Music Council asked me to speak on 'The Attitude of the Press toward American Composers,' with special reference to ways in which it could be changed for the better.

I decided that I could not do better than make use of notes which — for lack of a convenient soapbox! — had been stored away in my files. Although we had progressed beyond that social era in which children were obliged to take the word of their elders on all matters without question, it occurred to me that as adults we were still prone to adhere with some awe and even fear to the idea that the opinions of critics simply cannot be questioned. Why, I asked myself. On what basis could such omniscience be imputed to a critic who, after all, is mortal, fallible, like the rest of us?

When I finished speaking before the Council, someone raised the question as to whether or not composers were often just as arrogant as some of their critics.

'I have come to believe,' I answered, 'that sometimes the true artist uses a seeming arrogance as a kind of protective coloration for sensitiveness, whereas, in reality, he may be a deeply modest individual. How many of us have heard a composer assert at some time, "I am as great as Beethoven!" ' Of course members of the Council laughed. A few were sure I was joking, until I told them about a young composer who said to me earnestly, 'If I don't believe I'm as great as Beethoven, I can't compose.' I was certain that he meant as great *potentially*; at the same time I could see what might seem to an outsider presumptuous and even absurd could serve a very real purpose in his inward artistic growth.

One must agree in all fairness that, if critics are often hard on composers, it is not always easy to be a critic. Lawrence Gilman was once persuaded to list the qualifications necessary for being a critic and did so as follows:

> . . . the constitution of a traffic policeman . . . the nervous system of a coal heaver . . . the hide of a rhinoceros . . . a measure of philosophy adequate to survive the realization that you can claim no disinterested friends in that professional world, which views you either as a ruthless destroyer or as a useful builder of reputations . . . a willingness to accept the fact that your praise of artists will be regarded as their due, and your dispraise as the natural result of ignorance, animus, dyspepsia, or all three. . . .

One December Sunday morning in 1943 I read in Virgil Thomson's forecast for the new music year that 'The League of (yesterday's) Composers, official merchants of (yesterday's) modernism, is quietly burying itself under the funeral monuments of its Twentieth Anniversary . . . Happy New Year . . .'

That morning I had many telephone calls from our directors, inquiring if flowers were in order for the League's funeral, or perhaps better yet a large bottle of saccharine, tastefully gift-wrapped, to the author of this surprising bouquet!

Of course the League survived; so, it must be noted, did the critic. And our files contain abundant proof that composers were not the only ones to suffer in those days from the cantankerous attentions of some critics. Several conductors, having incurred the displeasure of music editors for bravely present-ing contemporary music, were to discover that music pages no longer had any space in which to mention them or to publish news releases concerning their programs. Sometimes the logic was hard to follow; for instance, whereas room could be found in October to note a classical program to be heard in February, no room was available for mentioning an October performance of some *modern* works!

There is a factor which seems to me indispensable to progress in any field, whether art, or science, or business. That is the will-ingness to acknowledge the need of exploration, or experiment-ing, for the very reason that we do not as yet know all there is to be known. To my mind the critic who admits, for instance, that discoveries are still to be made in music, and who then helps questing minds forward in the search, is meeting an im-portant responsibility.

Why is it that, only in rare instances, will a critic risk admitting that he, too, having matured, has experienced a change of opin-ion? I remember the glow of respect I experienced for one music critic who said, writing on the subject of Copland's Piano Con-certo, that 'It was an extraordinary experience (for this re-viewer),' pointing out further that he had not liked this music when he first heard it played sixteen years earlier, but now he found himself completely reversing his opinion, since the music was greatly to his taste.

One could wish, of course, that the composer had not been damned sixteen years earlier, with all the implications of a public inclined to follow blindly the critical lead.

Perhaps some day the critics may adopt a Lord's Prayer of their own: 'Give us this day our daily opinion, and forgive us the ones we had yesterday.'

# 8

## *Music and Electricity*

JULIAN CARILLO, a Mexican composer and inventor, arrived in New York in 1926 to give a demonstration of his compositions with new musical instruments. Having been interested from its inception in establishing a platform for experimental music, the League of Composers arranged a Town Hall concert program to present Carillo's inventions, instruments capable of quarter, eighth, and sixteenth tones around which he had composed music.

The program opened with a *Sonata Casi Fantasia* for a guitarri, an octavina, and an arpa citara — all original instruments, played by three Mexican musicians the composer had brought here with him. To this new ensemble he added cello, horn, and violin.

Though Carillo himself conducted his first number, the fractional tones did not seem to register with the audience, who remained visibly uninterested. The composer-inventor had also been asked to demonstrate each instrument separately and, by playing a scale on it, to demonstrate the modulations from quarter- to sixteenth-tone. As each of his performers in turn played the ascending and descending scales, the reaction of the audience changed and there was spontaneous hearty applause.

114

Whereas it had been difficult for listeners to distinguish the unfamiliar intervals in ensemble, as each instrument played them in scale, solo, they could be comprehended and enjoyed.

Once again the League was the butt of humorously derisive comment from the critics. For example, *The New Yorker's* reviewer regaled his readers and presumably himself, by commenting,

> In the *Sonata Casi Fantasia* quarter, eighth and sixteenth tones were trotted out by a denatured horn, a fiddle, a cello, a guitar and *two strangers*, respectively called the octavina and the arpa citara. The octavina looks like a broomstick plunged into a triangular mandolin; the arpa citara is a naughty piece of the old-fashioned zither which used to be heard in our best kitchens, when fronts of houses were of brownstone and steps were straight.

Obviously it is not easy by the usual critical standards to gauge the value of new physical media of art — nor even the reactions of the average concert-going audience.

Another innovator, or composer-inventor, was Harry Partch, who was brought to our attention a few years ago. We introduced him to our members at an afternoon concert in which he demonstrated instruments he had both designed and constructed. He played, he sang his compositions, he talked about his inventions. One was called the chromelodeon, another the flex-a-tone, another the kithara. This latter he described as 'a modern evolution of the ancient Greek instrument.' The chromelodeon, he said, 'is a reed organ adapted to a forty-three-tone-to-the-octave scale.' To present his compositions in an ensemble he added tin flutes and tin oboes to his instruments.

When John Cage arrived on the musical scene we had heard about the 'prepared piano' but not about his orchestra. He had invented a dozen or more strange-looking, strange-sounding, seemingly strangely named instruments or devices for an ensemble for which he had written some compositions himself and also ordered other works by some of his colleagues. To arrive at the effects he sought he made use of thunder sheets, bells, cowbells, temple gongs, automobile brake drums, anvils, tin cans, buzzers, rattles, rice bowls, bongos, button gongs, flower pots, and — somewhat more scientific-sounding — an audio frequency oscillator.

A recent composition by Cage was 'An Essay into Silence' with the sub-title '4'33.' It was 'performed' by a young pianist who simply sat at the piano in absolute silence for four minutes and thirty-three seconds. It had been reported as creating peculiar difficulties 'since the public cannot always be sure whose music is *not* being played!'

Henry Cowell, who has — at intervals — belonged to the experimental group, writing for a John Cage orchestra, invented his own system of cluster-tones. He has also utilized the conventional instruments in every type of ensemble and has made his place among creative musicians of this century with his classical contemporary works, many of which have been played by major symphony orchestras. Thus his case somewhat resembles that of Josef Haydn, who became interested in writing a series of musical pieces for musical clocks which, of course, were built not by a musician but by an inventor. Probably in the eighteenth century these clocks were also a radical invention. It is almost superfluous to add that of course Haydn's fame was established not as an innovator, but as a great composer of classical music.

The composer-inventors of the early 1900's, around whom the term 'futurist' grew up, seemed to have been the precursors of the above-mentioned musicians. Marinetti, the Italian, led a group of writers, painters, sculptors, and musicians in forming a Futurist movement, seeking new forms and media. A musician named Russolo, a friend of Marinetti, claimed that the world was weary of the orchestras of the day which, he said, were capable only of producing five kinds of noises, those of stringed instruments (bowed or plucked), brass, woodwind, and percussion. Employing the slogan 'the glorification of noise,' Russolo set forth that 'the noises of the twentieth century are what the Futurist orchestra is designed to produce.' In 1915 he gave a concert in Milan and, although there is no detailed description of the instruments used, they were listed as 'three groaners, two exploders, one thunderer, three whistlers, two rustlers, two gurglers, one shatterer, one scraper and one snorter.' One can only imagine the aggregate noise, imitating groans, gurgles, scrapes, and snorts! Oddly enough some Italian critics were sympathetic; in a Milan newspaper review one wrote, 'The ensemble playing was almost perfect throughout, and the public was not only impressed but delighted by the beauty of the sounds that the "noisicians" produced.'

Despite the critics' efforts to comment, more often than not in sarcastic vein, despite the lack of understanding shown by the public whenever an interesting innovator appeared on the scene, the League held firmly to its principles with regard to the experimentalists. Therefore it is encouraging to read the statement by Arthur Berger [1] to the effect that '. . . there was therapeutic value in the early experimentalists . . . even freshness in doing a parlor stunt in public, for the expedient did clear away cobwebs, and made audiences more receptive to the major trends of Schoenberg, Webern, Bartók and Stravinsky.'

In the 1930's there was a great resurgence of interest in experimental developments with electrical instruments. Leopold Stokowski was working feverishly with electrical engineers at Columbia University to conquer many acoustical problems with special reference to radio and recording. At rehearsals of the Philadelphia Orchestra a corps of engineers set up all kinds of electrical apparatus with which they worked while Stokowski manipulated his expressive hands.

Programs of 'space-controlled' instruments were being heard in chamber music programs. The Theremin was 'played' by Clara Rockmore and Lucy Rosen, the chief disciples of the inventor, Professor Leon Theremin. John Hays Hammond, Jr., had built into his house in Gloucester, Massachusetts, a re-

---

1. A composer, former associate music critic of the New York *Herald Tribune*, now teaching at Brandeis College.

markable great pipe organ which was of enormous interest to
his friend Stokowski. Wilfrid had completed a color organ, used
by several conductors in conjunction with symphonic concerts.

An invention that commercially had become the most successful among such instruments was the Hammond Organ (not
to be confused with the organ designed by John Hays Hammond,
Jr.). Within a short time of its first appearance, the Hammond
Organ was being used extensively in schools and churches.

I felt the time was ripe for the League to gather together
some of these recent inventions and give a demonstration for
our subscribers. I conferred with Carlos Chavez, the Mexican
composer and conductor, who has made outstanding contributions to the development of music in Mexico. At that moment
he was engaged in writing a book about electricity and music.
Through him I met Dr. Alfred N. Goldsmith, a great electrical
engineer and today technical advisor to the RCA organization.
Dr. Goldsmith was extremely interested in the new field which
he felt was being opened up for electronics in music. He agreed
quickly to co-operate with us. 'I do want to help those composers
belonging to the "inventive group" to find interesting new instruments for use in their compositions,' he told me; 'I have
already given some assistance to Stokowski, and recently also
to Chavez. Do you know him well?'

'Oh yes, Chavez and I are old friends,' I replied; 'I was a
member of his first honorary board for the symphonic concerts
he organized in Mexico City. We played some of his compositions just last season on a League program.' I elaborated a little
to Dr. Goldsmith about our work, and our plans for the demonstration of electrical instruments at Town Hall.

'I think,' he said approvingly, 'that I can interest a number
of inventors and perhaps even some manufacturing companies
in your work.' He rang for his secretary and immediately dictated
a letter which set forth, in part, 'An attempt is being made by a
prominent organization, influential in the musical field, to bring
together scientists and groups who are developing electrical musical instruments and advanced methods of reproduction of

music by electrical means . . . for . . . composers who may find musical merit in such instruments or reproducing devices. . . .' Before I left, Dr. Goldsmith brought out a file on inventors of such instruments, suggesting a few names to me.

'Do you know the work of Benjamin Meissner?' he asked. The name was completely new to me. 'Well, then,' he said, 'you must go out to his laboratory, in a little town in New Jersey; there you can choose a few of the instruments he has invented, and they will make a fine addition to your demonstration.'

Minna Lederman joined me and we explored obscure towns of New Jersey until we finally located Mr. Meissner in a large ground-floor shop which he had turned into his laboratory.

He was entirely hedged around by electrical tympani, violins, guitars, and a group of unfinished instruments on which he was at work. In the back of the shop was a grand piano which he had developed into an instrument that he called an electronic piano. It combined the qualities of piano, organ, and the string section of an orchestra. He played a few chords for us; it seemed in fact as he claimed it to be, an orchestra in itself. We were astounded by the orchestral quality of its tone; we were quickly convinced that this instrument would be the *piéce de resistance* at our demonstration.

Mr. Meissner was delighted to hear about the Town Hall program and promised to bring his new electrical piano, and also a professional pianist who could play contemporary music on it. Even in this planned, so-called scientific demonstration we wanted only modern music performed; our primary purpose was to interest contemporary composers in these new fields for their future creative work. Before leaving the laboratory we selected an electrical violin capable of great amplification of tone, adding to the variety of the instruments which would demonstrate this new field of music and electricity.

As we knew no one who had actually played contemporary music on an electric violin, we decided to ask Nicolai Berezowsky, a composer and able violinist, to take part in our experimental venture.

Berezowsky, normally very calm and serene on the concert platform, looked very pained that evening as he played a melody by Ernest Bloch. When he started out from the wings he whispered to me, 'I'll be damn glad when this ordeal is over!' He looked pale and kept fussing with the electrical cable hanging over his shoulder from the instrument, and I could see that it irritated him. Although for Nicolai the work was not difficult, he winced often as he played, and I began to wonder if the audience were aware of his discomfort; his unusually strained behavior rather puzzled me.

He finished the piece and was about to go out for a second bow when he smiled and murmured, 'Thank God that's over and I wasn't electrocuted!' Later he added, 'Claire, if it hadn't been for the League, I believe I'd have stopped playing. All the time that electric wire hung over my shoulder I kept wondering, *What if it should break? I will be electrocuted right here on this platform!* You've no idea how jittery that instrument makes me feel — no more electric violins for me! The good old-fashioned kind of violin is all I'll ever need to play on!'

The program also included a demonstration of the Theremin by Clara Rockmore, in several works by Ravel and Korngold. This was followed by Joseph Schillinger playing the Hammond Organ. The last instrument to be introduced on the program was Meissner's marvelous electric piano. It was to create the great climax to the evening.

Meissner had invited Anton Rovinsky to demonstrate the orchestral qualities of his new piano, and the pianist began his group of pieces with Ravel's 'L'Oiseau Triste.' Instead of the orchestral tones I had heard in the laboratory, strange sounds began to issue from the piano. The pianist paused, inspected the socket and wires and, shrugging his shoulders in doubt, commenced again. This time the sounds which came forth were like the loudest static on a poor radio and again he was obliged to stop. By now we were very puzzled because all who had listened to the rehearsal in the afternoon had been most enthusiastic about a seemingly extraordinary instrument. The pianist made one more attempt to play the Ravel composition, but when the squeaks and squeals continued tumbling from the piano, he got up and walked off the stage.

Equally puzzled by the bad behavior of his cherished creation, Meissner inspected all the electric wires and connections, but he, too, shrugged his shoulders and walked out of the hall, completely baffled. He then followed the wires to their main connections and discovered that during the demonstration the building elevator had been in operation, carrying passengers to another auditorium. The static had been caused by the elevator; the reason the rehearsal had gone well was that the elevator had not been in use at the time.

Dr. Orestes H. Caldwell of the Rockefeller Institute had accepted our invitation to say a few words about music and electricity, following the demonstration of the various instruments. He began by explaining, 'This unusual electrical piano is not really a temperamental prima donna; the disturbance you heard was due to static set up elsewhere in the building.' But by this time many people in the audience had lost interest and were wandering out.

At times our fan mail berated us for our very advanced music. And so I was very pleased the next day to find a letter at the office which read, 'Bravo, League of Composers! Your concerts are by a good margin the most interesting musical events in New York. I hope that you will have some more electrical instruments next year.' It was signed 'An Enthusiast.' Evidently, the Town Hall elevator had not lost us our entire public!

Shortly after that particular evening of electrical music, my attention was called to a complete orchestra of electric instruments, organized by my nephew, Tom Adrian Cracraft. This ensemble had given a program of classical music in 1939 for the International Congress of the American Musicological Society.

When I told Stokowski about the new group he became very much interested, so I arranged to introduce him to the originator of the Cracraft Electronic Orchestra, as it was called. As he looked over the sixteen instruments including electric violins, celli, violas, a bass viol, also a guitar, piano, and tympani, Stokowski told Tom that he saw great possibilities in this small group. In certain ways he believed that the effect might equal that of the average orchestra of a hundred men. We began discussing a plan for a performance by the Electronic Orchestra under Stokowski's direction, and he grew more and more enthusiastic as he talked about future possibilities.

But the interest was destined to be short-lived. One day, soon after this meeting, I received a letter from Stokowski as follows:

> Dear Claire, Regarding the electric orchestra, I have been requested by the Musicians' Union not to form an electric orchestra. Of course such advances as electric orchestras cannot be stopped forever; but it will be difficult to continue the idea in the near future — anyway for a time. With friendly greetings, Leopold.

Nevertheless the Cracraft Electronic Orchestra did continue to give sustaining programs over NBC, commercial programs over CBS, and also filled other engagements. As a result of World War II, conditions changed over the networks; and also there was a great shortage of electrical materials, so eventually the Electronic Orchestra was forced to disband.

Not long after that the union took notice of another experiment, this time in a theater orchestra. The late Kurt Weill had introduced the Hammond Organ into a Broadway show entitled *Johnny Johnson*. The strong tonal volume of this instrument replaced five live-players; the Musicians' Union ordered the management to engage the five theater orchestra men, even if they had to sit in the cellar throughout the performance and play pinochle.

During this period of instrumental experimentation, I was invited to Schirmer's to hear another new instrument. As my interest in these new mechanical developments was always in relation to the composer, I wondered what this invention would offer.

It was another piano. Unlike Meissner's, it did not attempt to combine orchestral qualities but seemed notable chiefly for producing a volume of sound which, booming through the Schirmer corridors, almost deafened us. When I raised a timid question as to its purpose the astonished demonstrator answered proudly, 'Why this instrument can be heard thirty miles away!' I could not help wondering if he saw its usefulness as some variation of the primitive drum used for war signals, for it seemed to me highly unlikely that any composer would be intrigued by writing for a thirty-mile range of sound! I quickly lost interest in the virtues imputed to the instrument by its inventor, and as quickly, forgot his name.

On the whole, however, many composers enjoyed this lively period of investigating and experimentation. Some of the more liberal critics conceded that no combination of instruments was too outlandish to be tried at least once; even if results were not uniformly successful, some residue of good would probably remain.

Leonard Burkat [2] has made an interesting study of the various approaches by which to experiment with music, among them 'with media of performance, with musical sound, rhythms, forms and techniques.' New ideas, new inventions call for additions to our musical vocabulary. This has happened in recent years in radio and in recording. A few years ago, who ever mentioned 'high fidelity,' or considered tape-recorded music? The science of music draws closer to the art of music, each entering into the other, in the same way that, in medicine today, the art of medicine is part of the science, and vice versa. It is interesting that the Massachusetts Institute of Technology — also other technical training centers — has recently successfully introduced music as an elective in the curriculum. Perhaps our music schools also will begin to include laboratories for acoustical studies and other scientific aspects of value to musicians.

In a fairly new field, many composer-innovators — among them Otto Luening, Vladimir Ussachevsky, and Edgar Varèse

---

2. Musicologist and author, who is a member of the staff of the Boston Symphony Orchestra.

— are seeking new effects with electronic means. For instance, Vladimir Ussachevsky has briefly summarized for me the new developments with the tape recorder. He says,

> Composers in Europe and the United States became interested in magnetic tape as a means of transforming, and creating, new sounds. Since the post-war experimental period, these composers have been fashioning musical compositions out of materials they create on tape. The French 'Musique Concrète' group, initiated by Pierre Schaeffer, produces musical abstractions on tape by means of a 'montage' of sounds derived from nature, and man-made sounds too, from some percussive-music sounds. In Cologne, Germany, a group of composers is producing music from an electronic sound generator not unlike the electronic organ, connected directly, however, to a tape recorder through a system of filters.
>
> Among American composers Otto Luening and I compose 'tape music' which primarily utilizes sounds from musical instruments which we transform, creating a new sound vocabulary, a procedure I initiated in 1952 independently of the European groups. We have used the tape recorder as a solo instrument with the symphony orchestra.

In the early 1930's, the League presented some of the first all-contemporary programs of chamber music over the National Broadcasting Company. We were also encouraged by Davidson Taylor, then program director of Columbia Broadcasting System, to give programs over their network. Due to Mr. Taylor's interest and vision, CBS commissions were arranged in co-operation with the League for new works to be written direct for radio. Mr. Taylor had a profound conviction that the composer with something to say could say it on the air to thousands of people capable of comprehending a new work. He regarded writing for radio as 'a challenge to clarity and cogency on the part of the composer.'

As a result of his enthusiastic support and co-operation, one of the important works commissioned was an opera, written for radio by Randall Thompson and titled *Solomon and Balkis*.

After several broadcasts it was performed with full stage by small theatrical and/or operatic groups in various parts of the country. Taylor's faith was encouraging. Then, as indeed today, we needed more men in the field of radio to champion the cause of the living composer.

The first National Conference on Educational Broadcasting was called in Washington in 1936, in co-operation with the United States Office of Education, and the Federal Communications Commission. There were representatives of over 350 educational institutions, 109 government agencies and broadcasting companies, libraries and museums. Twenty-five delegates represented foreign countries. The U.S. Commissioner of Education, John W. Studebaker, opened the sessions, and there was a welcome by the Secretary of the Interior, the Hon. Harold L. Ickes.

I had been invited to take part in the panel discussion on music and broadcasting. The panel included people from the three major broadcasting systems, several music critics, and representatives of musical organizations. Each was asked to read a paper. Necessarily, my paper dealt with contemporary music.

After three days of conferences we felt very hopeful about the foreseeable development of music through the medium of radio; we felt that we were going to reach a great new audience. Hence I applauded vigorously Mr. Ickes' statement that in radio educational programs we 'should be alert to avoid that regimentation of minds which might result from imposing the same ideas, the same thoughts upon large groups of people. Radio,' he concluded, 'has a magnificent chance to solve some of the problems of child education as well as of adult education.'

Today the crusading era for contemporary music on radio, especially with live music, has long since passed. Now the situation is chiefly economic. The question is, Is there a commercial sponsor for a program?

During the period when the League gave annual series of

broadcasts, it was heartening to receive so many letters from college students, who inquired about our special programs and told us how much they enjoyed them.

A particularly happy occasion was WQXR's celebration of our twentieth anniversary. A composer-teacher was introduced on each program in the series. Following the talk, his composition — a piece dedicated to the League — was performed. We were very proud of 'salutes,' from Harvard University by Walter Piston, from Mills College by Darius Milhaud, from Columbia University by Douglas Moore, from Sarah Lawrence College by William Schuman, and from others.

There are today a few exceptions to the generally depressed radio situation for the live composer. One is the annual Festival of American Music, over station WNYC, which was inaugurated by the late Mayor La Guardia. In this American Festival, the League has gladly co-operated with Mr. Seymour N. Siegel and Mr. Herman Newman. Another recent exception, of immense value to the composer, is the series of broadcasts over CBS of the Louisville Orchestra's *premières* of its commissioned works, conducted by Robert Whitney.

In the late 'thirties, the film industry began to call upon contemporary composers to write serious scores for films. Immediately, we felt it was part of the League's responsibility to focus attention on the newer use of modern music in documentary and Hollywood feature films. It had been rumored earlier that Hollywood did not want the type of composer whose writing, by and large, was for the concert hall; according to the Hollywood concept the score for a movie was good only when people were not aware of it.

I asked for assistance from the Association of Documentary Film Producers and the Film Library of the Museum of Modern Art in assembling a program of excerpts from six documentary films. The scores were by Marc Blitzstein, Paul Bowles, Aaron Copland, Roy Harris, Douglas Moore, and Virgil Thomson.

Again there was the feeling of excitement about a new experiment.

This first evening of films presented us with fresh adventure in a new field in the arts. The films had been selected either for general educational worth or for their government use. For example, *Roots of the Earth* had been made for the Soil Conservation Service of the U.S. Department of Agriculture. *Valley Town* had been filmed for New York University's Film Institute. *Power and the Land* showed the influence of electricity from dawn to dusk on the farm. Other selections were field scenes from *One Tenth of a Nation*, a flood sequence from *The River*, and traffic scenes from *The City*. Each film brought its important message.

The composers acted as commentators on their scores. The success of the evening warranted a second film evening, with excerpts of fiction films from Hollywood's leading studios. For this second series the composers were George Antheil, Aaron Copland, Louis Gruenberg, Bernard Hermann, Werner Janssen, and Ernst Toch. These men had written the music for some of the outstanding films of the day, including *Of Mice and Men, Citizen Kane, The General Died at Dawn,* and *Juarez.*

We distributed questionnaires to the audience, believing it would bring out interesting audience reaction to our unusual series. We were amazed at the total ignorance about music for films which came to light.

Even here, at a League gathering of musical people, the composer seemed to be the forgotten man. In this audience of 400 people in the Museum of Modern Art, only 120 could fill in the titles of three film scores by composers whom they knew by name. The balance could not conjure up any names at all!

In contrast to this distressing ignorance there was a heartening tally of 384 who preferred (or perhaps believed theoretically) that original music be written for films, in contrast to 12 who preferred arrangements of classics.

Other questions showed the need to educate the public in

listening more carefully to the music of films, inasmuch as music bade fair to take a greater part than ever before in the film industry.

The League added another demonstration of a new type of film in 1949. It was called *Experiments with Sound and Music,* a recent development by Norman McLaren; he produced sound synthetically by painting graphs with a brush directly on the film. In contrast to this very experimental film we presented an excerpt from a film called *The Assassination of the Duke of Guise* with a score by Camille Saint-Saëns. My impression of our audience reaction that evening was that they felt the Saint-Saëns work was a little too old, the McLaren film a little too new.

For a short time the scene looked promising for the serious composers who were being called to Hollywood as well as for those who already were writing music for the documentaries. Perhaps music for motion pictures would no longer be a patchwork quilt of themes from *Carmen* or from the *Symphonie Pathétique.* The public was beginning to weary of Great Master motifs which had been classified to accompany silent pictures; the categories from Sentimental to Sinister, from Lovely to Licentious had outworn their usefulness.

Notwithstanding the number of important contemporary composers participating in the film world, the music critics remained supremely uninterested in the early film scores by men whose works they heard in symphonic repertoire. One day Louis Gruenberg sent me a letter from Hollywood, asking, 'Do you think you could get the New York music critics to come to a preview of *So Ends Our Night?* The music I have written for it is not a potboiling job. I am actually pleased with it.' Only a short while before Louis Gruenberg had been, in effect, the Musician of the Year; that is, he had written the opera based on Eugene O'Neill's famous play *Emperor Jones* which was presented at the Metropolitan Opera House.

With the United Artists office I arranged a preview of the film with Gruenberg's music. We set the time at 4 p.m. on a Monday afternoon to avoid conflict with any scheduled concert. All the

New York and Brooklyn critics were invited to see and hear *So Ends Our Night.*

One critic came. Their general lack of interest equaled the neglect of the film producers. On their mimeographed information sheets about the producing staff for the picture, names appeared in profusion — stage director, producer, wardrobe designer, hair styler, photographer, sound engineer — all in big, bold type. The name Louis Gruenberg, the composer, brought up the rear, in small letters.

Lawrence Morton, a composer of film music and also editor for *The Hollywood Quarterly,* was one of the first musicians to observe that film music has been regarded less as a legitimate field of musical activity than as 'a pasture, where serious composers occasionally graze for fattening.' He believes that 'the semicultivated taste of the public, and the unfortunate influence of producers and directors invades the music departments, causing the miscasting of composers or their being hired out of nepotism or other favoritism rather than for individual ability and style. Too there is the danger of distortion of sound, by engineers who seemingly cannot let a piece of music "ride" without fiddling with the controls. This, added to overemphasis on box-office "exploitation," the prevalence of cliches, the absence of courageous experimentation' — these conditions, argues Mr. Morton, have created a mediocrity which is to be condemned. Defending his attitude about some of the Hollywood composers he said, 'I have not been shielding Hollywood composers out of a mistaken sense of loyalty; only have I been careful not to throw the baby out with the bath water.' His figure of speech obviously implies his belief that there is much room for growth in some of these Hollywood musicians; at the same time that the 'baby' is worth saving to grow up.

One day recently I chatted with a friend, Arthur Mayer, about music and films. He is one of the leading figures in the film industry. 'What ever happened,' I asked, 'to the progressive attitude shown by Hollywood toward some of our good contemporary composers in the late 'thirties and early 'forties? There must be some reason for not using more of these men today. After all, their works are found on symphonic programs, they are recorded, even occasionally broadcast. It goes without saying that these composers would like to receive an occasional Hollywood assignment.' I pointed out that Aaron Copland had even received an Oscar from the Academy of Motion Picture Arts and Sciences for his music for the film *The Heiress*. Why shouldn't other men be discovered who also could write well for films?

Arthur Mayer has the great advantage of understanding the film business and also of appreciating the point of view of the artist. Above all he has an acute awareness of the pulse of the people.

After a few thoughtful moments he replied, 'It is true that our picture producers ransack the corners of the world to acquire the services of gifted authors, directors, and performers. Yet they do seem singularly uninterested in the accomplishments of modern musicians. Of course there are exceptions to this as to all other generalizations. A recent exception is Leonard Bernstein's fascinating score for the film *On the Waterfront*. 'I suppose,' he continued, 'many reasons could be cited for the sharp decline in Hollywood's appreciation of musical originality and vitality; for example, the inflated popularity with movie audiences of a few, loudly touted, thoroughly conventional composers; economics, growing out of the use of musical directors under contract to major studies and undoubtedly holding musical prejudices.' Mayer also mentioned the high pressure and artistic difficulties a good composer must meet in working for films. Somehow I felt that was begging the question; after all, composers both in this country and in Europe have contributed to film music and have survived, preserving their artistic integrity.

'Primarily,' Arthur went on, 'the culpability, it seems to me, lies with the public rather than the producer. The ears of the producer may not be closely attuned to other than reminiscent and conventional harmonies, at the same time they are marvelously sensitive to the melody of the box office and cash register!' He grew a bit more intense, exclaiming, 'Now Claire, if the

music-lovers would only talk less about the need of modern music, and more frequently patronize the occasional good films
which have the courage to present it, then perhaps good pictures
and good music would be synonymous.

'Speaking of their being synonymous, what about the story of
the woman who liked to close her eyes when she went to a film,
so she could listen to the music undisturbed by the picture! Perhaps not everyone can absorb several arts at one time, even
though you and I agree that with good films there should be
good scores.'

Our discussion wandered on to the need of larger acclaim for
the good film score. I referred again to Bernstein's music for *On
The Waterfront*. 'Did you perhaps notice, Arthur,' I asked, 'that
one of the picture weeklies ran three pages of stills from the
picture when it opened in New York, without one mention in
the cutlines about the composer, not even his name?'

We could both agree that a need existed for better promotion
of good film music. How will it be brought about? By some
clever 'merchandising' method? Some form of musical Rotary
Club? By the hard, discouraging, unremitting labor of a society
such as the League of Composers?

I wonder.

# 9

## American and Soviet Operas

'WE MUST do something together next year,' Stokowski had called across to me as we left the Metropolitan Opera House after the performance of *Le Sacre du Printemps* that April evening in 1930. It was obvious that he had been pleased with the production, and I felt, despite the many clashes of personality and technique, that he had enjoyed working with us in the past two seasons. I did not realize at that moment, however, that the next year would find us embarking on a far more ambitious production, a double bill of two major works, Stravinsky's *Oedipus Rex* and Prokofieff's *Pas d'Acier*.

For both works we needed the full Philadelphia Orchestra. Stravinsky's opera-oratorio called for a large men's chorus and soloists. It had been staged in Paris by Diaghilev in 1927. In the United States it had been heard only in concert form, conducted by Dr. Koussevitzky with the Boston Symphony. This was to be the first American staged performance of *Oedipus Rex*, with the American *première* of Prokofieff's ballet, which called for a full *corps de ballet* and solo dancers.

In any of our plans for stage productions a first step was always a reading of the piano score for the principal artists. We arranged with Stokowski and Bobby Jones to meet at my house,

132

to hear the music, discuss our general ideas, and also select the artists.

As Jones listened to the reading of *Oedipus Rex*, he remembered those beautiful marionettes Bufano had built for us in 1925 for de Falla's opera. 'This music makes me long to design some great archaic figures,' Bobby remarked, standing up and making a sweeping gesture of great height. 'I think I could do something on a heroic scale in interpreting this music. I'd like to ask Bufano if he would use my designs and create some extraordinary and majestic puppets.'

Both Stokowski and I were delighted at the prospect of a unique inspiration for this Greek drama which Bobby volunteered also to translate into English from Jean Cocteau's French text. To lose no time I called up Bufano immediately, and as I expected, found that he would be happy to work with the League on another major production, with a new opportunity to make marionettes of great size. When he had agreed to embody Jones's design in twelve-foot figures he laughed, 'One thing — where are we going to find our rehearsal hall this time?'

'I'll begin the search right away,' I replied. The task of finding space for preparing our productions was becoming more and more complicated. Estimating roughly, it was apparent that this time the puppeteers would need at least six feet of height over and above the twelve-foot archetypal figures, in order to manipulate them smoothly.

Neither combing the real estate advertisements nor weeping on the shoulders of friends produced any results; we began to feel very worried about rehearsals for Oedipus & Company.

Meanwhile, Stokowski relieved our situation in regard to space for the ballet dancers, by securing the wonderful cork-floored gymnasium of the Dalton School for us in the later afternoons; this boon came through his friendship with Helen Parkhurst, principal of the school at the time.

One day an artist-friend of Bufano's offered us his barn in Leonia, New Jersey, for two months at a very low rental. 'Let's snap it up!' we chorused for we were feeling desperate. At that moment all that interested us was a barn's height, which surely would allow the puppeteers to work without knocking their heads against the ceiling.

That March was notable for wintry days, and naturally there was no heat in the barn. Bufano called me often. 'My puppeteers' fingers are numb from cold,' he would cry on the phone; 'how can we expect them to work out here?' I did not know how to answer him but I felt very sympathetic with his troubles.

I went out to Leonia to watch the puppeteers at work. Not only their fingers but also those of the pianist were red from cold. Then suddenly it began to rain! 'Cover up Jocasta!' yelled Bufano to an assistant; 'hurry up and move Oedipus to the other end of the barn — at least over there the roof doesn't leak!' Undersized as he was, Bufano quickly shoved the piano out of its rained-on position; in five minutes everyone was back at his post, deep in rehearsal.

Word of a somewhat unusual type of rehearsal reached magazines and newspapers, and interviewers came knocking at the door of the Leonia barn, interested in questioning Bufano and Jones, surrounded by Greek figures. Often rain from the leaky roof fell on reporters' notebooks but that only added to their interest.

Undaunted by atmospheric difficulties while he co-ordinated puppet movements with Stravinsky's music, Bufano achieved a great beauty in motion for these plastic figures of unusual dignity, designed by Jones. Hundreds of hours of rehearsal with puppeteers and pianist went into this unique conception, which was to replace the human figure on the stage.

Margaret Matzenauer had previously sung the role of Jocasta, under Koussevitzky's baton. Stokowski suggested my writing her, to ask her to join us in this stage *première*, even if it meant coming from California where she made her home.

She accepted immediately, but wrote, 'Please, please do not make me wear a costume, I am much too stout.' I thought she would change her mind when I replied that the famous Robert Edmond Jones was designing the sets and the costumes, and that 'each one of the singers will be in a simple robe, seated on the stage; the action will be carried out by a group of puppets.' In a brief letter it was not easy to describe our plans in full.

'I am bringing a simple black dress and I promise you I shall not wear any jewelry, but please, no costume,' she wrote me again before her arrival.

'Madame Matzenauer has asked for a piano rehearsal with you,' I told Stokowski shortly after I received several calls from the great diva.

'She is a marvelous musician,' he said blandly, 'she does not need me to coach her; she can wait for the orchestra rehearsals.'

I received several more calls from Madame Matzenauer, each of them emphatic and to the point. Some of them I relayed to Leopold. 'Are you her personal entrepreneur?' he finally inquired with a sly smile. We laughed together but it was on my mind that the matter of the prima donna's costume remained still to be settled.

The dress rehearsal took place in Philadelphia where the series of productions opened. The chorus took seats with the soloists at the front of the stage, all dressed alike in gowns and hoods of Persian blue, and a dim light gave a very subdued effect, contrasting well with the heroic figures on their fifteen-foot elevation above them. And then — out walked Matzenauer in the threatened black dress! For a moment she stood by the empty chair awaiting her; looking at Stokowski, she then said, 'Please let me stand; I sing so much better that way than sitting down.'

But now Stokowski was a man of the theater as well as a musician. Conformity was a requisite. He waved both hands and it could only be taken as an order, 'Down.' With a deep sigh Matzenauer sank into the chair. Having observed this much, I could tell that she was going to lose the battle about her costume.

In the intermission I said apprehensively, 'We shall have a scene tomorrow before the opening unless you *order* Madame

Matzenauer to finish out this rehearsal in costume.' Giving me
a knowing look he walked over and spoke to her. I heard her sigh
again; then she disappeared into the wings.

As the second part of the rehearsal began, there, seated, in
complete harmony with the scene, was the great Margaret
Matzenauer — in the required blue robe.

I knew, when Lee Simonson accepted our invitation to design
Prokofieff's ballet, that there would be moments of having to
count to a hundred before answering him. He was well known
to be a great stage designer — and also somewhat temperamental. But I had made up my mind never to let him catch me
off guard, with a possible resulting explosion of nerves. I had
been fully warned that although his taste might prove extrava-
gant it would always be beautiful.

'We are a very poor organization, Lee,' I protested innumerable times during the early days of our preparations.

'But Claire,' he would come back at me each time, 'I am giving you my time free.' Obviously there was no answer for that,
and I really felt grateful to him.

Lee Simonson had helped Edwin Strawbridge to create a brilliant choreography for the scenario of *Pas d'Acier* (Age of
Steel). In the text Lee wrote, 'The rhythm of steel is perhaps
the triumph of the machine, and implies the mechanization
of labor. This scenario is a satiric and skeptical commentary on
the rhythm of machine industry, with its large-scale efficiency.'
He used a large projection screen on which were thrown shadows
of the temples which slaves had erected; then silhouettes of
steel girders appeared, and finally gigantic shadows of the arms
of labor, swinging hammer and sickle. At that time the sickle
was not suspect as a symbol of Russian force; in this ballet it
was accepted purely as a symbol of labor, without political reference. Below the screen the dancers moved, in the roles of
groups of laborers. Simonson's words described it, 'in the weary
rhythms of archaic slave labor and, as the ballet progressed, they
were incited and animated by the efficiency experts. The rhythms

changed to those of modern machine industry, faster, more precise, and always monotonous.'

This immense Stravinsky-Prokofieff double bill called for rehearsal of orchestra, dancers, singers, chorus, puppeteers, décor, and lighting. Necessarily each detail needed to be planned with precision. For all of us it had been a period of intensive work; for Stokowski, Jones, Bufano, and myself it had been a pleasant period also. In promises of harmony we four had worked faithfully through trying weeks of rehearsals. I could always count on them to arrange their time carefully, with full awareness of the problem of union overtime, for these were artists who were meticulous in all their planning. Lee, on the other hand, being busy also with Theatre Guild affairs, constantly kept us guessing about all his schedules, even to costume tryouts and plans for the lighting rehearsal.

Finally the dress rehearsal for *Oedipus Rex* was over. Jocasta, Oedipus, Tiresias, all had been tucked away for the night, ready for the opening next day. As choreographer, Strawbridge had put the dancers through their final preparatory paces in the Philadelphia Opera House, when Simonson arrived in Philadelphia at eleven in the evening, to run through his lighting rehearsal with the stage crew, and the dancers on stage. He had come from a New York rehearsal of one of his shows.

He dismissed the dancers at four in the morning, asking them all to return at 10 a.m. for a final run-through — the very day of the opening performance! At that point the dancers balked, refusing to show up. I realized that counting now would do no good. We were forced simply to overrule Lee, and we sent the dancers home to sleep until time to report for the performance. That time it was Lee who needed to count to a hundred. Arthur Judson and I spent some sleepless hours thinking about union overtime bills.

It was fortunate that the sharp eye of our stage manager had not been dulled by lack of sleep during the long drawn-out rehearsals of these difficult productions, or we should have met with calamity at the opening performance.

On the Friday afternoon of the Philadelphia *première*, half an hour before curtain time, he noticed a frightening slant to the theater bridge high in the air. A main rope, holding the bridge on which the puppeteers manipulated the Greek figures, apparently had been cut by a knife, not quite through but enough to make the depending bridge extremely dangerous. Was it sabotage? So far as we knew, all complexes — including the Oedipus — had been confined within the framework of Greek history. Among carpenters and electricians there had been visible interest and devotion in their work with Bufano, Jones, and Stokowski. Yet this vandalism had come close to a tragedy.

Everyone on the stage clustered around to look. Someone remarked thoughtfully, 'I believe this Oedipus production can be an even greater success than the ballet.' Someone else said, in a tone of disbelief, 'Is it possible that any human is jealous?' As for myself, it looked as though the theater were suffering a plague of gremlins.

Mystified as we were, there was no time to solve the riddle. The rope was replaced. The stage manager called authoritatively, 'Curtain!' To this day no one knows with certainty the answer to the mystery.

The ballet, *Pas d'Acier*, had many novel and attractive features and was well received. But, we all agreed that artistically it could not equal the production of *Oedipus Rex*.

At each performance in Philadelphia and in New York there was a tremendous ovation as the great figures were swallowed up in darkness. Never in the League's history had there been a performance quite like this one. These works of Stravinsky and Prokofieff were both important, not only in the framework of contemporary music but also as Stokowski said, 'because of Stravinsky's ideas, and Prokofieff's dynamic power.'

Jones's design and Bufano's skill in puppetry had found a mobile form, in which these figures, monumental in size and abstract in style, made one vividly conscious of a new value, that 'livingness of light' so well described by Jones in his book

*The Dramatic Imagination:* 'We use light as we use words, to elucidate ideas and emotions.' [1]

The Princeton Glee Club comprising the 'Oedipus' men's chorus trained by the late Alexander Russell, their Director, for the Philadelphia performances had conscientiously studied their parts. This was their first experience appearing under Stokowski's baton in a stage performance, and they seemed a bit nervous. They jiggled about in their chairs, awaiting the fateful rise of the curtains for the afternoon *première* at the Metropolitan Opera House production in Philadelphia. Stokowski sensed their state of nerves and at the very last minute came out in front of them and said quietly, 'You have all done a fine job in learning this difficult music. I know we are going to have a superb performance.' He added spontaneously, 'You are good!' The boys grinned appreciatively, relaxing just enough. One of them, quick on the uptake, volunteered, 'We think you're pretty good yourself, Sir!' With both hands Stokowski waved his thanks, disappearing to enter the orchestra pit and conduct a performance that was truly magnificent.

We had invited the Harvard Glee Club to take part in the New York performances. They had already been coached in this work the year before, when they sang under Dr. Koussevitzky's baton with the Boston Symphony. Our April dates conflicted with their spring vacation, but their manager wrote that they had no objection to missing two days of vacation time in order to meet our plans. In my letter to their manager I had suggested as an added incentive that the boys might like an extra day in New York before rehearsal, which came the same day as the performance. Evidently I did not comprehend vacationing college boys as well as did their manager for he wrote me firmly, 'We will bring them all down on the overnight boat from Boston, arriving just in time for the rehearsal. We would not like to give them free time in New York just before this

---

1. Duell, Sloan and Pearce, Inc., New York, 1941.

important event.' I felt rather sorry for the boys because they would have no time out for any 'joyrides.'

They were unanimously excited over singing under Stokowski at the Metropolitan Opera House, however, and not at all resentful about missing either the two days' vacation or a New York spree.

After they were back in Cambridge, Dr. Archibald Davison, the renowned founder of the Harvard Glee Club, wrote me, 'It will be a long time before we forget the pleasure we took in the performance of *Oedipus Rex* in New York. The boys still talk about it. We are certainly indebted to you and the League, for the opportunity of taking part in such a distinguished program.'

During the months of intensive preparation for these spectacular productions, I asked myself frequently why I stepped into ventures of such proportions, full of hazards as they were, artistically and financially. In sleepless hours, I would have visions of the huge opera house with every seat empty! In the morning I would rush to inquire about the ticket sale from the veteran box-office manager, Mr. Earle R. Lewis, who would tell me cheerfully, 'We're almost sold out.' Each season we were sold out, weeks ahead of the performances, and letters and mail orders came from as far away as California and Mexico, begging us to reserve seats. The day after we closed we always experienced the same regret, that we had not planned on more performances. But so many of the artists had volunteered their services that we simply could not ask them to spare more time. Over the years I was to receive many inquiries as to whether or not we could give just one more of these great evenings which, regretfully, had been missed.

In the late 'twenties there was no parallel to our type of production. Fundamentally, we all were giving our services to the cause of contemporary music, with the ambition to present important new works with new ideas in décor, lighting, and stage direction. Our aims were reminiscent of the group described by Alexandre Benois in his *Reminiscences of the Russian Ballet:*

> It is now accepted that what was afterward known as the Ballet Russe was originally conceived — not by the professionals of the dance, but by a circle of artists linked by the idea of art as an entity. Everything followed from the common desire of painters and musicians to see the fulfillment of their theatrical dreams, a burning craving for art in general.[2]

This was our common desire too.

At the time Stokowski first volunteered to direct Stravinsky's *Les Noces* I felt that we should invite a permanent advisory group interested in music and stage to join us. We planned an afternoon tea-meeting, and I invited to my home a group of stage personalities of my acquaintance, among them stage designers and directors, for the purpose of meeting Stokowski, to hear about some of his new ideas. Present were Norman Bel Geddes, Martha Graham, Theresa Helburn, Doris Humphrey, Charles Weidman, Richard Hammond, Leonide Massine, Rouben Mamoulian, Agnes de Mille, Donald Oenslager, Lee Simonson, and Nicholas Roerich.

That February afternoon turned out to be blustery. Two or three guests had just arrived when my maid rushed into the drawing room and announced to me excitedly, 'Mrs. Reis, there is a fire in the pantry!' I ran out to find a little curling flame creeping across the ceiling. A short circuit, probably! I called the Fire Department. The voice on the other end boomed at me, 'Shut off your electric current in the cellar!' and I hurried to do as I was told.

The memory of a fire in our house when it was in process of being remodeled made me apprehensive, so I put in a second call for the fireman. Meanwhile, smoke was filling the drawing room and, as we had not yet located any candles, everyone was

---

2. G. P. Putnam's Sons, New York, 1941.

milling around, chatting in the dark. I recruited two early guests, Norman Bel Geddes and Richard Hammond, to bring up a large fire extinguisher from the entrance hall. They dashed to do so but, being inexperienced, when they tried to play it on the ceiling they seized it by the wrong end, soaking their own clothes instead. Where under the sun were the firemen, I wondered. Hurrying into the hall to watch for them, suddenly I was relieved to see a dozen of them come filing in. Immediately they took command, shouting, 'Bring a ladder!' 'Do——' this, 'Don't——' do that. One of them exclaimed impatiently to me, 'Lady, you'll have to get us a ladder — we're not ladder-men.' I rushed to get the maid's help in locating a ladder, which she trundled to the scene of the short circuit.

Just at that moment one fireman caught sight of the state of Geddes' and Hammond's clothing, which was awash with sulphuric acid. 'Better get out of those suits as fast as you can,' the fireman instructed them; 'they'll rot right on you if you don't soak 'em in fresh water quick.'

'Go upstairs to my husband's closet,' I called to Norman and Dick, 'and I think you'll find some golf clothes and sweaters you can get into.' Geddes was twice as broad as Arthur, and Dick was twice as tall.

More guests were arriving. Trying to keep track of what was going on in that direction I heard a voice announce, 'I don't think we've met — I'm Lee Simonson,' and a voice, 'I've seen you on the stage; I am ——' and so on and so on. They were all behaving exactly as though they were in the habit of arriving for tea at houses that were on fire; inasmuch as all the guests seemed to be managing beautifully, I decided I could return to the firemen. By this time they had hacked open the ceiling, cut the house wires, and were clumping down the stairs on their way out.

Candles appeared. My guests settled calmly around the tea table. Stokowski launched unconcernedly into his ideas for music and stage, with discussion of some of our plans for the future of the League. Everyone listened intently and in no time everyone around the table was expressing an opinion, or making an offer to help.

I had just received a letter from Otto H. Kahn and I read it in part:

> In Mr. Stokowski's highly experimental work in connection with the League of Composers, it would seem from many indications that a new form of art is seeking to find expression . . . Our times, our spirit, our reactions, are groping for some manifestation in art commensurate with the vast changes which, of late years, have come into our daily lives . . .

I had hardly got out the last word when a man, putting his head in the pantry door, broke in on our discussion to say, 'I'm from Consolidated Edison, here to put on the lights again. Where's your cellar so I can connect up the juice?'

Stokowski's dramatic sense of holding attention made him unwilling to be interrupted. 'Go away and come back tomorrow!' he ordered, waving his hand in a gesture of dismissal. 'Besides, we like the candlelight.'

'Excuse me,' I interrupted, 'but my family will want the electricity tonight.' My domestic life was important to me if it was not to Stokowski! I ran after the Consolidated Edison man who had vanished dutifully, like a musician banished from a Stokowski rehearsal.

The lights came on again. We blew out the candles and finished up the tea party with enthusiasm for future plans and a genuine desire by all to co-operate.

Stokowski took his departure without ever once having mentioned the fire or having given any sign that he knew about it. As Mamoulian left he said, laughing, 'Ask me again, Claire, when you're going to have a tea with a fire.'

Dmitri Shostakovich's name was hard enough to pronounce, and rather harder to spell. Artur Rodzinski, with the Cleveland Orchestra, had produced the *première* of this composer's opera *Lady Macbeth of Mzensk*. He appealed to the League to bring it to New York.

Since the depression we had not undertaken stage productions of Metropolitan Opera magnitude and we were glad of another opportunity to sponsor a major performance, in 1935. It was too expensive to bring the entire Cleveland chorus here in addition to a large cast of singers and the Cleveland Orchestra. We therefore invited members of a local chorus to take part in the New York production. We were not prepared, however, for the political reactions with which we were suddenly confronted by the White Russian chorus, a group which we needed because they sang in Russian.

This was the first Soviet opera that had come out of Russia since the Bolshevik Revolution. There were phrases in the text which the White Russians found 'objectionable' — whatever that meant!

I came into rehearsal one day to find everyone simply sitting around, not singing a note. As Rodzinski greeted me he said, 'We will begin soon again.'

'But what is going on?' I asked. The singers seemed to be marking out words on their music sheets, and inserting others in their place.

'We have had a sit-down strike,' said the irritated conductor, 'but we are now changing certain words and rephrasing part of the text which they say is "too Bolshevik"!'

During our musical adventures in the past we had encountered considerable varieties of difficulty, but this was our first political tangle. When we announced the opera as a Soviet opera — which it was, in point of fact — we were requested by the chorus to omit the word 'Soviet.' We were requested not to send any official invitation to the Soviet Consul or to the Soviet Ambassador at Washington.

In the light of the interest shown at the *Lady Macbeth première* in Cleveland, and despite banning of the term 'Soviet,' there was a great curiosity in New York about this presentation. Jascha Heifetz, who had heard the work on a trip to Russia, was quoted frequently as saying, 'One of the high points of my Russian trip last year was a performance in Moscow of *Lady Macbeth of Mzensk*, a dramatically exciting and musically most interesting work!'

The Metropolitan Opera House was packed to overflowing with all the regular boxholders and the League's entire formidable list of patrons. In an orchestra seat that evening was Igor Stravinsky. He listened to the opera intently. A leading critic, who had not spared either Stravinsky or the League when we gave some of his works a few years earlier, wrote in his review for the next morning, 'How unfortunate it is that a great composer like Stravinsky sat in the audience unobserved, listening to this commonplace music by Shostakovich. How much more important it would have been had the League of Composers chosen to do one of Stravinsky's works.' Can one ever please a critic I asked myself.

Several months after this performance in New York — although *Lady Macbeth* had been in the permanent repertoire of both the Moscow and Leningrad opera houses — Russia banned this work as 'unworthy of the Soviet culture,' and it was withdrawn completely from circulation.

In this connection it is interesting to recall that, at a meeting of distinguished American and foreign artists at the Waldorf-Astoria in 1949, Shostakovich was present, and the blunt question was put to him, 'What do you think of Stravinsky?' It was revealing to hear his bloodless, robot-like voice as he said, 'Stravinsky has lost touch with the masses, therefore he is not a great composer.' I could not help thinking of all the great men the masses had not understood. I realized too, how a personality like Shostakovich's could become warped, by being exposed to a political party possessing the power to mold, indeed to denounce, the artist's creative spirit.

At the conference, one of the speakers that day had asked me to wait after the speeches and questions, and he would introduce me to Shostakovich. 'Talk French to him,' someone said.

When I observed Shostakovich entering the hall, with a man

in front of him and a man in back of him, the three taking their seats on the dais only after everyone else was seated, I doubted whether anybody would be able to get me within speaking distance, in any language.

At the end of the meeting the chairman said, 'Will the audience kindly keep their seats until all the guests have left?' The ceremony at the beginning was reversed, and Shostakovich was conducted out of the hall, with the same man in front of him, the same man behind him. Only a short ten minutes before, he had been talking about Stravinsky who had 'lost touch with the masses, and was therefore not a great composer'!

Financial conditions continued unfavorable for elaborate new productions by the League on a Metropolitan Opera House scale. I was delighted when Stokowski showed interest in a semi-dramatic interpretation of Schoenberg's *Pierrot Lunaire*. This work had been heard in the United States only in concert form.

Again we enlisted Bobby Jones and, with Stokowski, worked out the dramatic ideas for a Town Hall event. The small ensemble of instrumentalists, with Stokowski conducting, was placed on the far left side of the stage, practically in darkness except for hooded lights on their music stands. Stokowski had said, 'Let's have the music for the ensemble photostated on black paper, only the notes in white.' He had been quite emphatic about this. 'I want to have the little instrumental group in almost complete darkness,' he kept reiterating.

Jones had designed a semi-sphere suggesting a crescent moon, which was in the center of the stage. Pierrot (Mina Hager) was in a stylized Pierrot costume, sitting on this moon and, in contrast to the musicians in semi-darkness, in a fairly bright light.

At the dress rehearsal Stokowski came suddenly to the front of the stage, calling, 'Claire, would you talk to me for a moment?' He added in a whisper across the footlights, 'Will you please send somebody out to buy a few yards of black cloth? We *must* cover the orchestra men's collars — their white shirts spoil the effect of darkness. I think this is so important!' Perhaps he had whispered to me for fear the men would object if they suspected what was in store for them.

In a few minutes the messenger came back with several yards of black sateen. We cut out triangles of the material and before the men could collect themselves to protest we had tied the black bibs around their collars. The only illumination was the bright light shining on Stokowski's hands as he conducted and gave Pierrot the necessary cues; the instrumentalists were completely invisible; Stokowski was much pleased, with both the bibs and the black music sheets.

During the preparations for each stage production there always seemed to be moments when we were in the position of the moth with the flame; but if we were burned often — chiefly by some of the critics — we were lured on to further trials through combining music with ballet, or pantomime, or drama. At the root of all our efforts was a desire to encourage composers to write more works for music and stage. The few performances that the League could sponsor as an example to others, together with the very limited record of contemporary operas performed by the Metropolitan or other opera companies, were discouraging for composers, if only in cost of time. A way needed to be found whereby writing for the medium of opera or ballet might assure a definite series of performances.

In 1939 the American Lyric Theater asked the League to join it in its first stage productions. New operas and ballets were aims of this society, in addition to the challenging fact that a permanent lyric theater had never been established in the United States. Among the directors on the board were Walter Damrosch, Angier Biddle Duke, Robert Edmond Jones, Lincoln Kirstein, Nelson Rockefeller, Thomas J. Watson, Jr., Mrs. Lawrence Tibbett, Carleton Sprague Smith, and myself, with Edward R. Wardwell as President.

As the League anticipated giving a chamber opera by Douglas Moore and Stephen Vincent Benét, called *The Devil and Daniel Webster*, we joined forces with this new organization. Their share in the early plans was to produce an opera based on the

music of Stephen Foster. Together we agreed to add three
ballets from Ballet Caravan, under Lincoln Kirstein's direction:
*Pocahontas* by Elliott Carter, *Filling Station* by Virgil Thomson,
and *Billy the Kid* by Aaron Copland. The program looked very
promising.

Ely Lilly, a magnate of pharmaceuticals, had offered a hundred thousand dollars to any person or group who would produce an opera based on Stephen Foster's melodies. Already Mr.
Lilly had given memorials to Foster in several cities. He also
wanted an opera to be written and produced — regardless of
the libretto — for Stephen Foster's music had been the great
passion of Mr. Lilly's life.

Between Clarence Loomis, the musician, and Sara Newmeyer,
the librettist, an opera was completed.

We ran into unforeseen difficulties with the manager of the
American Lyric Theater. His sudden illness forced us to post-
pone the opening, not once, but several times. Postponements
have many unhappy aspects. We began to wonder if we would
open this new theater at all.

One day I received an urgent message to please call on Mr.
Arthur Packard, then the director of one of the Rockefeller
foundations.

'Mrs. Reis,' he said, 'as the Lyric Theater seems to have col-
lapsed, I am told by Robert Edmond Jones that you are the only
person who could take over the work and bring it to a successful culmination. Now I believe you should.'

'Why, Mr. Packard,' I said, greatly surprised, for I had no
anticipation of any such request, 'it is very gracious of Bobby
to think well of my work, and it is true that we have done a lot
of things together, but although I am chairman of the executive
board I could not take on this managerial job, which would not
only require full time in the theater but all kinds of night work
too.' As I sat there, puzzling about Mr. Packard's share in our
calamities, he answered my next question before I could ask it.

'You will understand, Mrs. Reis,' he said, 'I am interested in
seeing this become a success; one of the Rockefellers is on your

board and has contributed money to the project. As your League of Composers is a partner in this new venture of the Lyric Theater, I do think you should step in and take over this job.'

I explained to him then that I had a husband, children, and a home preventing me from taking on any full-time job; that while I would gladly help to pull us out of some of the present difficulties, it would also be necessary to find a professional producer or theater manager.

Mr. Packard seemed a little disturbed, even surprised at the discovery of my private life. We decided soon, however, that Bobby Jones's second suggestion — namely Richard Aldrich, well known on Broadway as a producer — was an excellent one.

For some weeks nobody connected with us thought we would ever open this theater. Nevertheless, although we postponed the opening from early March until the middle of May, Fritz Reiner, John Houseman, and many other artists whom we had corralled in the interest of a brilliant season did stand by.

Despite the many able people on our board, we greatly misjudged our timing, in regard to weather as well as to rival entertainment. The World's Fair of 1939 opened the week we launched our gala production. Moreover, an unseasonal summer heat descended on the city, sending crowds to the World's Fair in preference to mazda-heated Broadway.

*The Devil and Daniel Webster*, brilliantly conducted by Fritz Reiner, was the League's contribution to the Lyric Theater; it met with great success and has since had frequent presentations in all parts of the country. Douglas Moore's letter of confidence showed his appreciation of those strenuous days, when he wrote me, 'I shudder to think of what would have happened if you had not stepped in. All along, I had a comfortable feeling that, with you a part of it, things would turn out all right.' He little realized how many shudders some of the rest of us had over the near collapse of the entire production!

Ballet Caravan's share of success was in large measure due to Lincoln Kirstein, who has now absorbed some of that program in the New York City Ballet Company. *Filling Station*, created by Virgil Thomson, has become one of the very successful ballets in its repertoire. *Billy the Kid*, by Copland, has frequently been repeated, by other companies.

Despite the fact that the stage production of *Oh Susanna*, with Stephen Foster's music, was handsomely carried out by Robert Edmond Jones and José Ruben, neither critics nor musicians liked this operatic version of Foster's music.

But Mr. Lilly was happy! His wish to hear an opera based on Foster melodies was completely satisfied. For this occasion he brought a carload of guests from Indianapolis to New York in a private car. He reserved one whole floor in the Waldorf-Astoria hotel. His guests attended the show in full evening regalia, complete with orchids and boutonnieres. Having spent a hundred thousand dollars to satisfy a cherished personal desire, Mr. Lilly had no regrets.

The underlying reason for Stephen Foster's untimely death prompted me to appeal to Mr. Lilly the following year for financial aid — perhaps some commissions — which might help to save some living composers we knew from the specter of the same tragic fate.

Our theme, 'The forgotten man in music,' had not brought us success with patrons of our Metropolitan Opera productions, in previous years. I hoped for a sympathetic response in this instance. But Mr. Lilly was not interested in the composer of today, nor in his difficulties in earning a livelihood. He was not even moved by the fact that the tragic career of Stephen Foster could easily be duplicated in the lives of many composers. Mr. Lilly was interested in Stephen Foster melodies.

The League of Composers continued its search for wider opportunities for composers of opera and ballet. Finally a new project emerged, 'The Composers' Theater.' We called upon the resources of music and drama departments in universities and colleges, conservatories, and museums to help in building up producing units for the lyric stage. Each unit could use its own orchestral and/or dramatic group, its own chorus and soloists. The stage designs, or completed décor, and costumes would be rented out by the League to any unit in the co-operating centers of production.

The plan was simple and within a few weeks fifteen to twenty universities and colleges had accepted this suggestion of a 'Composers Theater.' Among institutions that showed positive interest were Harvard, Yale, Columbia, Smith, Vassar, Princeton, Bennington, Bard, Western Reserve, Duke, the Juilliard, Eastman, and Curtis Schools of Music, and others.

A first production in this new project was at Converse College, at the Spartenburg Festival. A *Tree on the Plains*, by Ernst Bacon, with libretto by Paul Horgan, was premiered, and later repeated at Columbia University and in several other cities.

Sponsored by the Music and Drama departments of Columbia University, Benjamin Britten's opera, *Paul Bunyan*, with libretto by W. H. Auden, followed soon after.

The project had made a fine beginning; there was real hope for the needed series of performances through this means, for educational institutions seemed genuinely interested.

But then came 7 December 1941 and the onset of World War II for the United States. One after another, the universities wrote us students were leaving for the armed services, music and drama departments were greatly curtailed. For the time being the attempt to create a national movement in the universities had to be shelved. Shortly after the war was over Douglas Moore, professor and head of the Department of Music at Columbia University, established a similar plan there with the assistance of the Columbia Theater Associates and the Alice M. Ditson Fund.

Although some projects of the League of Composers have been short-lived, nevertheless they have left an imprint in many cases, giving others an objective and the impulse to reach it. I was reminded of this by Lincoln Kirstein, formerly the Managing Director of the New York City Center of Music and Drama. At a party where we were bidding farewell to the City Center

Ballet Company at the end of the season, Lincoln said, 'You must know that your League of Composers really is greatly responsible for what we are doing today, because you started some of the great ballets in this country with Stokowski; we have just carried on from there.'

'That is a nice compliment, Lincoln,' I answered, 'and do you remember an article that you wrote for *The Hound and The Horn* way back in 1931? You expressed the hope that Stokowski and the Philadelphia Orchestra with the League of Composers would find painters and brilliant choreographers who would collaborate. You even mentioned George Balanchine at that time. I think that in your mind then the greatness of Diaghilev was to be carried on by us. Well, YOU have certainly done it, by creating the great ballet company you have brought to the Center.'

As we continued our talk about the creative spirit in the arts I was reminded of the early days at the Center when I had asked Stokowski and Robert Edmond Jones to meet Newbold Morris, the chairman of the newly formed City Center of Music and Drama. He had quickly agreed with me that the great artists' creative talents would bring a wealth of experience and prestige to this new organization. Within a short time Stokowski had volunteered his services and formed a City Center orchestra, and with Jones they had produced a Christmas Festival for music and stage which was an unforgettable experience.

It is my belief that the same high standard of creative achievement of the ballet company should become a constant, not a sporadic share of the City Center's productions. It is conceivable that a great Lyric Theater of America can arise in time. A few distinguished operatic *premières* such as Rossini's *Cenerentola*, Menotti's *Amahl*, and Nicolai's *Merry Wives*, and a few other world *premières* have called forth talent and vision.

Fortunately the City Center's Ballet includes in its repertoire a very extensive list of American and European commissioned works. Directed by Lincoln Kirstein and choreographed chiefly by the inspired artist George Balanchine, this company has achieved a unique place in the world. Moreover, the new interpretation of the classical ballets added to the contemporary ballets has opened the City Center's doors to a new vista in American culture, and a new era.

For the composer at least there is a hope for the future, as he turns his talents in the direction of music and stage. To help him on his way, however, he needs the poets and playwrights, the stage designers and the stage directors to co-operate with him. Most of all he needs to see his work produced on the stage, just as he needed — and still does — the experience of hearing his symphonic works performed.

Until recently the operatic scene in America has seemed very inadequate, especially in comparison with the great number of opera companies in Europe. Without government subsidy — which in many of the European countries helps to meet the deficit — opera on a 'grand' scale still remains an unsolved problem in this country. It becomes apparent that a hope for the future of American opera lies in finding the way to give more performances with smaller units in smaller auditoriums than the Metropolitan Opera House.

When Tullio Serafin, the famous Italian conductor of opera (formerly with the Metropolitan Opera Company), returned recently to New York, after a long absence abroad, he said that the greatest changes he observed were in the operatic field.

'Across the country I find new ideas are circulating,' Serafin commented, 'an expansion of opera activity bubbles with youth and vigor, a desire to perform and to hear the less hackneyed works (whether it be a seventeenth-century opera or a contemporary work) and a welcome change of attitude that the native talent is at last coming fully into its own. I am convinced that opera's days of future glory lie right here in America, where the windows have been firmly opened and the fresh air let in.'

# 10

## Composers in Wartime

AT THE BEGINNING of World War II the composers on the board
of the League frequently discussed their ideas about contributing as a group to the war effort. While many of them were beyond the draft age, everyone had a natural desire to do something to help in the world crisis.

The newspapers were propagandizing the importance of
maintaining our cultural life for those fortunate enough to be
far from the battlefields, and special mention was made of
preserving the educational institutions for those who would return after the war.

President Roosevelt issued a statement to the effect that, while
it was obvious that the war effort was the primary task of everyone, amusement and recreation would help to maintain human
efficiency by bolstering morale, relieving people of the strain
of war and work. Sports, motion pictures, music, drama, and
dance, all having beneficial value in wartime, were therefore
commended as necessary.

We kept in touch with many composers already in the service; their letters inspired us often in sustaining the League's musical activities. One letter came from Elliott Carter, a very talented young composer, who had been an active member of

154

our board. He was in New Mexico, about to join the armed forces. 'I am finishing my symphony now, and about to join the Army,' he wrote. 'I hope you all realize how important it is to keep up your efforts in behalf of contemporary music, especially now; the League is giving us one more tangible thing to fight for.'

We heard from some of the musicians already drafted, about their difficulties in finding a place where their particular skills and talents could prove useful in the armed forces. Often they pointed out that painters' technical abilities were being absorbed for the art of camouflage. Could not similarly useful opportunities for the composer-musician be uncovered? Surely those who could play or teach a band instrument might well be used in the war machinery? Through many of the letters ran evidence of frustration at finding that the desire to contribute creatively in a time of world catastrophe was looked on often as of little practical value.

In Washington at least eight Government agencies in building programs around the war effort included music. Among them were the Office of Civilian Defense, the United Service Organizations, the National Education Association, and the Joint Army and Navy Committee on Welfare and Recreation, the latter set up as a co-ordinating program of musical activities within the armed forces.

The chairman of this group's sub-committee on music was Dr. Harold Spivacke, who is also the Chief of the Music Division of the Library of Congress. I wrote Dr. Spivacke, asking if he thought it would be of value to the Army and Navy Committee on Welfare and Recreation for me to assemble detailed information on the background, training, and experience of composers of draft age. My idea was that their earlier training might be channeled to certain technical departments rather than KP — to which we learned, with consternation, that some of them were presently assigned. After conferring with his committee, Dr. Spivacke sent me a letter of approval, asking me to get this project under way as promptly as possible.

I drew up a questionnaire to set forth the composers' general education, instrumental training, ability to arrange band music, original compositions for films, radio, and plays, and any other experience in the entertainment field. I sent out an urgent request for names and addresses to the American Society of Composers, Authors, and Publishers and they co-operated immediately by making their lists available. Within forty-eight hours, 1500 questionnaires had been mailed out to composers of draft age.

Soon Dr. Spivacke wrote me, 'We have made use of the answers to the questionnaire you sent out and have found them very helpful. They are now housed in the office of the Joint Army and Navy Committee.' Naturally, he could not give us amplifying details.

I had also been in correspondence with the Chief of Special Services of the War Department, conveying the earnest desire of many American composers to be of active assistance. He replied,

> The desire to serve one's country through the medium of music has been emphasized throughout the ages. Undoubtedly the creativeness of modern composers will be influenced by the mighty forces at work. However, no provision has been made by the Army for the official encouragement of musical composition. Perhaps the League of Composers may serve as the co-ordinating medium for the correlation and necessary publicity concerning the work of its members which has an inspirational effect. [Signed] F. H. Osborne, Brigadier General, Chief of Special Services.

I felt that the words 'inspirational effect,' coming from a military mind, might portend an important new influence for composers. Meanwhile, though composers were proving their abilities somewhat in band music, they were also encountering some strange situations wherein military music and militarism did not always seem to be in harmony.

Lehman Engel, a very talented conductor, was one of the composers who had quickly been recognized by the Navy as both an excellent band leader and a qualified teacher. He was placed in a Mid-Western training school.

One day he was asked to conduct the band in a concert. The commanding officer made a point of being present. Lehman finished the program and turned to the Lieutenant Colonel, hopefully awaiting some approving comment. The superior officer carefully looked over the band complement, from first row to last. Turning then to Lehman he said curtly, 'It does sound good, but it certainly looks all wrong. We will have to change things right away. Now, just look at that big fellow over there. Why is he playing that little instrument — piccolo, I believe you call it, don't you? And look at that little man in the corner, why should he be playing that big bass drum?'

Amazed, Lehman could only explain that when these men were inducted into the Armed Forces they were already playing specific instruments and their physical size had no bearing on their talent. The fact was that nothing was wrong with the band; the Lieutenant Colonel and musicians just used different measuring rods.

As the war accelerated we tried to find more and more ways to relate our efforts for music to war activities; those were days when no one with any conscience could continue to live in a rarified atmosphere.

It seemed clear that our organization had a double job: to help the morale of our colleagues still in civilian life as well as those taken into the service and already in the fighting ranks.

For a concert to be given at the New York Public Library we prepared a program of works by composers then in the armed forces. We introduced a work by Ulysses S. Kay, a very talented Negro, and he was given special permission by his commanding officer at a Rhode Island camp to attend the concert and hear his Piano Sonata played. He was called to take a bow and as he stood there in his Navy uniform, I thought what a poignant memory he would carry back to camp with him, and perhaps on into battle.

On that same program were works by other men who by this

time were overseas. We mailed copies of the program to them and their response to our thought of them during those war days was touching indeed.

We had letters from men in the services from all parts of the world, asking us to mail them copies of our magazine *Modern Music*. A lieutenant wrote from an Army hospital, 'If you have any free copies of past issues — or, even better, of current issues — of *Modern Music*, we hungrily beg for them.' A soldier at Camp Robinson, Arkansas, asked if we could notify him of any networks carrying contemporary music programs. 'Here in Camp Robinson,' he wrote, 'I find the lack of music, especially modern music, pretty painful. There are thousands of people like us, dislocated from the big cities and spread out in all the camps and hospitals, glued to our radios. We *need* your help.' Naturally we made every effort to meet such requests, to pursue every means of fitting our activities into the war effort.

Correspondence reached us even from the Royal Air Force headquarters in the Middle East, asking us to recommend 'the finest American overture or symphony.' This request was from a young professional conductor who was preparing programs to be given in Egypt and in Palestine. His letter ended, 'It may surprise you to learn that there is a really keen and intelligent demand for music of high quality in these parts of the world, and an audience which would be interested in first-class performances of first-class American works.' To his question as to 'the finest,' I answered that we were glad to send him lists of composers' names, though we would not indicate any *one* as the finest. As we were broadcasting some American contemporary works to our American outposts, perhaps some of these programs would come to his attention.

During the war days it was encouraging to receive a letter from Charles Thomson, who was Chief of the Division of Cultural Relations in the State Department. He believed that music's wartime role was 'to maintain the sanity of the people all over the world.' He wrote, 'Music is one of the great satisfactions of life that cannot be touched by rationing or priorities, nor sunk at sea, nor seized by conquering armies for their own use; therefore, music remains truly international.'

Our concerts in New York proceeded all through the war, and we were glad to hear from the New York Defense Recreation Committee that they could use thirty or more tickets for each concert for men in the city on leave. As the war continued Mrs. Julius Ochs Adler, chairman of the recreation committee, found more and more men interested in music, and during the Christmas holidays we doubled the number of free tickets sent them for our programs.

At a meeting one day with a group of young music lovers who had recently formed an associate committee to help the League's varied activities, we took up the problem of music in wartime. Pierson Underwood, an able young musician and chairman of this committee, remarked on the fact that so many soldiers and sailors were to be seen strolling in Central Park in those days, obviously looking for recreation and entertainment in the open air. 'Why don't we give them some good music to listen to when they sit on the Mall, or row on the lake?' he said. In an instant we all seemed to be talking at once, suggesting ways and means of making the music pleasant to hear. There ought to be loud-speakers, with controlled carrying power; motor trucks could carry instrumental ensembles around the Park — all kinds of fantastic ideas were put forward. We finally got down to cases, deciding that the first step was to ask city authorities if they would sanction our plans. Meanwhile we would investigate the problem of artists who might volunteer to help us entertain the servicemen on furlough.

I set out to help the young committee by going down to City Hall first to talk to Newbold Morris, then President of the City Council. I was referred to him by Mayor La Guardia.

Mr. Morris seemed very much interested and called Robert Moses, the chairman of State Council of Parks and New York City Commissioner of Parks, who asked me to come right over to talk with him.

Mr. Moses was even more enthusiastic, and he quickly offered

us a variety of places for the proposed concerts, a new pier on
the East River, an amphitheater on Riverside Drive. He made
several other suggestions, believing wholeheartedly as he did in
more and more recreation, more and more use of parks.

Meanwhile we decided to use various foreign music groups
with their folk music and dance for the main part of the programs and also to introduce into each concert at least one contemporary work, sometimes more than one. I felt timid about
revealing to Mr. Moses our planned modern slant for these programs but noticed as we talked that he did not even raise an
eyebrow at the mention of modern music. And he seemed unusually pleased that we would use foreign groups and their folk
music.

After considering the acoustical problems of concerts in the
open air, we concentrated on the Mall in Central Park, and
Prospect Park in Brooklyn. The series was called 'Wartime
Concerts for Soldiers and Sailors,' and at the request of Mayor
La Guardia and Robert Moses we continued them a second
season.

The hard-working young committee, steered by Mr. Pierson
Underwood, Mrs. Stephen Duggan, Jr., Miss Sally Dodge, and
Mrs. Martha Norton, scoured the city for talent. Between the
Bowery and the Bronx they unearthed the Radischev Russian
Chorus and Dancers, an African group under Effiem Odok of Ni-
geria, the Puerto Rican Choral Singers, and the Chinese People's
Chorus led in Chinese guerilla songs by Liu Liang Mo. There
were music and folk dancing from Lithuania, Greece, Italy,
Scotland, and Czechoslovakia. We remained faithful to our
original intention and contemporary music was heard on each
program.

During these wartime park concerts several incidents qualified
for our file of 'concert calamities.' What organization does not
encounter its jinx at one moment or another? Fortunately all
our near-calamities had happy endings.

One day when Sally Dodge was combing the lower East Side

for local talent, she found Mr. Liu Liang Mo rehearsing a chorus in a laundry. He told her that the group was made up of printers, restaurant workers, and laundry men who just liked to sing. At the request of the Generalissimo, Chiang Kai-shek, Mr. Mo had taught Chinese soldiers to sing while marching, something which had not previously been their custom. Describing his experiences he said, 'A singing army is a fighting army,' and he felt very proud of a new method by which he had trained soldiers to sing.

We wrote up his story in brief, with a few program notes. But just half an hour before the concert was to begin Sally happened to glance at a program and, with an expression of horror on her face, ran over to show us a printer's error. Instead of reading, 'A new form of Chinese singing,' the printer had set it to read, 'A new form of Chinese sinning.' In all our many adventures in musical projects we had never gone so far as to feature vice. All of us seized pencils and changed every program. The concert ran smoothly, and 8000 people were in the audience.

It proved fortunate that our final rehearsals for these programs were always held at five o'clock on the Central Park Mall for, the following week, we encountered another situation calling upon all the ingenuity of our young associates to prevent a real calamity at concert time.

Leon Barzin and the National Orchestral Association had volunteered their services for a concert. As they arrived in the Park, wind was blowing the leaves about and an early spring gale seemed a definite threat. Mr. Barzin inquired for music clips for holding the sheets on the music stands.

There was an instant of stunned silence from the members of our young committee who were new at preparing open air concerts. No one had known anything about music clips. Rising to the emergency someone said, 'If we run we can get to Woolworth's before it closes, they'll have something we can use for clips.' Off dashed Pierson Underwood and Mrs. Duggan, plan-

ning when they got to the store to divide up the aisles until
they found some articles on a counter which would serve the
purpose.

At 6:05 p.m. Mr. Underwood came racing back, his pockets
bulging with bobby pins. 'These were the best substitutes I
could find,' he gasped; 'I would have taken clothespins, but I
guess they'd be too light.' He had underestimated Mrs. Duggan.
She arrived on his heels and — practical housekeeper that she
was — spilled forth from a paper bag a collection of mouse
traps! 'These'll hold the pages tight — tight as a mouse!' she
cried, implying considerable experience with mice in country
houses. And so it was that the mouse traps proved both a novel
and highly effective way of anchoring the pages during the concert on that windy evening.

We heard about recently organized bands and orchestras in
some of the armament factories near New York; they were a
valuable addition to recreational projects in the factories. We
did not have much information about their aesthetic standards,
however, and several of our Associate Committee members took
a day on Long Island to investigate. They reported back to us
that some very good musicians were available. Within a short
time, the Sperry Gyroscope Company accepted our invitation
to send its band to play in the two parks. Fifty-five men and
women from the plant — including two Ph.D.'s, a former chauf-
feur, and an all-engineer section which played the horns —
proudly made their debuts under the joint auspices of the Department of Parks and the League of Composers, and were not
only applauded but also cheered by huge audiences. As one of
the concerts ended, a comic in the crowd was overheard to say,
'That conductor sure is a wartime man. He must be conserving
lumber, he won't even use a baton!'

'I find this a very exciting evening,' someone remarked to a
critic. I looked around. It was the great artist, Wanda Landowska; she seemed to be enjoying herself hugely. People began to
recognize her and were gathering around when a big police-

man strode up and ordered everybody to make way for a car, approaching along the Mall. 'Move on! Move on! Quickly, ladies, make room!' he cried, 'let the truck pick up the band instruments — all these guys have to get back to work. Don't you know there's a war on?' Landowska had vanished and the crowd scattered obediently.

The League decided to commission a series of eighteen short pieces, each work to be written on a war-associated theme. I asked Dr. Artur Rodzinski, then conductor of the New York Philharmonic Symphony Orchestra, if he would like to play these works, one at the opening of each program, as a gesture of support in the war. He accepted gladly, saying in a statement to the press,

> These commissions serve three important purposes. One: a strong and moving reminder to our country that the preservation and furtherance of our cultural resources is a duty and a privilege of the first importance, in times as critical as our own. Two: these works will create a living musical record of various aspects of this war, with its accompanying social manifestations. Three: composers resident in the United States will be encouraged and stimulated, for all too rarely they are given the opportunity to be heard.

When Dr. Koussevitzky heard about these eighteen works to be written, he called me on the telephone, saying, 'I would like to have half of that group of short pieces on war themes, for *premières* with the Boston Symphony. 'I'd be delighted to ask Dr. Rodzinski,' I replied; 'I'm sure he will divide them with you.'

But I was mistaken. Dr. Rodzinski said, 'This project was accepted by me for the eighteen concerts with the Philharmonic next season, one on each program, and I want them all as *premières*.'

I felt powerless to change his mind. He was right in that we had begun the idea with the New York Philharmonic Symphony, of which he was the conductor. On the other hand, Dr. Koussevitzky had been such a good friend of so many composers, as well as an old friend of mine, that I really wanted to give him half of the group.

In our desire to enlist a large number of composers to write on war themes, we felt that the series had value for the audience, too, as part of the morale effort of the times. Many of the composers described some of their own emotions or experiences from World War I or II in the program notes they sent with their compositions. For instance, in connection with 'The Anxious Bugler,' John Alden Carpenter wrote for the program, ' "The Anxious Bugler" may stand for any man anywhere who finds himself a soldier. He works and sweats, and sometimes he fears. He also has his hopes, with home always in the back of his mind; and at times the stern voice of God is in his ears.'

'To a Lone Sentry' was the title of Norman Dello Joio's composition, and he wrote, 'Sentries walk their posts at night. The man alone has only thoughts for company. Great distance makes these thoughts vivid. The strong ties of friends and loves become painfully real to a man alone. Recapturing both the sad and happy memories of a once peaceful life helps to pass the time of the sentinel's solitary vigil. To the lonely sentries stationed over the world, I dedicate this work.'

For a humorous march, 'Soldiers on the Town,' the composer Nicolai Berezowsky wrote, 'An attempt to portray soldiers on leave on a week-end pass, anywhere, any town.' The Negro composer, William Grant Still's composition was called 'In Memoriam — The Colored Soldiers Who Died for Democracy'; his program note read in part, 'The first American in our armed forces to be killed in World War II was a Negro soldier. My thoughts turned to the colored soldiers all over the world, fighting under our flag, and under the flags of countries allied with us. Our civilization has known no greater patriotism, no greater loyalty, than that shown by the colored men who fight and die for democracy. Those who return will, I hope, come back to a better world.'

Other titles were 'Destroyer Song' (dedicated to the U.S. Navy) by Douglas Moore; 'Invasion' by Bernard Rogers; 'War Song March' (sub-title 'They Are There') by Charles Ives; 'Before the Battle' by Werner Josten. 'Fugue on a Victory Theme' by Walter Piston was based on an adjutant's call used in the U.S. Navy which had impressed Piston greatly in 1918 with its spirited simplicity. Roger Sessions' piece was called 'Dirge.' Henry Cowell's was 'American Pipers' and dedicated to the A.E.F. men stationed in Ireland who had seized the opportunity to study the bagpipes and learn the Irish folk tunes.

All these works presented a great challenge. Olin Downes's opinion of this plan was that

> This is a great creative opportunity, nor will the composer be to blame if expression of the essential simplicity and conciseness eludes him. The time set for his task is of the briefest, the theme of the greatest. No situation could be more calculated to take the 'serious composer' out of his real or fancied aesthetic seclusion, and force him to stand creatively on his own feet, and address his fellow man in terms of sincerity and reality. And that is needed in Art. It will be needed in Music, even after Victory and the Armistice.

During the season, seven or eight works were performed, some of which received genuine approval by public and press. Among them was Bohuslav Martinu's 'Memorial to Lidice' which was repeated several times during the war years.

In the late spring, a letter from Dr. Rodzinski announced that he would play the remaining works the following year, merely that, with no further explanation. I thought very often about Dr. Koussevitzky's wish to take half of the series, and of the great disappointment of the men who were not played, 'because of the orchestra's strenuous schedule.' Besides this, the late Macklin Marrow, then Director of the New York branch of the Office of War Information, had agreed that live recordings of all these works would be made during their initial performance and shipped abroad for additional broadcasts from our various output stations in all parts of the world, to be heard by the troops, by the civilian populations of Allied and neutral nations, and even by those in some of the occupied countries.

As I talked with Macklin Marrow one day in his office, about the wonderful work being done by the American Overseas branch of the O.W.I., Macklin said, 'Perhaps you have not heard, Claire, that we now have a collection of music of all nations, including symphonic works by American composers, also folk music from all parts of the world, a collection larger than any that has been made elsewhere.'

I was feeling very unhappy at the moment about this matter of having only part of our war series played by the Philharmonic, so it was a good pickup to know that our American composers were being so widely introduced to the peoples of foreign countries.

Macklin smiled, saying, 'You probably cannot realize how some of these far-off countries look upon us, and not just musically. But let me tell you what we're doing. For instance, in some little European towns, they only think of Chicago as a city of gangsters because of our periodic headlines and radio reports. Well, this is the way we begin our broadcast. We say, "You are now going to hear one of the finest orchestras in the country, the Chicago Symphony Orchestra. It comes to you from a city of many millions of people, a city of wonderful museums and other cultural institutions." ' He paused and we both laughed at his sales talk — as though I were in need of being converted to the respectable advantages of Chicago and its great orchestra!

While we had been developing our own new wartime projects for composers, we had made efforts to learn of conditions in other countries. In Russia, for many years prior to the war, there had been great activity in musical groups and clubs, both in amateur and professional circles. When Russia entered the war these musical groups turned their talents immediately to the entertainment of the troops, and also to keeping up morale for their families at home. The composers were accustomed to writing war songs; too, there had been a symposium in Moscow, lasting five days, led by composers, poets, and other USSR artists, to discuss war themes, especially war songs.

In England, prior to the war, there had been little if any affiliation between government and artists. It was all the more amazing to note the immediate success of CEMA, the Council for the Encouragement of Music and Art. Established in England in 1940 to encourage music and drama, it was supported chiefly by government subsidy to protect the interests of artists and to provide war-harried men and women with entertainment at small cost. In small communities and in factories, local projects were developed; assistance was given to theaters, orchestras, and entertainments provided in parks and other public places. In addition, during the darkest days of the war, Dame Myra Hess's wonderful mid-day concerts helped heroically to keep up the people's morale.

In the spring of 1942, the annual meeting of the League's Board and the National Committee of Composers was held at the home of Mrs. W. Murray Crane. Talks were given by Aaron Copland and Robert Edmond Jones. The topic was 'The War.'

Each man differed in approach, but what each said was very true. In part, Copland said,

> To talk about the composer's role in wartime — well, composers are always in the war. They struggle to write a piece of music, struggle to get it accepted, to have it heard, sometimes have to struggle to find time just to write a piece, for usually they have to do other things in order to earn a livelihood. So the composer lives continuously in a wartime atmosphere.
>
> But this great war only makes the problem the more serious. We have offered Washington the services of the composer to write background music for war films, to arrange music for army bands, to write songs or production numbers for the entertainment of troops — yet to date very little has come of it. The composers want to help in the war effort. Music has an important contribution to make in the final orientation between ourselves and the people of other countries.

Robert Edmond Jones began by saying,

> This is the first time I have stood up in public to talk since
> Pearl Harbor; the words do not flow quite so easily, because
> it is hard to talk about art in wartime when people are lay-
> ing down their very lives. Perhaps some sincere thoughts on
> this subject may be of value. The entire world is concerned
> with real things, but we should not forget that there are
> other things which are just as real, although you cannot
> touch them with your hands. They are the intangibles,
> ideals, freedom, brotherhood, truth — all intangibles, but
> real.
>
> Art is like these things; it is also intangible, but real. Art
> is created by people called artists. Perhaps they understand
> some things more than the rest of us can. There never has
> been a greater need to encourage, to help, to push artists,
> in order that, being inspired, they may inspire us.
>
> Perhaps all art is meant to remind us how important
> people are.

When the war ended, Minna Lederman resumed her correspondence, for the magazine *Modern Music*, with many of the
European writers with whom communication had been interrupted during the critical years of hostilities. Occasionally between 1941 and 1944 an article would come to us from France
or from England, giving news of composers, or concerts, or
operas. In 1942 Marc Blitzstein, in the Air Force, had written
from London. 'The big town is jumping. There is frenzied activity in all fields.' Then, during the most devastating bombings,
he composed 'The Airborne Symphony.' Marc told me that this
is the only instance of a musical work's being created as an actual
assignment by an army to one of its enlisted soldiers, during a
war, and in the very zone of war-operations.

Robert Ward, an active member of the League's board and
later Director of the Music School Settlement, sent a very
different sort of letter from Fort Ord in California, where he
was stationed. He stressed the problems of the composers' lives
in the Army, quoting the Dean of the Army Music School in
Virginia, who had said cogently, 'This School was originally
organized to make musicians of soldiers; now we must make

soldiers out of musicians.' Drastic changes in the curriculum now required well-trained musicians to gain — not just band experience — but the necessary instruction in the non-musical functions of the band leader.

We found new problems in postwar music, both theoretical and real ones. Help was needed in the relocation of musicians and the resumption of musical activities that had been curtailed. Discussion of former political sympathies of musicians became a new battleground in itself. Because of widespread interest in the fate of many artists, Minna arranged a symposium in *Modern Music,* on 'Artists, and Collaboration.' She solicited the views of several distinguished composers, former Europeans now living in the United States. Some were all-forgiving, others realistically severe.

Arnold Schoenberg wrote from California, 'Those who acted like politicians are politicians and should be treated in the same manner in which politicians are treated. Those who did not so act should escape punishment.' With leniency toward his colleagues, Schoenberg continued, 'But considering the low mental and moral standard of artists in general, I would say — treat them like immature children — call them fools, and let them escape.' To the contrary, justly regarding musicians as responsible human beings, Darius Milhaud's viewpoint was, 'I don't see why artists should not be treated as ordinary citizens. For example, Mr. X is a composer who has written a few works in which you may find a certain gift. He became a Minister in the Laval cabinet. Now he is arrested, accused as a traitor, a German spy. I hope he will be shot.' [1]

Bohuslav Martinu, Vittorio Rieti, and others added many divergent points of view to a very stirring problem. Ernst Krenek repudiated Shostakovich for acknowledging the right of his government to impose aesthetic demands upon art for political use.

---

1. *Modern Music*, League of Composers, New York, Vol. 22, No. 1, November-December, 1944.

The symposium opened up many arguments but few solutions.

As a further means to resume our European contacts, I was advised to call on the Secretary of the United Nations Information Board, to offer our services in renewing relations in other countries. The Secretary was British and had just come back from England.

As I began to talk with him, he seemed little interested in considering any aesthetic values among postwar plans. He could only talk to me about the grim picture of war as he had seen it in England, and the reality of the distress of the people. 'I've lived with these people, who are hollow-eyed from lack of sleep from the bombings, their clothes threadbare; I've seen their homes with gaping holes in them. These people don't want music,' he said grimly. 'Every human being in civilian life has been doing duty several nights each week in addition to their long day's work,' he continued. 'That is England. The people need rest, they need physical care.'

I talked about the English spirit about which we had heard so much throughout the war. 'Just remember,' I said, 'what Dame Myra Hess's concerts did for morale through the most severe bombing period. I hear now, too, that the Philharmonic Orchestra is filling its London concert hall with people in real need of music. Our own League, for instance, has had so many letters from boys in the Army asking us to keep up our musical work, "to keep the home fires burning" until they return.'

I then showed him a letter from Stokowski written during the war; he had asked for the names of some new American compositions, saying, 'I am playing American music in one-quarter of all my programs, because I feel strongly that, for musical and patriotic reasons, we should play the best modern American music, particularly during the war.'

The Secretary began to think further, and said reflectively, 'Perhaps when I speak of only the grim side, I should not assume that that is the entire picture today.' To my surprise he suddenly changed the tone of his voice, continuing, 'I do wonder now, as we prepare for Flag Day here, whether we should allow the flags to be carried by beautiful girls with beautiful legs, or should we only look at the flags. What do you think?'

I assured him that I believed there was morale value in the flags, and also in the beautiful girls — marching with their beautiful legs!

Shortly after the war ended I met a well-known Italian lawyer, Piero Sereni, a friend of G. Francesco Malipiero, of whom we talked. 'I have never met him,' I said, 'but I feel as if I knew him, for we had so much correspondence in the earlier years. You know, Malipiero arranged the "Sette Canzoni" for the League for chamber orchestra; Tullio Serafin conducted it for us in Town Hall.'

Mr. Sereni became more interested, saying, 'I hope to see him next summer, and I'll tell him about our chat.' As he was about to leave he said, 'Did you know that Malipiero has not written any music lately, for he could not afford to buy coffee in Italy? Without coffee he simply cannot write.'

'But that is dreadful!' I exclaimed, 'I shall send him some at once.' I thought of the limitless cups of coffee available to almost anyone in the United States, and how much it was missed by those deprived of it when it became a war luxury.

I wrote immediately to Malipiero and sent him two five-pound cartons of coffee.

A few weeks later, after my packages had arrived in Asolo, Italy, he wrote me,

> Dear Mrs. Reis: It was for me a real emotion to receive your letter and see the headline 'League of Composers' again. After the terrible cataclysm of this inhuman war, it seemed to me as if it would never be possible to find each other again, to come into touch with the friends of the other side of the Atlantic. Your letter and package were therefore very precious to me, and I thank you. [He wrote a little about his recent opera, then his letter ended.] Coffee to me is Life; without challenging Balzac or Paul Valéry, I really cannot work without it, and during the last six years it has been almost impossible to obtain. How can I thank you enough —

I am really grateful. Thank you again for that cheering
letter. Always yours,

G. Francesco Malipiero.

One more consequence of the war, one more composer's need
— this time it was coffee.

# 11

## *Evenings of Tribute*

THE FIRST reception given by the League of Composers to a
visiting composer probably was unique in that it was the only
one among all these evenings that could possibly be described
as jolly. This, thanks to Harold Bauer, was chiefly due to a spur-
of-the-moment impulse.

Late in 1923, shortly after his arrival from London, Arthur
Bliss had joined our board of directors. The League arranged
an evening in his honor, and he consented to give an informal
talk for the occasion. It was some time after this reception-
lecture that we adopted the custom of prepared programs of
music for these special evenings to honor composers.

A capacity crowd gathered to hear Mr. Bliss's first address in
the States. He finished by a quarter to ten but it then appeared
that the audience felt reluctant to leave at such an early hour.
When Mr. Bauer, the president of the MacDowell Club, had
thanked Mr. Bliss for his talk, he sensed that the audience was
somewhat unsatisfied and, feeling a responsibility for making
the evening a success, the great pianist turned suddenly to the
piano, sat down, and launched into the 'Blue Danube Waltz.'
The reaction to this was quick and gay: chairs were pushed back
— even knocked over! — and in a minute, in true Viennese

style, everybody was whirling in the waltz in a contagion of gaiety stemming jointly from Johann Strauss and Harold Bauer.

Although it was the only occasion when there was dancing, this first Composers Evening set a pattern for the many that followed, and a stamp of distinction has always marked them. I believe it has been due to the fact that composers, well known in their own right, especially appreciated the public banding-together of colleagues to do them honor.

We learned that Serge Prokofieff was coming to the United States again in 1937, on tour. We wanted to give an evening officially in his honor and I wrote him about our plans, addressing the letter in care of the Union of Soviet Composers, USSR. Although this was the address from which I had heard from him in recent years, several months passed without my receiving any answer.

A telephone call from Dr. Koussevitzky at Boston added to my growing anxiety. 'I hear,' he said, 'that for some time you have been trying to reach Prokofieff. I have too. I am now worried about him; he has always answered my letters heretofore.'

'Is it possible,' I asked, 'that he has another address which we could find? Nobody here seems to have heard from him at all.' We agreed to continue trying to find him through other channels, and a few days later Dr. Koussevitzky somehow managed to get the address to Prokofieff's apartment in Moscow, which he sent to me.

I cabled Prokofieff, asking for a date on which to present an evening of his compositions, with the added request that he himself participate in some of his works for piano. In its abrupt style his reply was completely 'Prokofieffian.'

'Date accepted. Will play a few notes. Prokofieff.'

As he arrived in New York only very shortly before the day set for the program, in February 1938, I waited in great suspense for the interpretation of his 'Will play a few notes.' Meanwhile I took the risk of printing in the program 'Mr. Prokofieff will play one of his recent works.' I could only hope that at the last moment, in a quixotic mood, he would not elect to play a Czerny exercise or a Russian anthem!

Happily, his 'interpretation' was to play three times during the evening, and he gave every evidence of thoroughly enjoying the whole thing, including his part in it.

I had one moment of fearing, however, that the occasion was going to be marred. Following the opening number, a Sonata for Two Violins, brilliantly played by Roman Totenberg and Nicolai Berezowsky, Prokofieff leaned over to me and whispered, 'I am so eager to hear this next work.'

'Why particularly?' I whispered back. 'Is it a favorite of yours?' One could not always be sure, with composers, which were their favorites among their brain children — that is, except when it happened to be their very latest! In this instance that was not the explanation.

'I am curious to hear this work,' remarked Prokofieff to my amazement, 'because I never wrote any "Aria of the Fata Morgana" in *The Love of Three Oranges!*' Now he was laughing.

I felt greatly embarrassed and murmured, 'But your own publisher gave us this title!" At that moment, however, Madame Maria Maximovitch commenced singing and, although Prokofieff continued smiling to himself, I could not enjoy her lovely voice at all, for fear of what might happen next. Fortunately, the audience acclaimed this excerpt from his delightful opera so enthusiastically that he seemed to forget all about his little joke with me, so I began to breathe easily again.

Although never a man to enjoy torrents of chitchat, at the reception following the concert at the Cosmopolitan Club one could see that he was genuinely pleased with the honor paid him and happy to meet many of his colleagues again.

Frankly intolerant of people who bored him, Prokofieff was spontaneously candid about anything and everything in life that interested him. He never bluffed, never troubled to conceal his real opinions. It was during his last stay in the United States that I had another opportunity to talk with him and to admire his innate honesty once more — even if at times it bordered on the brutally frank.

I took him to the studio of the Hammond Organ Company for his first hearing of their instrument. Their public relations director had been asking me to try to interest Igor Stravinsky in writing a special work for them; but not only was Stravinsky in Hollywood, but also it developed that the electric organ did not appeal to him.

At this particular time, however, several conductors of symphony orchestras were introducing the instrument in their concerts. Hans Kindler, with the National Symphony in Washington had made use of it in Liszt's *Faust* Symphony and said, 'This is the marvel of our modern scientific and artistic achievements.' Naturally the Hammond directors believed that if so eminent a composer as Stravinsky would write a new work especially for the instrument, its aesthetic standing would catch up with the commercial success it had achieved in churches and public schools.

As Prokofieff happened to be staying in New York for a short time, I had suggested him to the Hammond people; they were delighted to have me bring him to their demonstration studios and said they would be prepared to select him as the composer to be commissioned. I had asked Aaron Copland to join us, since he and Prokofieff were good friends.

As we entered the studio it seemed to me that one could not see the walls for the solid line of Hammond officials, clad identically in suits of dark blue. With utmost and unsmiling ceremony Prokofieff was taken down the line and introduced to each in turn.

That formality out of the way a young man dashed to the organ, sat down, and plunged into Chopin's 'Butterfly Etude.'

Prokofieff stood it patiently for a few moments but about halfway through he interrupted the young man saying in his abrupt, outspoken manner, 'Yes, yes, you have a fine technique. But now let me see, what does the organ do?'

Supremely undaunted the young man launched into a Bach

fugue. Before he could get far into that, Prokofieff interrupted again, saying a bit more sharply this time, 'I did not come here to hear Chopin and Bach. I want to know what the organ can, and cannot do.' This rather disconcerted the young performer, but it was all too evident that he did not know what Prokofieff was interested in learning.

Now several of the executives were whispering nervously together. One whispered aloud, 'Send for the engineer!' When the engineer arrived on the scene, Prokofieff was ready for him with a barrage of challenging questions, of great importance to him musically.

The engineer, however, was able to describe only in terms of engineering how the instrument was constructed. When Prokofieff put a question to him concerning staccato potential, it was obvious that the engineer was unacquainted with the term, hence rather stumped to demonstrate this or, in fact, any other musical quality in the instrument. That made two puzzled people, first the pianist, now the engineer.

By this time Prokofieff was growing irritated. Having a genuinely inquiring mind, he was searching for factual information about a new medium for composition with an instrument that seemed to have enormous possibilities.

One by one the executives began slipping out of the room. The demonstration, it seemed, was at an end. As Copland and I went downstairs with Prokofieff he said, with the greatest sincerity, 'These new mechanical instruments have enormous possibilities for a composer, but as artists we must thoroughly understand them, not only scientifically but also musically. If this instrument could be sent to me in Russia with a man who could explain it to me, and if I could have six months or a year to study it thoroughly, I would be glad to write a work for it.'

The next day I conveyed his message to the director of public relations for the Hammond Company. To my amazement he explained that the executives were greatly disappointed in Mr. Prokofieff, who not only had asked a great many extraneous questions but also had not shown any positive ap-

proval, for which they had hoped, for this commercially successful instrument. They had therefore decided to abandon the
idea of commissioning a composer to write a work especially for
the instrument.

That seemed to make it unanimous; the performer, the engineer, and now the executives had completely misunderstood
Prokofieff's honesty of approach, and the searching value of his
questions had been lost on them. Perhaps the opportunity had
come too soon, for a type of collaboration which today, in the
development of new instruments, is being recognized more and
more by scientists and musicians alike.

How clearly Carlos Chavez perceived this when he wrote in
*Toward a New Music*, 'The collaboration of engineers and musicians should produce in a few years a material appropriate
and practical for huge electrical musical performances. . . . Our
epoch of electricity shows the way to immense new developments, in the form and media of art.' [1] I have often wondered
whether any of the directors of the Hammond Organ Company
ever had occasion to read Chavez's challenging statements on
music and science.

Chavez's book asking for the collaboration of engineers and
musicians was written in 1937. Today in 1955, almost twenty
years later, a meeting of engineers and musicians has been held
at the American Institute of Electrical Engineers to hear a
'music synthesizer' — a new electronic demonstration by the
Radio Corporation of America. As a result, the need of a new
musical dictionary was suggested by Alfred Wallenstein, the
musical director and conductor of the Los Angeles Philharmonic
Orchestra, who believes that this compilation is necessary in
order to establish communication between engineers and musicians, both of whom are now related to the new art of electronics. As Mr. Wallenstein has said, 'The vital importance of
this dictionary is that each profession must clearly understand
what the other is talking about.' Prokofieff's unfortunate results

---

1. W. W. Norton and Company, Inc., New York, 1937.

at the Hammond Organ Studio would probably never have occurred if he with the engineers and artists had found a basis of communication.

Long before our misadventure in the Hammond studios, there was another instance in which Prokofieff showed the frankness of his nature, this time to the point where his wife had to suppress his conversation. This was in 1931 when he was in New York for some concerts. Although he had made his home in Paris for some years after the Russian Revolution, and traveled extensively as a composer and pianist in North and South America as well as in Europe; and although he had become a Soviet citizen in 1925 and frequently returned to Russia; nevertheless he felt the urge to be a free citizen, to continue his concert career without restrictions.

I arranged a luncheon so that he could meet a few of his colleagues in a thoroughly informal way. He and his wife seemed very happy to come. We were twelve at my long dining room table. Prokofieff sat at the head of the table and every head turned to him; each guest was anxious not to miss a word he said.

Conversation drifted from one subject to another as lunch proceeded, and a chance question about music in Russia found our guest of honor fairly overflowing with comments about conditions of the moment in the Russian concert halls and conservatories of music.

Characteristically, Prokofieff's intelligence and forthrightness caused him to be now voluble, again abstracted, but he was never ambiguous. His comments became rather incisive and suddenly Madame Prokofieff, a most attractive Spanish singer, interrupting from her seat at the far end of the table in a loud, almost impassioned voice, cried 'Serge! You forget, you intend to go back to Russia!'

He glanced at her, startled. Then, with a grateful smile, he broke off his sentence, recognizing the wisdom of her reminder and falling back on discretion.

Fortunate it is for the world of music that Prokofieff's prolific musical talent found free expression for the greater part of his lifetime, before it became necessary for him, as for many others, to bend to the dictates of Communist masters. As a *New York Times* editorial said at the time of his death, 'He belonged to the ages before he belonged to the Kremlin.'

As conditions grew more difficult in the early 'thirties, more dangerous for those who would not accept the totalitarian regimes, many artists were fleeing Europe. When important composers arrived in the United States, we in the League greeted them with all possible acclaim. In whatever way we could, we wanted to help them to make a new life in this country, to forget as far as possible how much their creative life had been interrupted, indeed often gravely disrupted.

The character of a man, the experiences suffered in his own homeland, his adjustment to the New World milieu — all these were bound to be factors in the orientation of such European composers as Schoenberg, Hindemith, Krenek, Bartók, Martinu, Milhaud, Weill, Toch, Pisk, Rathaus, and many others. Some adjusted; some became oriented with ease; others found life here difficult, or never, in the real sense, found a true second home on this side of the Atlantic.

It is part of understanding the changing status of composers to observe the careers of several during the years when they were adjusting, or trying to adjust, to this new life. For instance, Darius Milhaud, Paul Hindemith, as well as Kurt Weill are three renowned composers whose work has born fruit in this country, yet whose reactions to their problems as *émigrés* in the United States varied greatly.

In the case of Paul Hindemith, I surmise that he never realized any genuine happiness in this country; eventually he relinquished his position on the musical faculty at Yale University and returned to live in Europe.

It was important for him to come to the United States in 1937. Under the Hitler regime his compositions had been removed from most programs, not because he was of Jewish faith, for he was not, but because he was a modernist whose work was disapproved automatically by those in power in Germany.

Though well-merited acclaim was given him here, it was not in Hindemith's temperament to put down roots in this country, and it seems certain that the years he spent here did not give him the spiritual satisfaction which one naturally seeks. Even though he was able to write many works and have them performed, he may well not have been able to escape the feeling of being a wanderer in this country. In a sense Hindemith's predicament vaguely resembled that of the great Austrian author, Stefan Zweig, who never felt able to adjust in a new world. Zweig never overcame his sorrow about his homeland and his life ended tragically.

In Europe Hindemith returned to an environment in which he would work and find peace. In Switzerland he is teaching less, composing more. Great master, great teacher that he is, in his mature years some changes of personality are evident. His approach to people seems instinctively to have become more objective; but before he can open up his rich personality in any group, he requires time. I have been told that in earlier years in Europe he did not give the impression so much of being a distant person, the aloof teacher, as he has more recently been described; there was a large following of students who felt uncommonly close to him. The seeming change in him may well be accounted for by a desire, not to be denied, to return to Europe, to recapture a life he had enjoyed in earlier years. Perhaps the quality of shyness about his personal contacts became in itself a barrier to finding the closer ties with new people which might have made him feel at home in a new land.

That his tendency to aloofness became firmly established was evident by the austerity of a letter he wrote me, answering an invitation from the League of Composers in 1937, to do him honor and welcome him with a program of his works.

'Many thanks for your friendly wish to give an evening reception to me,' he wrote. 'I am truly not a great friend of official honors, and until now, in Europe, I have gone out of my way to avoid them. I realize, however, that in this instance I must not refuse. With my kindest greetings, Paul Hindemith.'

The reception to him was at the Cosmopolitan Club. The program included his own performance of the Sonata for the Viola Alone together with some of his wonderful songs from *Das Marienleben* and other chamber music works. To our subscribers, his name and some of his compositions were familiar, so the occasion was one of keen interest and genuine acclaim.

He expressed his happiness about the program and the interpreters of his works; yet it was evident that this salute to him from his colleagues, and the reception bringing the musical elite to meet him, caused him a difficult evening, for his nature could not produce the quick response to a stream of people in contact with him for the first time. Totally missing was that *Mon cher collègue* atmosphere which was so evident, for instance, in Stravinsky's approach to crowds surrounding him at the memorable reception given by the League in his honor.

Darius Milhaud arrived in 1940 with his wife and son to find refuge in New York. Although he had visited the United States several times previously, he had never come here to settle for a period of years, for never before had he been forced to leave his own country, war-torn though it was, because of his Jewish origin.

On the Milhauds' arrival at Hoboken they were met by Kurt Weill and his wife, Lotte Lenja, and driven to my house for lunch. The Germans had taken the Milhauds' little summer home in the Paris suburbs and also had turned their beautiful old homestead in Aix-en-Provence into a hospital, destroying many tapestries and other family treasures. Now their Paris apartment had been given up, and they sought a new life here.

We had only just begun lunch when their son Daniel stopped eating. His mother explained that the child was overexcited by the lightning changes in their lives since leaving Paris. Daniel asked pathetically to be excused from the table, and went upstairs to my room where he dropped off to sleep.

In view of the many difficult circumstances the Milhauds had lately endured, I felt particularly happy to be able to give Milhaud a package of welcoming letters to read after lunch; they had been forwarded to my house to await his arrival.

'Just look at this!' he cried to his wife Madeleine. 'Here are two letters from colleges, inviting me to go on their faculties.' A moment later he glanced up from another letter, saying to me, 'Why Claire, here is confirmation already of the broadcast you were telling me about!' In France in those days things were not happening with such celerity! With Davidson Taylor, then program director of CBS, I had arranged for a broadcast program of Milhaud's music soon after his arrival, which he was to conduct; the note was Davidson Taylor's gracious confirmation of the event, welcoming Milhaud and his family to this country.

At just this moment the telephone rang and it was a long distance call from Dr. Thaddeus H. Ames, then treasurer of the League of Composers, who wanted tentatively to make arrangements for Milhaud and his wife and son to rest for a week at the Ames's country home in Connecticut.

Milhaud shook his head in bewilderment, murmuring, 'There never was a country like this for welcoming a foreigner! Here am I, a refugee, arrived just today, and already I have two positions offered me, my works are to be broadcast, and so much hospitality is already prepared for us!' He seemed quite overcome by it. It seemed to me on the contrary that all this was little enough compensation for a man — one of the most renowned composers in the world, beloved in his own country — now forced to flee almost like a criminal, seeking refuge in a strange land, from the heavy hand of Hitler.

But there was more. The doorbell rang, and a gathering of newspaper reporters came upstairs. I had arranged for their interview to take place after lunch. Tired and overstimulated as he was, Darius seemed pleased with the interest shown in his arrival by the press.

An hour later the Milhaud family was on its way by automobile to the Ames's home in Lyme, to rest for ten days from their arduous experiences.

The evening which the League gave to honor Milhaud's music included the American *première* of 'La Cantate de la Mére et de l'Enfant' with Madeleine Milhaud, an extraordinary *diseuse*, reciting to the rhythm of the music. There were also excerpts from his opera, *Christophe Colombe*, which had had a successful *première* in Berlin in the days when Milhaud as a composer was acceptable in Germany.

Milhaud was obliged to sit in a chair at the reception following the program, because of his rheumatic condition. The effect of his graciousness on everyone was contagious; once reaching his side no one wanted to leave, and I had great difficulty in introducing all the people anxious to meet him. In consequence, the reception lasted longer perhaps than any given previously for composers. The measure of Milhaud's grateful thanks was charmingly expressed in a letter to me shortly afterward in which he said, 'Every letter I send you must be a thankful hymn.' It seemed to me not only to show his appreciation but also his real desire to find happiness in a new environment.

Six years later, in December 1946, we gave a program entirely devoted to Milhaud's Cantatas, performed for the first time in the United States. Milhaud conducted, and commented on his own work; again Madeleine Milhaud was the gifted *diseuse*. Milhaud elected to sit on the stage and talk very informally, with the result that it turned out to be a most successful experiment with a new type of program. 'Where else,' cried Milhaud joyously, 'could I give a program just of my Cantatas? It is only in this League of Composers that there is the opportunity to have an evening of this kind.' I could not help thinking to myself, Yes, but where are we to find many such composers, so able to hold the interest of an audience in a program of such a type; where, also, find the composer with the capacity not only to conduct but also to talk well about the music.

In his book, *The Musical Scene*, Virgil Thomson describes Milhaud as

one of the most facile and turbulent talents of our times
. . . one of the most completely calm of modern masters
. . . who, by adding depth . . . and penetration . . . and
simple humanity to his gamut, has become the first composer
of his country, and a leader in that musical tradition which,
of all living musical traditions, is the least moribund.[2]

Milhaud has proven his cosmopolitan qualities. He remains
a beloved character both in the United States and Europe, sharing his time between one winter season at Mills College in
California and the next winter at the *Conservatoire de Musique*
in Paris; between times he spends the month of August at the
Aspen Institute of Music in Colorado.

He understands the Latin and the Anglo-Saxon pupil equally
well, and has the affection of all his students. His supremely human qualities and wisdom have added to his stature as a great
master. He knows how to accept with a mischievous smile some
of the world's little foibles, whether women effusively desirous
of pushing his wheel chair in order to get to know him better,
or the student-composers leaning on Milhaud's genius, with the
hope that some of it will brush off.

Upon one of Milhaud's arrivals in New York, I asked the Customs Department to have him met at the dock by a special
inspector. I impressed upon the port authorities that here was
an important musician who needed help; at the time he was in
a wheel chair.

The special inspector met us and together we waited until
the Milhaud baggage was assembled, sixteen pieces of it — but
where was the seventeenth?

While Madeleine searched for it, Darius sat calmly in his
wheel chair. It was a mercilessly hot day in July but a nice
breeze blew on the French Line's open pier.

Suddenly someone remembered that Kurt Weill and Lotte
Lenja would be coming to greet the Milhauds but, as they had
no pass, they would have to wait outside the barrier.

Nearby the inspector was waiting for the missing piece of

---

2. Alfred A. Knopf, Inc., New York, 1945.

luggage to be found so he could begin his work. 'You mean
Kurt Weill of *Street Scene?*' he exclaimed, overhearing us; 'I'll
go and get them through the gate right away.' In a moment he
was back with the Weills who were overjoyed to join their
great friends. All of us launched into a lively conversation about
new operas and films in Europe and the States.

When another hour had passed, with no sign of the missing
piece of luggage, it was decided that it should be left until the
next day. Again the inspector spoke up, saying, 'Oh do wait a
little longer; it's much cooler here than uptown anyway, and
your conversation is so interesting! I love music and all you've
been talking about is a great treat to me!'

Milhaud, however, was growing tired, and we decided we
should leave. Darius put his hand in his pocket for money with
which to reward the inspector for his patient attentions; I intervened hastily, telling him that it would not be allowed. 'I am
sure, though, that the inspector would enjoy having your signa-
ture on a photograph of yourself,' I said.

Milhaud stared at me, smiling in bewilderment. '*Un auto-
graphe!*' he exclaimed, '*pourquoi moi?*' There was nothing
feigned about it; he was simply an innately modest man.

At the end of 1935 Kurt Weill had arrived from Europe. He
was another composer who had left Germany to find a new
home in this country, one more European intellectual escaping
from Hitler's tyranny. Before leaving Europe he had spent two
years in France, and arrived in New York with the great stage
producer Max Reinhardt.

Although the League of Composers had not found it possible
to produce Weill's operas, we were well aware of their important
place in the opera houses of Germany. He had appealed to a new
German public with music that was simple enough — even
jazzed-up enough — to be intelligible to the masses. In 1927
at the famous Baden-Baden Music Festival his opera *Mahagonny* had created a new interest for musicians and music
lovers who gathered there. This opera — his first attempt to

blend jazz and blues rhythms — gave the public a certain shock; at the same time there was a simplicity to the work that gave it a truly popular appeal.

Of course, it was in order for the League to plan an evening in Weill's honor shortly after his arrival here. He chose for the occasion a program of great variety. There were excerpts from an opera, excerpts also from what he called an 'operetta.' His wife, Lotte Lenja, with her marvelous talent and charm, had interpreted many of his works in Europe; she offered us her co-operation. Though her singing voice is slight, her personality is so remarkable that her presence on the stage makes itself felt immediately.

The program included a chorus from *Die Burgschaft*, solos and chorus from *Mahagonny*, and *Three Penny Opera* (*Drei Groschen Oper*),[3] and closed with excerpts from the operetta *A Kingdom for a Cow*.

As far back as 1932, the late Jerzy Fitelberg had written in the League's magazine, that it did not seem possible to carry the style and development of Weill's opera *Die Burgschaft* and *Drei Groschen Oper* farther; 'but Weill is a genuine creator, and will find a new path along which to guide opera. Today he is probably the only real opera composer in Germany, a fact that is generally accepted and which explains the great interest that awaits all his further development.' As it turned out Weill found his 'new path' in this country, though perhaps it was a path that did not always add to his stature in the best phase of his musical talent.

That evening in honor of Kurt Weill proved a great success musically; an enthusiastic audience at the Cosmopolitan Club brought him and Lotte Lenja forward to take innumerable bows. For me, only one thing marred the evening in retrospect; it was a telephone call the next morning from Olga Samaroff, with whom I had enjoyed a long close friendship. We had been colleagues in various musical activities — the Town Hall Music

3. This opera, in the production revised by Marc Blitzstein, was one of the great successes in the 1953 season in New York.

Committee, the Schubert Memorial, and the League of Composers — and, since she was always open minded and far seeing,
I had often sought her advice, and she had been helpful in many
ways. This was the first time she had ever taken me to task.

She explained that she had brought several people to this evening for Kurt Weill, with the hope that they were potential
patrons for the League. 'Claire,' she cried on the telephone,
'how could you have a League program presenting a mixture of
classical opera and popular operetta? I have never before known
you to lower the League's musical standards!'

'But Olga,' I tried to explain, 'not only has the League always
quite frankly aimed at representing all the contemporary composers of note at these evenings, we have tried to present them
in their various styles. Weill — famous not only for light music — chose this program himself because it represented the
wide range of his work.'

I was not absolved. Olga assured me that we had lost the
potential patrons; being purists, they could not accept the musical 'mixture' they had heard. Those were still days when, to
many people, there was simply no meeting ground between serious and so-called light music. I think we should always bless the
name of George Gershwin for breaking down many of the bar-
riers.

A few years later I recalled Olga's scolding, when Kurt Weill
wrote the music for the New York World's Fair exhibit called
'Railroads on Parade.' Many critics dwelt on what a fine example of music it was, written for a specific purpose; some went
so far as to claim it was as important as a symphony written for
performance in Carnegie Hall.

Kurt Weill, as a man of the theater, came very quickly in
contact with theater groups in the United States. Perhaps his
easy ability to blend into the American scene may have lost to
him certain of his earlier traits. Seemingly his music for *Street
Scene, Lady in the Dark*, and *Knickerbocker Holiday* might well
have been written by a native American composer.

However, the original Weill is in evidence in his folk opera,

*Down in the Valley.* At a program given as a memorial to him in 1951 I sat with Nicholas Nabokov,[4] who had been a personal friend and great admirer of Weill's music when he knew him in Europe.

'How very different, how far apart, are the two styles of the music we have heard tonight,' Nicholas reflected. (The program had included excerpts from some of Weill's earlier works as well as recent compositions.) 'How completely integrated is Weill's music, written in Europe before he came here, and what a pity that he lost some of that quality when he took on the coloration of the American scene — or, should I say, of Broadway?' I felt compelled to agree with him, that the great success Weill had achieved in this country — doubtless because of his ability to blend with it — seemed at the same time to have weakened the reservoir of a profound creative talent.

When Dr. Koussevitzky suggested in 1925 that Béla Bartók might write a new work for the League which he would like to conduct in a world *première* in Town Hall, Bartók had very quickly sent us a new work for chamber orchestra and vocal quartet, called 'Village Scenes.' This was in the early days of the League, before we had found the means of raising money to pay for commissioned works. Bartók undertook this labor out of respect for Dr. Koussevitzky, and as a generous gesture toward his unknown colleagues in the League of Composers across the ocean.

At the time very little of his music had been played in this country. Dr. Koussevitzky even repeated 'Village Scenes' at the close of the program; it was a delight to see that almost the entire audience was sufficiently interested to stay, vigorously applauding the repetition. It gave me a feeling of confidence that evening — there was a public eager to know the work of a great man.

---

4. Nicholas Nabokov, composer and author, has been the director of the Festivals sponsored by the Committee for Intellectual Freedom, which were held in Paris and in Rome in 1953 and 1954.

Then for some years we were out of touch with Bartók. When he left Hungary in 1940, a voluntary exile, we immediately planned an evening in his honor at the Museum of Modern Art. Two great Hungarian artists — a Metropolitan Opera singer, Enid Szantho, and the great violinist Joseph Szigeti — were delighted to help us and happy to interpret Bartók's chamber music. Both of them revered this great master.

Szigeti played the Rhapsodie No. One which, interestingly enough, Bartók had dedicated to him. Miss Szantho sang a group of his famed arrangements of Hungarian folk songs. The program concluded with the composer playing selections from *Mikrokosmos,* a *première* performance in the United States. The evening proved a great success and a letter from Bartók later showed his deep feeling.

In 1942 we invited Bartók to join the League's National Committee of Composers. He was having difficulties at the time in becoming an American citizen. In May he wrote,

> I wanted to be in a position to give you a clear picture of the prospects of becoming a citizen or not. . . . It appears that there are some difficulties for me as a Hungarian citizen, in going to Canada, because of a declaration of war by Canada on Hungary . . . There are negotiations with the American Consul in Montreal . . . but again a postponement . . . I applied for reexamination of my case in Washington. Apparently they are still examining the case. As you see, I am still very far even from the 'first paper.' This probably constitutes an obstacle to becoming a member of your National Composers Committee.

We assured him immediately that Europeans domiciled in this country, even if their citizenship was not established, were eligible to this committee. He seemed relieved and pleased, and joined the group.

A short time thereafter Minna Lederman invited Bartók, André Schulhoff, and me to lunch at the Café Lafayette. As always Bartók was very cordial in manner, yet extremely quiet, a man of few words, shy and simple. There was an ascetic quality about him which even seemed to intervene in his choice of the famous Lafayette food.

One felt about Bartók that at all times he was deeply involved in his creative life, completely dedicated to his composition, not a man to promote himself in any circumstances at any time. Yet, notwithstanding this aloofness, one could feel very warmly toward him because of a great sincerity and an innate cordiality.

In 1946, a few months after he died, we gave another evening of his compositions, for the benefit of the Bartók Fund. This time the Budapest String Quartet, Andor Foldes, Arthur Balsam, Tossy Spivakovsky, and — again — Enid Szantho, all volunteered their services to honor his memory.

Bartók's life contained many elements of tragedy. Only once in his lifetime was the famous piece, Music for Strings, Percussion and Celesta played. Ironically it was played five times in the three years following his death! This was only one of many unfortunate situations.

Royalties from performances of his works during the last year of his life amounted to just $500. The year after his death I was told that royalties were close to $10,000.

A small social skirmish took place in late 1934 on the arrival of Igor Stravinsky in this country. The question was whether the League of Composers or a leading patroness of the New York Philharmonic Symphony Orchestra (rejoicing in a ballroom in her own home) should have the pleasure of giving the first reception for him.

The emphasis of the League's evenings honoring renowned composers was always on the privilege of welcoming a colleague, by presenting a program of his works. Over the years, many of the distinguished composers whom we entertained spoke particularly of their happiness and appreciation for being feted by colleagues, instead of being a 'centerpiece' and lionized socially.

The skirmish was brief, the League won out over the patroness who, for the most part cleverly, had built up her social life by entertaining famous artists.

Accordingly, we planned a program for Town Hall in January 1935. Since we wanted to give this event signal distinction, we included on the invitation a large list, a committee of eighty composers, to welcome Stravinsky. Although Walter Damrosch was not a composer whose works we played, as the dean of musicians in this country we felt that he should be invited to join this Composers Committee, and perhaps say a word of welcome to Stravinsky at the reception.

But Dr. Damrosch had evidently found himself unable to accept the Stravinsky of later years. He wrote a frank letter which we accepted in good spirit from a man of his years:

> I highly appreciate the compliment of your invitation but I do not feel I am the right man for this particular job . . . I share with most of my musical colleagues an intense admiration for the master who wrote *Petrouchka, The Fire Bird*, etc. But I have absolutely no sympathy for the later Stravinsky. To me the change of heart which demonstrates itself in his later compositions is so terrible, and the results so unsympathetic, that I do not feel that I should make the speech of welcome. I would have to ignore, or prevaricate, and I cannot do either. I do hope you will understand, and forgive me.

To my surprise, Dr. Damrosch came nevertheless to the concert and reception. Whenever possible throughout the evening he helped me to introduce famous musicians to *Mon cher collègue*, as he continued to allude to Stravinksy all evening, regardless of the fact that for the composer's recent music, Damrosch could have 'absolutely no sympathy.'

I planned a dinner with a few composers in our home at the start of the evening honoring Mr. Stravinsky, wishing to establish an atmosphere of felicity. He accepted gladly, asking me if he might bring with him Samuel Dushkin, the young violinist who had been touring with him.

The week before the dinner, *The New Yorker* had published a profile on Stravinsky. I was so busy preparing for the concert that I did not have time to read it, but my maid Emma did. A most faithful and efficient person, Emma, who vicariously enjoyed a musical coterie, came to me one morning, saying, 'Mrs. Reis, you must order red wine for the dinner for Mr. Stravinsky this Wednesday night.'

'Whatever for?' I said. The choice of food I planned indicated a white wine.

Emma showed me *The New Yorker*. 'Because,' she said, 'this article says he drinks only red wine.'

On top of everything else I had to do, this seemed too much. 'Now Emma,' I exclaimed, 'that is just something dreamed up by some reporter — like that story last year about the German philosopher, here on a visit, who would only go out to a dinner if he could be sure of champagne to drink, and of a seat next to a blonde.'

Emma was displeased with my attitude which, I could see plainly, she expected would get me into trouble.

The afternoon of the day of the dinner and program, I came in from the final rehearsal at Town Hall to be met at the door by Emma, who had a triumphant gleam in her eye. 'There was a telephone call for you, Mrs. Reis,' she said, adding importantly, 'from Mr. Stravinsky.'

Heavens! Was he ill, or something equally dreadful, creating a crisis?

'What did he want?'

Emma had faultless politeness, but did I just imagine a moment of delicate gloating in her voice as she said, 'He just wanted to let you know — that he drinks only red wine!'

'Great heavens, have we even got any good red wine?' I cried.

'Yes, Mrs. Reis, we have,' said Emma calmly. When I had time to think it over I could see — such was Emma's interest in this fabulous bit of detail — that if we had not, by this time she would have ordered it on her own responsibility.

I flew downstairs to our wine cellar and picked out the best Burgundy it offered. This I had Emma place in front of Stravinsky. Not to be outdone in my own home, I served the rest of my guests the white wine, which certainly was better suited to what we ate. It was a great night for Emma, however; passing and re-passing Mr. Stravinsky, she never missed an opportunity to replenish his glass of wine — red.

At the concert Mr. Stravinsky expressed delight with our selections and the interpretive artists for his program. The compositions included a String Quartet written in 1914; songs written in the eleven years between 1908 and 1919; and a first New York performance of an aria from his opera *Mavra*.

Not only was Town Hall crowded to the doors, but also approximately the entire audience of 1400 people did its best to crowd into the Town Hall Club lounge for the reception. I did not realize until the next day that some people had looked in at the reception and, discouraged by the enormous crush around Stravinsky, had gone away.

Among them was a particularly irate subscriber to the League's concert series. Promptly at the office I received a letter instructing me to return her membership fee, which she said she had paid 'particularly in order to meet Mr. Stravinsky, and he was not there!'

I wrote her as pacifically as possible that of course he had been there; perhaps she had not realized that he had been hidden from many by the enormous crowd because he was a slight little figure, only five feet tall. I naturally regretted that she had not been able to touch the hand of the great composer but nevertheless advised her to stay with us, for there would be many more such occasions, and other great composers whom she would have the opportunity to meet.

Stravinsky expressed profound appreciation to the League following that evening. Shortly thereafter, it seemed logical to invite him to become a member of our National Committee of Composers, the *honorary* association of American and European composers. We were disappointed when he declined the invitation, writing to me in part,

> . . . I am sorry to inform you of my refusal to become a member of the National Board of Composers. This attitude of not belonging in any capacity to any musical organization, be it in Europe or America, is of a long and unchange-

able standing, and you will, I hope, understand my position in this instance. With my sincerest wishes of success in all endeavors of The League of Composers, and with my kind regards, Sincerely yours, Igor Stravinsky.

Originally this National Committee had been an Advisory Board, made up of men who in the early years actually helped us by recommending works little known in this country and by contributing articles to our publication, *Modern Music*. Over the years this advisory body had been replaced by the National Committee and, although not active, it represented prestige value for the society. Men of great stature, colleagues of Stravinsky in Europe, were on the present list, Milhaud, Martinu, Weill, Bartók, Schoenberg, and also many of Stravinsky's personal American friends. As I thought over this letter, his many works that we had premiered in the United States came to mind. In this country in the 'twenties and 'thirties, there was no other society which was giving performances of his *Les Noces, Histoire du Soldat, Oedipus Rex, Le Sacre du Printemps*, with such renowned conductors as Stokowski, Monteux, Tullio Serafin, and with a long list of eminent stage designers, directors, and soloists.

No one must deny the right of an artist to be completely the individual, free of group affiliations if he pleases. Nevertheless, an association of artists needs to call upon the individual at times to further the cause of benefit to the many. In this instance, as with many organizations, the prestige of some of the names listed was of distinct help to the League's growth. Yet a great man, whom we had wholeheartedly recognized in the early history of contemporary music in this country, would not change his principles and give us the support of his name and his influence.

Like so many of the others, Arnold Schoenberg, coming to this country for the first time in 1933, had left Germany to get away from the Hitler regime; he, too, had remained a refugee in France for some months before coming here.

One day, at a directors' meeting of the League of Composers, we spent a long time discussing what we should do, not only to honor this great composer but also to satisfy him. We had heard that he was not easy to please, and we were anxious that the welcome we gave him be one he approved.

I had had correspondence with him over the years when he was living in Berlin. In our files were several letters showing irritation due to misunderstandings with his publisher over not having received royalties for a work we had presented in one of our concerts. He had also been troubled about the quality of performances given in New York; somehow he had developed an idea at that time that, in the United States, new compositions were not sufficiently rehearsed.

We decided upon a carefully chosen all-Schoenberg program in Town Hall, and were fortunate to secure the Pro-Arte Quartet, renowned for its remarkable interpretation of contemporary music. A reception honoring the composer would follow the concert.

Just before Schoenberg sailed from France, I received a letter from him, giving his approval of the program; he seemed delighted to accept our plans to welcome him.

I invited Mr. Schoenberg and his wife to meet a few colleagues at my home for dinner before the concert; by having some composers there to greet him informally, and with some good food and wine, I hoped we would establish that just-right atmosphere of warmth and friendship which would prepare him happily for the Town Hall event.

This was one of the rare times when I felt worried about a famous person whom I had not met. So many people went out of their way to warn me about his being difficult! I prepared myself to tell him — if necessary — that it was not we who had been at fault about the payment of royalties in Europe, and also to explain that the *première* of *Pierrot Lunaire* was rehearsed twenty-two times! As it turned out, however, I need not have worried.

From the moment Schoenberg arrived at our home, he beamed

upon us all. The heavily lined face of this stockily built man
turned red as a rose as we toasted him with a welcoming cock-
tail; all the rumors that had reached me about a man of prickly
disposition were dissipated.

At the dinner table, in halting English with French to rescue
us intermittently, he told me he was fifty-eight years old and a
grandfather of two children then eight and eleven. His own
child by this present marriage was just two. We strolled around
among subjects of painting and the drama, and he told us he
had written a play he hoped some day to see performed. The
conversation was perfectly easy; he was in a most genial mood,
smiling occasionally across the table at his timid young wife
of only twenty-eight, who at that time spoke very little English.

Leaving for Town Hall, I took Schoenberg in my car with
several guests while my husband took Mrs. Schoenberg with
the remainder of our party. On the way, Schoenberg suddenly
became extremely agitated. 'I want to sit in the same box as
my wife,' he whispered to me; 'we have only been married three
years and she has never been apart from me.' It seemed very
charming, almost naïve. When we reached Town Hall he paced
nervously up and down in the lobby, refusing to go to the box
until his wife arrived; at once his mood quieted down, and soon
the concert began.

It opened with Schoenberg's Third String Quartet performed
magnificently by that great Belgian group, the Pro-Artes, followed by a group of piano pieces brilliantly played by Nadia
Reisenberg.

As the applause broke out, Schoenberg's broad smile convinced
me that he had a great personal capacity for happiness, a quality which certainly had never been correctly interpreted from
across the ocean. He expressed great pleasure with the quartet
and the pianist in the first part of the program, and I felt that
one more hurdle had been taken successfully.

During the intermission I took the composer to the top of the
staircase to see the crowd which was now milling about in
the lobby. His eyes sparkled; from our box he had not realized

the size of the audience. Again that naïveté, quite surprising and delightful, was revealed when he said with a rising inflection, as though he couldn't quite believe it, 'All these people have come here to hear me?' There was a real emotion in his voice. It struck me that this great composer was really unaware of the exalted position he had achieved in the musical world.

The program following the intermission included a group of songs, interpreted by Rita Sebastian. We had had an emergency that day and had been compelled to substitute the accompanist at the last moment.

Suddenly I noticed Schoenberg fidgeting in his chair; his neck seemed to fairly stretch, like that of Alice in Wonderland — upwards, toward the ceiling! In panic I wondered if he were ill. As I peered at him closely, he half turned his head and whispered to me, 'She is accompanying the singer in the wrong clef!' I started to whisper an explanation about the emergency accompanist — the song ended — a burst of applause drowned out my words. The composer had to rise then to take a bow, but he sank back into his chair in deep silence after a slight wave of approval in the singer's direction. He seemed to be digesting the dissonances (fortunately only a few bars) improvised by the substitute accompanist and assuring himself that they were no fault of the composer!

The audience had not been aware, however, of any departure from the original score. Perhaps that, in itself, disturbed Schoenberg. At any rate, the Pro-Arte Quartet and Ruth Rogers, soprano, safely closed the program with the Second String Quartet with Voice, which brought salvos of applause to composer and artists.

At the end of the evening, when Schoenberg had shaken hands with hundreds of people who crowded into the reception, I believe he was too exhausted to give another thought to right or wrong clefs. Although the party for him was by invitation only, one woman appeared with a little boy of ten, asking if she might come in, since her son intended to become a composer. 'If he could only shake hands with Mr. Schoenberg,' she pleaded, 'it would be an inspiration for him all his life to re-

member this event.' Schoenberg chanced to overhear her remark and, beaming once again, shook the child's hand, wishing
him well. How often have I regretted that I did not learn their
names, for perhaps today that boy is one of the many composers
carrying on the Schoenberg twelve-tone school.

As our honored guest left the party, clinging tightly to his
wife, he shook hands repeatedly, and with emotion spoke over
and over again of the memorableness of the evening given him
by the League. A few days later I received a letter expressing his
gratitude about an occasion that seemed rare in his career.
'May I tell you,' he said in part, 'that for me this was a truly
great joy. I had the feeling during the evening that there are a
great many people here who are not altogether without an understanding of my work.'

My correspondence with Schoenberg continued at intervals.
Often his letters gave me an unexpected glimpse of his sense of
humor. When I wrote asking him to fill in a questionnaire for
the revised edition of my book, *Composers in America*, which
included some of the important European composers who had
recently settled in this country, he wrote, 'May I first congratulate you on the splendid idea of compiling a book on
American composers and including also such ones who did not
come with the Mayflower!' At other times an aggressive, even
fighting spirit dominated his letters. For instance, I consulted
him about a performance the League wanted to give of *Verklärte
Nacht*. He had heard it played by one of the outstanding and
very popular quartets whom we proposed to engage for this
occasion and with two instrumentalists. The following defensive
letter naturally changed our plans:

> Hearing the broadcast of my *Verklärte Nacht* . . . was a
> great disappointment to me. I did not like the performance
> at all, though I must admit that, in spite of many accidents
> and much disorder, (in this performance) the quartet from
> a standpoint of instrumental ability was very good. But this
> is the only good I can say about them. Imagine, my style
> of 1899 is not familiar with them! How can they perform
> my style of 1942?

We were unable to give full-scale receptions for many of the men of music who came to this country during the 'thirties. We tried nevertheless to be of help by placing their works on some of the League's programs as soon as possible after their arrival in the country. Among composers who had been friends with some of our board from the earlier days in Europe were Jerzy Fitelberg, Nicolai Lopatnikoff, Bohuslav Martinu, Paul Pisk, also Karol Rathaus, Vittorio Rieti, Ernst Toch, and Stefan Wolpe; it was stimulating to meet with them again in New York, and by giving attention in various ways to their compositions, we tried to assure them that we welcomed them as colleagues.

Not being a composer, I abided invariably by the program decisions of the composer-committee. News of my position in the League seemed, however, to have traveled abroad. Yet when a foreign composer, with whom I had only had correspondence, came to call on me for the first time, I was not prepared for his arriving at my home with a new manuscript in hand which he had already dedicated to me! As I always emphasized in our board meetings that we must be objective and never be influenced by personal factors in the selection of works for our programs, I was quite embarrassed as to how I could accept this work graciously. Obviously I could not feel personally flattered! Nor could I very well turn around at our next League meeting and ask the committee to include it in our next concert. I decided that the better part of valor was to keep the incident to myself.

The music of Villa-Lobos has been described as 'lushly colorful.' His many works based on Brazilian folklore are largely responsible. Someone once asked him to define the term folklore. 'I *am* folklore!' he said blandly.

In the simplicity of its melody, much in the background of his music suggests the quality of Brazilian popular music. Although a very prolific composer, with an estimated thousand or so works to his credit, on a visit to New York, when we gave an evening in his honor, so few chamber music works were available as mentioned earlier that we actually found it difficult to make up a program which we felt would be up to the stature of this important composer. Like Béla Bartók, Villa-Lobos' studies in the folk music of his country had been very extensive; in order to secure indigenous Brazilian themes, he joined scientific expeditions into the interior of the country for research, and recorded the music of the Indian tribes.

Between the years 1938 and 1937, Carlos Chavez, a native of Mexico, transformed the orchestra of the musicians' union in Mexico City into a symphony orchestra of the first rank. He was not only their conductor — today he is a guest conductor in so many countries — but he organized the Department of Fine Arts in the Secretariat of Public Education in Mexico; at the same time he directed the National Conservatory of Music and became the most renowned musician of his country.

During those very active years with government executive positions in the arts, he never ceased to compose. Many of his works have been played all over the world. (He is at present completing an opera commissioned by the New York City Center of Music and Drama.)

Chavez's interest in the potentialities of electrical music brought him a commission by the Secretary of Public Education in the United States, and the report he made led to his writing the book entitled *Toward a New Music*.[5]

In 1937 we heard from Chavez that he was coming to New York on a visit. As we always consulted the distinguished composer whom we were honoring about the works he preferred to have performed, I had written Chavez at Mexico City. He had replied, 'I think that the best person to make suggestions for the hour of my music will be Aaron Copland. Let me, this time, be just a little piece of the audience. I regret that I will not take part in playing anything of my own.'

---

5. W. W. Norton and Company, New York, 1937.

The program of chamber music which we arranged included 'Tierra Mojada,' sung by the Madrigal Singers conducted by Lehman Engel. At the last moment Chavez did consent to take part in the concluding number, a Sonatina for Violin and Piano which he played most delightfully, and with Nicolai Berezowsky as violinist.

In the summer of 1954 I happened to be in Mexico City and at a party at Chavez's home we talked about some of those early crusading days in New York and in Mexico City. In his country he had been the pioneer for contemporary music, at a time when little was happening to encourage the contemporary composer. That evening he was eager for me to tell his guests how the League had started; in turn I wanted to know if he was still as active in promoting the arts in Mexico, in which he had achieved such remarkable results.

'I am not so young as I was,' he remarked with a smile. His slightly graying hair has added — not age — merely more charm to an already very attractive personality. 'Today I must give my time to my composition, except for the engagements I accept as guest conductor.' It reminded me of an encounter with Ernest Bloch, during which we had chatted about his earlier life and his leadership with the People's Music League Chorus, 'Palestrina on Twenty-third Street.' Bloch had said, 'Now I am in my middle years, and have so much to write; I must devote myself only to my composition.'

Some composers — Chavez, Bloch, and others — realizing in their middle years that their creative power is in full maturity, feel the need of the absolute creative life. Fortunate indeed are those artists who find life short for the fulfillment of their message.

During the period of World War II many Latin American composers came to New York. Juan José Castro, one of the outstanding Argentinian personalities, was entertained by us in 1941. He has become a prominent conductor as well as a composer.

In answer to our suggestion of having a program in his honor he wrote,

> I am deeply touched by your invitation and, believe me, I hesitated a long time before accepting such a great distinction, especially to give a program on which there will be only my music — that has scared me! I only did that once before, on my first visit to Europe, and then I was very young. Although I accept with great pleasure, it is also without full confidence!

But, as with all our 'composer-tributes' the evening turned out successfully.

Other Latin Americans whom we entertained at about this time were Albert Ginastera, Francisco Mignone, and Camargo Guarnieri.

After the evening in his honor, Guarnieri wrote from Brazil,

> The evening . . . will be a long-lasting memory and a constant reminder of the favor I owe. It is perhaps difficult for you to imagine how great a benefit it was to me personally, to hear my works realized so magnificently and under such fine auspices. The concert will always remain a great lesson and continue to be a true stimulus to more and greater effort on my return to Brazil.

Twice we deviated from these special 'composer evenings' to welcome two great figures in the contemporary scene in music: Nadia Boulanger and Serge Koussevitzky.

Boulanger — as she is customarily referred to, being famous enough to carry only a last name — has been the great force, the great teacher in Paris who has taught many of the most important composers from the United States, and is still teaching today. We were all very happy to greet her in 1938 when she came to New York and accepted the League's invitation to give a talk on 'The Relation of Old Music to Modern Music' before a large audience of composers, interpretive musicians, and music lovers. The reception following the lecture revealed not only how far her fame as a teacher had traveled but how greatly she had endeared herself to students and friends alike.

The evening to honor Dr. Koussevitzky, at the Modern Museum of Art, celebrated the fifth anniversary of the Koussevitzky Music Foundation, which he had created as a means to commission composers. Following the program, made up of some of these works, Dr. Koussevitzky made a very impassioned speech about composers, with a gracious gesture to the League. In part he said,

> For those of us who feel that the pioneers, the young talent in music, should not suffer through neglect, an organization like the League of Composers must win encouragement, sympathy, and support. By its very existence, it is dedicated to ease the path of the experimenter, and bring to the public the work of those new men who have the most significant message for their own generation.

Dr. Koussevitzky showed not only his own interest in contemporary composers in the early years, but maintained his close friendships with them, encouraged them to write and, on many occasions, even assumed the role of father toward them.

For example, in his early years Walter Piston, an unknown composer, had written one work.

'Why not more?' Dr. Koussevitzky asked him.

'Nobody will play it!' said Piston dejectedly.

'I will play it,' said Dr. Koussevitzky quickly. In time a second and then a third Piston composition were forthcoming, encouraged by the sympathetic conductor. Today Piston is one of the most important composers in the United States, holding a chair in music, which was given to Harvard's Music Department by Walter W. Naumburg.

Dr. Koussevitzky trained the young conductor, Leonard Bernstein, who as a very young man developed an extraordinary talent for conducting as well as composing. Bernstein soon became an 'adopted son.' Another Koussevitzky 'find' at a very early age was Aaron Copland. Immediately he showed his complete confidence in Aaron's potential talent, long before the young composer had established himself. He became another 'adopted son,' and in later years he was made assistant director of the Tanglewood School of Music, a position he holds today.

It was fitting that Aaron should want the League of Composers to arrange a public dinner in honor of Koussevitzky's Twenty-fifth year of association with the Boston Symphony Orchestra, an anniversary which coincided with his resignation as Music Director. The grand ballroom of the Waldorf-Astoria was crowded with more than a thousand people. Copland's speech that evening described well the attitude held by all composers toward this great conductor. 'The American boy's dream to be President of the United States,' Copland said, 'is no more than the American composer's dream to be "played by Koussevitzky." '

In anticipation of the occasion, I had written letters to composers all over the world, asking them to send personal expressions to Dr. Koussevitzky for an album from composers, which I wanted to have presented to him at the dinner, as a surprise. Replies came in quickly from every corner of the globe, even Jean Sibelius and the late Richard Strauss contributed warm congratulatory messages.

Naturally I had written to the five Russian composers in the Soviet Union whose works Dr. Koussevitzky had presented so frequently; Katchaturian, Kabalevsky, Miaskovsky, Prokofieff, and Shostakovich. Not one of them answered. Did my letters reach them? Were they forbidden to answer because Dr. Koussevitzky had been first a White Russian, and now was an American citizen?

There was only one other composer from whom I did not hear. When Schoenberg did not answer my letter, I wrote him a second time, reminding him of this important album of letters, and begging for a response from him to add to the collection.

Schoenberg finally answered curtly, 'How can I possibly send a tribute to a conductor who does not recognize my music by performing it?' [6]

The warmth of Dr. Koussevitzky's personality, his ability to

---

6. Nevertheless, at Dr. Koussevitzky's request, Schoenberg was asked by the Koussevitsky Music Foundation to write a commissioned work, and Schoenberg accepted.

maintain close friendships despite an extraordinarily busy career, always caused the artists' green room to be a scene of crowded animation after each of his programs. Not only did he like to see his friends there, he welcomed each one affectionately with a personal word. There was almost a naïveté in his enjoyment of their praise for his exhilarating performances. He found time for people, as well as for music.

As the number of the League's special evenings honoring composers increased over the years, I could not always have the opportunity to know our visitors personally. At times it struck me that one or other of the foreigner composers had quickly exhausted all their points of view in interviews with the press, and then had little left to say to me or even to many of their new colleagues. The receptions nevertheless always brought out a full complement of composers, interpretive artists, and music lovers who were anxious to know the renowned musician; and always there was a fringe crowd eager for the opportunity to tread on the heels of the great.

We entertained Francis Poulenc, Benjamin Britten, Ernst Krenek, Zoltan Kodaly, Georges Enesco, Florent Schmitt, and Gottfried von Einem. In earlier years Albert Roussel had visited New York and been welcomed by the League. I always made it a point to offer my piano in our home, in case the visitor wished to rehearse. I recall that Roussel seemed very pleased to have the seclusion of a home for his rehearsal. When I greeted him on his arrival at our house, he immediately suggested that I sit next to him on the piano bench, while he played. Despite his Gallic protests I wanted him to have the privacy I had offered him, and I withdrew. Before the concert he upbraided me for not staying with him! Nevertheless before he sailed back to France he presented me with a bronze medallion bearing a portrait of himself, which had been made by order of the French government. I have been told that these medals in bronze or silver are awarded as an honor to a few French artists, and are executed by *La Monnaie*, the bureau that mints the French

currency. According to a recipient of this medal, one is chosen
to receive it 'when you are a little known or a little old.' This
suggests the old lament, 'Must one be old — or dead — to be
honored?'

I feel saddened when I think that I never met Charles Ives.
Today he is recognized as one of the great American creative
musicians. He was a very successful businessman who founded
a large insurance company; yet, even before he was twenty years
of age, he felt impelled to write music.

I was only able to convey to Mr. Ives through correspondence how much I appreciated his encouragement in our League's
work. When I first wrote him, to obtain correct data about his
compositions for my book, *Composers in America,* he took the
time to add to my questionnaire a note of personal comment:
'If more Americans would take as much interest, and give as
much constructive help as you do, contemporary music in this
country would not have such uphill work.' It is a letter I have
treasured.

Although we performed his work over twenty-five years ago,
he was not well enough to attend a League concert. Nevertheless, at frequent intervals — always unasked — he would send
a check, usually $100 for the organization, accompanied by a
typical Ives line, 'I hope the League is being fully appreciated,'
and he would often send a contribution specifically to help the
magazine, *Modern Music,* invariably adding words of praise for
the editor, Minna Lederman.

Among the few musicians who early recognized Ives's genius
was Henry Cowell, who said, 'There can be little doubt that he
was the greatest American composer of his epoch . . . His
philosophy as well as his musical practice are becoming stronger
and stronger influences in the shaping of the creative musical
future of this country.'[7] A few years ago Howard Taubman,
Music Editor of *The New York Times,* succeeded in getting the

7. *Center Magazine,* N.Y. City Center of Music and Drama, September,
1954.

only newspaper interview with him which, due to Ives's enforced seclusion, had been granted in many years. Taubman wrote: 'It has taken America a long time to recognize that Ives is the most audacious pioneer in music this country has produced . . . in his vast output of symphonies, choruses, songs and chamber music, we have a living portrait of the land worthy to stand beside the literature of New England's flowering.'[8] And recently George Balanchine created a new ballet, *Ivesiana*, for the New York City Ballet Company; it was based on a group of Ives compositions, and Balanchine describes Ives as 'the most Yankee of American composers, prickly and independent!'[9]

It seemed fitting, as part of the League's twentieth anniversary, to have an evening to honor the American composers who had been associated with our League. Therefore in December 1943 we planned a program of works which were written to celebrate our two-score years of activity. The composer-committee for the reception included *all* the composers of our National Board, and they were received by a large gathering of interpretive artists and lovers of music who came to do them honor. The composers who wrote anniversary works for this program at the Museum of Modern Art were Roy Harris, Douglas Moore, Lazare Saminsky, Arthur Shepherd, Virgil Thomson, and Bernard Wagenaar.

Earlier in the month, as a salute to our anniversary, the Town Hall Endowment Series offered an evening of world *premières*, written by Aaron Copland, Frederick Jacobi, Darius Milhaud, and Walter Piston.

Again on our twenty-fifth anniversary, there were tributes from all parts of the country. Conductors of leading orchestras offered to repeat some of the earlier commissioned works.[10] Too, ten new works [11] — grants made in the League's name — were offered that year by publishers, patrons, the National Federation

---

8. *The New York Times Magazine*, October, 1949.
9. *Center Magazine*, September, 1954.
10. See Appendix, 253–4.
11. See Appendix, 253.

of Music Clubs, and the Goldman Band. Broadcasting stations joined in the celebrations, arranging contemporary music programs on radio in honor of the League. Impressive tributes, with concerts and receptions, were arranged by the Juilliard School, the Alice M. Ditson Fund of Columbia University, and the New York City Orchestra of the City Center of Music and Drama. Programs were offered by the National Gallery Orchestra of the National Gallery of Art at Washington, D.C.; in Boston by the Harvard Glee Club and the Radcliffe Choral Society; in Los Angeles, by the 'Evenings on the Roof' Society. In Europe, the Belgium National Radio Orchestra paid us the compliment of broadcasting the European *première* of one of our commissioned works.

It was heartening at the end of these twenty-five years of work, mostly uphill, to have so many honors paid by colleagues and fellow musical organizations. During the many celebrations I could not help wishing that we had been able to honor even more composers. True, we had given commissions to 110 composers; we had performed over 1200 compositions, of which the large majority were first performances. Six hundred and twenty-five composers and almost every nationality had been represented on our programs. Over the years *Modern Music* had published a series called 'American Portraits,' which included a great many American composers of stature. These articles were a kind of profile, combined with a general analysis of specific compositions.

As I looked over our files and scrapbooks, the name of the late Frederick Jacobi appeared, listed as a director as far back as 1924, our second season. His friendship had meant a great deal to me and to many others; even when his teaching schedule at the Juilliard School was heavy, he had remained a very active member, coaching, accompanying, judging scores.

Also the late Nicolai Berezowsky had been a real personal friend and popular member in our circle, giving his time to studying scores for us and playing on programs whenever needed, notwithstanding his intensive work with CBS.[12]

---

12. See Appendix, 254–5.

At the first meeting with Aaron Copland just after he returned from his studies in Paris with Nadia Boulanger, I invited him to play at our home before some members of the board. Paul Rosenfeld, although not a board member, was also invited. Later Paul recalled Aaron as 'a slim, be-glassed, shy and still self-assured young fellow . . . boyish but with a personality . . . He played and sang his own compositions . . .' The two works we heard that day were 'Passacaglia,' and 'The Cat and the Mouse.' Subsequently they were performed on a League program at the Anderson Galleries, where some of our early programs were given.

This was the first public performance of Copland's works. Over the years he has never hesitated to give the League credit for this first opportunity. When he received the Pulitzer Prize in 1945, in answer to my congratulatory letter he wrote me modestly, 'After all, you are an intimate part of my career, so you get the credit too!' For all his great stature he has retained an equal simplicity; to me this always is the true test of great talent.

Dr. Koussevitzky's early interest in Copland encouraged the League in 1925 to give this young man a first commission, and he had kept a watchful eye on him when Aaron first dedicated himself to composition.

Shortly after Aaron's return from Paris I had discussed with Koussevitzky whether or not to invite him to join our board of directors. 'Please,' the wise conductor advised me, 'leave Copland alone until he is an integrated person. For a few years he should not give his energy to anything but composition.'

'If you feel so strongly about this,' I said, impressed by the strong disapproval in his tone, 'we will not ask him now, but wait for some later time, when he has had more opportunity to mature in his own work.'

Before Copland joined the League, he and Roger Sessions organized a concert series called the 'Copland-Sessions Concerts'; but they found it encroaching too much on their time and abandoned it.

We were fortunate indeed that Copland became an 'integrated

person' at an early age. He joined the League in 1933 and, as a director, immediately became a real force. His influence and his judgment about works for performance, as well as his advice about the magazine, were invaluable, and his aesthetic opinions have always been sincere, never political.

At times Copland has expressed a great desire to 'find a new face for the League,' even a new name. This proposed plastic surgery on the society's profile was for the reason that characteristically Copland always wants 'to keep things alive,' in this case to prevent the League from becoming captive to the past.

We have had many discussions on these points. He even brought the matter to a vote at an annual meeting; at the time Aaron truly believed that if the society were renamed it would not *sound so old*. Fortunately my belief, in the value of continuity — so long as fresh blood continues to circulate freely through the organism — won out when the vote was taken.

When Copland was in Italy on a Fulbright Professorship and acting in the capacity of consultant at the American Academy of Rome, he wrote to me, 'Each time I go to a Santa Cecilia concert here, and read in the program that it was founded by Palestrina in 1566, and I realize that it is still going strong, the League does not seem too ancient! Anyhow, all your new activities for the 29th season sound good!' Since then we have not discussed the League's profile, or changing its name. In the merger which has now taken place, of the League of Composers and the International Society for Contemporary Music (United States Section), we shall use extra wide stationery, as a means of preserving both valuable names!

Our State Department paid Copland a distinct compliment by choosing him as 'Ambassador of Music' for a South American tour, to meet Latin American composers and to visit their schools of music.

He seemed to enjoy greatly an incident in Brazil, when he found his own photograph in a South American magazine; he wrote me, 'I am on the same page with George Gershwin . . . this is the first time that I made the same page as George!'

Aaron Copland always has had a profound interest in the American scene, as titles of many of his compositions show, 'Billy the Kid,' 'Rodeo,' 'The Lincoln Portrait,' 'Appalachian Spring.' Arthur Berger has commented, 'Even when Copland is not trying to do so, he writes music that is American, and — not least of all — music that is thoroughly inspired.' Darius Milhaud adds to this appreciation of Copland's interest in America, 'Copland has a feeling for the soil of his own country; he has a delicate sadness and sensitive heart.' [13]

With his usual modesty, when we asked Aaron if he would write a work for our twentieth anniversary, he was hesitant; only after several efforts on my part to get a positive answer did he finally say, 'I will, Claire — that is, if you really want it. Actually, I did not think you would care so much if I did or didn't write a piece, as you already have a list of so many important composers writing for the League's anniversary.' I assured him that we would feel the celebration incomplete if he failed us; and so he wrote us a work entitled 'Birthday Piece,' now called 'Danzon Cubana,' which Leonard Bernstein and the composer played at two pianos for the anniversary concert in Town Hall.

When I told Aaron that the League had decided to mark his fiftieth birthday by giving an evening to honor him, with a program of his works and a reception to follow, he was simply amazed. 'I certainly am surprised that the boys want to honor me!' he exclaimed; 'but of course I am simply delighted.'

Among the works given were Seven Songs from the Emily Dickinson Poems, also his Sextet, and an early song, written in 1924. Several times, while we discussed and planned this evening, I felt a curious resistance in him. As he has had such a forward-looking attitude about almost everything in life, and most of the time his personality has such buoyancy, I felt very puzzled by this new phase — or was it just a passing mood? I

13. Darius Milhaud, Notes Without Music, Alfred A. Knopf, Inc., New York, 1953.

remained mystified until one day he said suddenly, 'To think I am going to be fifty — isn't it terrible!'

'But Aaron, you don't look it!' I said cheerfully, feeling relieved to know the reason for his mood. 'Anyhow, why should you feel that a half century is such a long time, particularly when you have made such good use of your years?'

From the way he laughed, I thought perhaps he found some reassurance in my consoling remarks.

When Olin Downes devoted his entire Sunday editorial column in *The New York Times* to 'Copland at Fifty,' Aaron seemed to accept his age more philosophically. 'Copland has made himself the spearhead of the development of the modern American school,' wrote Downes; 'he has done this with an unostentatiousness and a desire for service to his art that will leave their mark on this whole period of native composition, and open the way for a greater future to come.'

Aaron's birthday program at the Museum of Modern Art was prefaced by a small dinner at my home. I invited him to draw up his own list of guests.

When the birthday cake came in, lit with fifty-one candles, including the traditional 'one to grow on,' all of us — Martha Graham, William Schuman and Mrs. Schuman, Irving Fine and Mrs. Fine among others — stood up to sing Happy Birthday. I handed Aaron the cake knife to cut the first slice.

'But how do I *cut* a birthday cake?' he said wistfully.

It seemed infinitely touching to me. I think when he was growing up, there had been no time for birthday cakes.

# 12

## *International Contacts*

'The purpose and aim of the League of Composers is the uniting of musical creative forces, promoting their art, sustaining an interest in their work. In its realm the League is in effect a United Nations.'

These words of Dr. Koussevitzky's sum up the task which, from the outside, I have felt was vital to our organization; a bringing together of many composers, many nationalities, many aspirations, many achievements.

In the early years, we were well aware of our musical dependence upon the European composers to sustain the contemporary scene. We had established some of our contacts in foreign countries through our 'composer-ambassadors,' as we called them — those musicians who traveled from the United States to the musical festivals in Europe, mingling with musicians from other lands. *Modern Music*, dedicated as it was to the 'critical analysis of contemporary music and the allied arts,' attracted to its pages reviews by the foreign composers and critics about new European compositions, and also material from the Latin American and Far East countries. Articles ranged from 'Art under the Soviet' to 'Music in Post-Empire Austria,' and included such other and varied articles as 'Magyar Explorers,'

'Dawn in Sweden,' 'Young Voices in Milan.' No issue failed to carry some material on new music centers, new musical personalities.

We were heartened in turn when the foreign periodicals began to review our magazine, and to request reciprocal articles about American composers. In many ways, it seemed prophetic of our intention, to reach other lands with our American music. Although the European headquarters of the International Society for Contemporary Music received a group of compositions each year from our United States Section of the organization, few, often no works were finally selected by the jury for the festivals in Europe in the early years. As a charter member of the Section, I had followed this disheartening record in which, over here, we felt quite helpless; clearly American composers were not yet accepted on a par with European composers.

Meanwhile, of course, we did keep abreast of what was going on in the European capitals. Works for chamber orchestra had become very popular during these unfolding years, both for concert programs and in the ballets and theater. Milhaud's 'Boeuf sur le Toit,' Hindemith's 'Junge Magd,' Malipiero's 'Sette Canzoni,' Stravinsky's *Histoire du Soldat* — whether from France, Germany, Italy, or Russia — all were frequently heard, and were very much a part of the international contemporary scene on the European continent.

Encouraged by Serge Koussevitzky, his programs for chamber orchestra under our auspices in 1924 and 1925 not only produced American *premières* by Prokofieff, Bartók, Tansman, and Honegger, but also brought out new American works by Copland and Gruenberg for chamber orchestras.

The American composers began to feel hopeful and by the next season we were able to present a whole series of works for chamber orchestra. In this category were Louis Gruenberg's 'Daniel Jazz' and 'The Creation'; Frederick Jacobi's 'Assyrian Prayers,' Richard Hammond's 'Voyage to the East,' and Emerson Whithorne's 'Saturday's Child.'

The symphonic orchestras in the early 'twenties, however,

were playing only the smallest percentage of American works, and these written by a generation well along in middle years, or by men who had died in the early part of the twentieth century.

It was not easy to discover unknown new American composers. Since very few major American compositions were being published, our search for new names and contacts necessarily depended upon acquaintances within personal circles. A European score and parts could always be rented through an American agency representing the foreign publisher; an American score was invariably handed to us personally, having generally been found through a friend of a friend of a friend, rather than a publisher or other agency. There was no recording, little collecting of royalties; the grateful composer merely blessed the friend of the friend of the friend.

At the close of the League's sixth season, I compiled a few statistics on the nationalities of composers whose works we had performed. One day at a board meeting I announced with pride, 'I'd like to play a quiz game with some of you composers; how do you think the American composer has fared on our programs?'

'Pretty badly,' said Mr. Saminsky promptly. He was forever berating us for presenting even a minor Stravinsky composition, 'because *he* does not need *us!*'

'I disagree,' said Richard Hammond; 'I've been observing the matter closely, and I think that American composers have fared pretty well with the League.' He had founded a music publishing house called Composers' Music Corporation, and was trying to develop a wider interest in American works.

After a few more guesses, most of them wide of the mark, I said, 'Here are the statistics for the past six seasons. Thirteen nationalities have been presented. In all, 116 works have been performed. There were 35 by American composers, 18 by Russian, 17 by Italian, 14 by German, 8 by English, 6 by French, 5 Hungarian, 4 Spanish, 3 Polish, 2 Dutch, 2 Czechoslovakian, 1 Swedish, 1 Mexican.'

There were exclamations of surprise. I added, 'I know most

of you are really amazed that in this short time we have actually discovered enough American works to double practically any of the other twelve nationalities represented.'

This report encouraged all of us, and set us on our mark to find other music by men of our own country. We genuinely felt that the League was called upon to render a crusading service for the American composer, and at the same time to further the exchange of music with as many other countries as possible.

By the end of the 1920's the League had become the most active contemporary music society in the United States. For some time, correspondence had been coming in to us from the various European chapters of the International Society, asking for an exchange of music. From Poland came the request for an exchange of concerts and also an offer to give American compositions over the Polish radio. From the Czech section of the International — ISCM, as it is called — we were asked for 'all news of your musical life and activity' to be published in their magazine *Rytmus*. This was a big order but we did our best to comply with requests.

A letter from Palestine asked for a copy of our by-laws as the group was setting up a Palestinian League of Composers. From Johannesburg, a South African League of Composers asked for a copy of our constitution, and suggested mailing to us some works by their members, with a view to having them performed; but they also prepared us in advance for the fact that they could only reciprocate by presenting American works 'in a much humbler manner.'

We were finding some difficulty in establishing exchanges, especially in settling financial considerations, since the European groups invariably held the popular idea that American sidewalks were paved with gold, and that a share in them was owned by music societies.

In Paris the Triton Society had become a center for contemporary music from all parts of Europe, including Soviet Russia. Many of the important composers, who in the early 'thirties spent part of each season in Paris, were either active or honorary members of this group, including Martinu, Prokofieff, Casella, de Falla, Bartók, and others.

I was about to depart for Europe, and a meeting was planned with the Triton Society's executive committee in Paris. They had been corresponding with us about an exchange of programs.

As my daughter Hilda and I stepped off the boat train at the Gare St. Lazare, a young man came up to me and said, 'I am M. Filip Lazar. I am the secretary of the Triton Society.' With true European hospitality he escorted us to the hotel. On the way he reiterated, 'We surely expect you tomorrow afternoon for a meeting with the Triton board at the home of Darius Milhaud. We have all been awaiting your arrival with pleasure.' I wondered how he had managed to find us in that mob of tourists at the station; and who could have given him some hint by which to pick us out?

The next afternoon I arrived at Milhaud's apartment on the Boulevard Clichy promptly at three o'clock. Honegger, Milhaud, Lazar, and Ferroud were already there. Missing from the executive committee were Francis Poulenc, Jean Françaix, Jacques Ibert, and Marcel Delannoy, who were away on vacation.

It soon became clear to me that, although the Triton Society was most eager to have an exchange of concerts with the League, we were in danger of running into difficulties.

'I should like to submit a list to you of American works from which you could make a selection for a program in Paris,' I said. 'Our organization feels that you would best know which works would most appeal to your audiences.'

Milhaud said quickly, 'I think your proposition is good.' Honegger agreed, 'I like the idea too; and you in New York will know also which French compositions to select from a large choice which we could send you.'

At that moment Lazar and Ferroud began to object strongly. 'We should be the ones,' said Ferroud firmly, 'to choose the complete French program and send it to you as it should be played. You should do the same with the American composers for us.'

Within the Triton group the discussion grew a little heated; it became clear to me that Milhaud and Honegger were talking objectively about the best means of exchange and, moreover, felt secure about their own work, whether performed in America or elsewhere. It was equally clear that Lazar and Ferroud hoped that their compositions would be on the program!

This matter was still unsettled when the group launched into a more crucial discussion, the financing of these exchange concerts. Again it seemed necessary for me to steer the discussion. 'I believe that each society must take care of its own compositions, including the expenses pertaining to any manuscripts or copying of parts. Likewise, the interpreters of each program must be paid by each society.'

I was not prepared for the somewhat shrewd and familiar argument then interjected by M. Lazar. 'But the Triton doesn't have much money, and America is such a rich country!' he said rather sharply. I then learned that he was also the treasurer of their organization, and had his problems in finding the necessary finances.

'It may surprise you,' I answered, 'to know that each season the League of Composers wonders if it will be able to continue for another year; organizations like ours have a very difficult time to find support, for there are really only a few patrons in the United States who have sufficient vision, as well as money, to realize the importance of our work.' The group expressed various degrees of astonishment but each person seemed eager to get into the discussion.

'Yet,' said Honegger, 'you cannot compare your strong organization and all you accomplish with a society like the Triton.'

I decided then that I could best break the tension which had arisen over our imagined strength and their weakness by telling them of a conversation I had had with the renowned critic, Pitts Sanborn.

He and I had been discussing the difficulties musical organizations faced in meeting their budgets. The American Music Guild and the International Composers' Guild had by this time closed their books due to lack of support. Sanborn had followed the League's concerts faithfully; he was also a staunch admirer of our magazine and Minna Lederman's editorship.

'It is too bad,' Sanborn said one day at the end of the musical season, 'really it is unfortunate to see the end of some of these musical societies; however, the League of Composers is like the Rock of Gibraltar; it will always go on.'

'You are certainly encouraging,' was all I dared to answer in reply. I did not want to tell him about our true situation, that every year we closed our books in April with such a small balance that I wondered if we could find the support for another season.

Evidently my French colleagues had also thought of us as a 'Rock of Gibraltar.' They expressed their complete astonishment that a society such as the League could be in need of financial assistance. I explained that each hurdle, however, was a further challenge to me to work out just one more season, despite the unending uphill road, the sheer fight to survive.

At that moment Honegger rose to go. He had sat through the meeting on a hot day in June, buttoned up in a leather jacket. Evidently as he grew more uncomfortable it reminded him that he was to go to the country, and it was time to catch his train. He had said very little during the last part of our conference. My impression was that he had little faith in what this new affiliation could offer. Milhaud, however, with his innately generous feeling toward all his colleagues, his buoyancy about life in general, was the most articulate in showing his desire to find some means of co-operation between France and the United States. We decided to correspond about our points of difference regarding both programs and finances.

In the fall I reported to our board about the Triton meeting. Our French friends' picture of our rich treasury caused great merriment. We decided that the League had better continue to plan its own choice of works, French included. After all, had we not always drawn our programs from the international scene?

Then, within the year Ferroud was killed in an accident. Lazar died shortly after. The Triton Society's correspondence with us also came to an end.

About this same time, Alfredo Casella had written from Italy that he wanted to establish an exchange of programs with the League. Although he had not been in the United States for about ten years, he wrote,

> I follow with great interest the magnificent activities of your League which, it seems to me, continually grows in a manner most advantageous to the culture of your country. I have recently conferred with our Minister of Propaganda. We would like to have a musical exchange between New York and Rome. We would give an American concert under the auspices of our society for new music, which is called 'I Concerti di Primavera,' and which gives its programs in April. I shall be glad, if you wish, to help to prepare and to conduct the exchange concerts of Italian music as I shall be in New York next winter.

Casella wrote again a little later.

> I am discussing with our Minister of Propaganda three other projects similar to the exchange of programs we would like to do with you. One is with a Viennese group, another with a Polish group, and the third is the Triton Society in France. These four concerts in Rome would make an interesting project under our society for new music.

Ministers of Propaganda under Mussolini changed frequently, as in other countries under dictatorship. We had accepted Casella's last plan for the Viennese, Polish, French, and American concerts. But then I heard nothing further from him. Although we tried to follow up the plans for exchange programs with other countries, they seemed generally to lead to an impasse. We were aware of the League's growing prestige abroad, yet we never felt that the European groups were as genuinely interested in our American composers as they were in planning exchange programs in order to have their own works played in this country. Paradoxically, we were conscious of the fact that we in the United States were considered still very young and immature by our European colleagues.

Yet we did not realize how far the League's name had reached until one day in the early 'thirties the League received a letter from Tokyo from the Honorable Secretary Yeinen Ynasa of the Japanese Section of the International Society for Contemporary Music, telling us that they were planning to hold a festival:

> We hope exchange of works may be realized between composers of the United States in next year. Friendship between United States and Japanese composers should be closer than others, as both of us are striving to produce something newer in music than from old traditions. We hope you to lend your hands along this line. We hope to write articles about American composers in our music publications and arouse interest for American music. We are too much influenced by present European music. Asking your future connections, Yeinen Ynasa.

We immediately forwarded some of our music to this Japanese society, with some of the back issues of *Modern Music*. Shortly thereafter the League received another 'hands-across-the-sea' letter, to which forty-seven signatures of Japanese composers were attached.

The letter read:

> Our society, 'Nippon Gendai Sakkyokuka Renmei' (founded April, 1930) is the association of the young Japanese contemporary composers, whose objects are the serious creation of music and the confirmation of our professional interests. [There followed the list of members]

| | | |
|---|---|---|
| K. Abe | K. Hashimoto | N. Itoh |
| H. Amane | T. Hattori | Y. Itoh |
| T. Etoh | F. Hayasaka | K. Kami |
| S. Fukai | N. Iida | K. Kishi |
| T. Go | Y. Ike | Y. Kiyose |
| S. Hamaguchi | T. Ikenouchi | B. Koh |
| T. Hara | I. Ishida | K. Kematsu |
| Y. Hasegawa | G. Ishii | H. Konoe |

| Y. Kozeki | M. Ohki | T. Tsuyuki |
| T. Kujirai | T. Ohnaka | S. Utsumi |
| Y. Matsudaira | T. Ohta | T. Yagi |
| S. Mitsukuri | K. Osamura | K. Yamada |
| M. Merita | H. Saito | N. Yamamoto |
| M. Moroi | T. Saito | S. Yamamoto |
| A. Norimatsu | K. Taku | T. Yoshida |
| Y. Ogiwara | T. Tanaka | |

We are ready and glad to hold out our hands to all artists endeavoring to create true musical works [the letter concluded], and wish heartily for the friendship and guidance of the comrades of the countries which are advanced in music.

Although at that time I was surprised that a Japanese society of composers would be so much interested in our American contemporary music, I have since learned that most of the young Japanese composers today prefer to write in the Western tonal idiom and style, and to use the instruments of the Western orchestras; moreover, most of the musicians in Japan have actually studied composition in Europe or with European teachers.

A few years of silence intervened after the first letters we received from the Nippon Society of Composers; this was during the era of Hitler's influence and later domination of Japan. Then the war canceled all teaching of Western music, although the Tokyo Orchestra continued to play some European music, but none by British composers, and certainly none by Americans.

A dispatch from Tokyo, picked up by New York newspapers in 1943, gave the League of Composers a clue to the type of propaganda Japan had adopted about music during the war years. It stated that all music of British or American origin was banned by regulations issued by the Tokyo government; and all American recorded music was being confiscated. Only foreign recordings of German or Italian origin were available.

Dr. Josef Rosenstock [1] who was the music director and con-

---

1. Dr. Rosenstock has been the director of the New York City Center Opera Company for a few years.

ductor of the Nippon Philharmonic Orchestra in Tokyo for ten years, was interned in Japan during World War II, and has told me, 'Music has a long way to go to recover the ground lost during the war. The American occupation has done a great deal of good for music in Japan; Japanese musical organizations have been revitalized under the aegis of the United States Army.' Moreover he predicts that 'the impact of new music and new audiences, crowded music schools, will all prove a rich era for music in Japan.'

Another letter from Japan, from F. Fujita in Tokyo, corroborated Dr. Rosenstock's observations. Mr. Fujita wrote,

> Through the kindness of Allied Forces, we Japanese are allowed to receive periodicals, books, et cetera, direct from abroad. I am now planning to write a book on American composers and their recorded music. May I have permission from you, Mrs. Reis, to quote passages from your book, *Composers in America?* When my book is printed, I shall see that a copy is forwarded to you. [Signed] F. Fujita, President, Long Playing Record Collectors' Club, Tokyo, Japan.

The Nippon Gendai Sakkyokuka Renmei Association of Contemporary Composers, he told me, was in existence, and active again since the war. They were seeking assistance in making contacts with contemporary music associations in other countries.

Although there had been years of interruption with our Japanese musical associates, I hoped that renewal of their request for 'friendship and guidance' would lead us again toward a conception of One World. The contrapuntal rhythms of war and peace lose their vibrations through friendships first cemented, then destroyed, then restored. The very powers which establish alliances at the turn of the wheel also determine enmities. Classically, music follows the pattern set by the political scene. Some countries which yesterday were joint defenders of a common culture today wrap themselves in an opprobrious silence; witness our experience with Russia.

The League had been asked early in 1941 by the Union of

Soviet Composers of the USSR Society to exchange new music with them. They had specified a few American composers about whom they knew, and asked us to send them other works of our own choice. In June 1941, I mailed about twenty scores by American composers to the Russian Composers Society. A week later Russia went to war with Germany. To this day we do not know whether the music ever reached its destination.

In our efforts to trace the music we inquired at the Embassy of the USSR in Washington. Mr. Basykine, then First Secretary, promised to inquire for us through the USSR Society for Cultural Relations with Foreign Countries. At the same time, he thanked us for answering an earlier request from the Embassy, to advise them on 'Lists of Military Band Music for the Use of the Red Army,' as well as selected American choral works which could be of interest to *Voks*. He ended this letter, 'I am wondering if there is any organization in the United States which would be interested in sending the military music you listed to the USSR, in exchange for Soviet musical works.'

In the summer of 1941 the League of Composers received a radiogram from Moscow — three pages — signed by six of the most distinguished composers in Russia: Prokofieff, Shostakovich, Glière, Miaskovsky, Muradeli, Khachaturian. It read:

> The entire multimillion Soviet people are experiencing creative upsurge and fighting enthusiasm in this hour of decisive battle against the worst enemy of mankind *Stop* The outrageously insolent Nazi rulers who have enslaved several European nations will meet an inglorious end in their mad venture against the Soviet Union *Stop* Composers of the USSR considering themselves mobilized for the relentless struggle against bloody Fascist barbarity which has plunged half of Europe into utter gloom and desolation appeals to American Composers with friendly greetings and an ardent call to muster still closer the international rank of defenders of culture in the joint struggle against the common foe by means of the great art of music.

The League's answer to this message of three pages was more in keeping with the terse — and economical — American manner of expression. We cabled briefly:

October 2, 1941

Your fellow American composers send warm greetings to your composers in profound admiration of the Russian artists and their valiant spirit.

Shortly after the League received another letter, this time from a member of the Union of Soviet (Russia) Composers, who said:

> The Union of Soviet Composers salutes you heartily. In these historical days with the Fascist Germany, our peoples are fighting together for the highest ideals of mankind. Our art also is a mighty weapon in this war, both songs and symphonies, which are dedicated to recent events, to our heroes, to our countries. We hope that there will be a permanent contact between our composers and musicians, between the League of Composers and Union of Soviet Composers a mutual understanding of our common aims and action. We salute you as our fellows and friends, and hope that nowadays our strength will grow in friendship as like as in our battle for democracy and social justice. May we take this opportunity of assuring that the Union of Soviet Composers would be glad to send out any regular information and all scores of Soviet music in which American composers might be interested.
>
> Yours for Victory
> V. Biely.

It is interesting to note that since receipt of that communication complete silence has prevailed between the Union of Soviet Composers and the League.

In the summer of 1943 the Russian Embassy at Washington informed us that a concert of American music had been organized in Moscow, and that material about the concert was being forwarded to us. However, we never received it. An article in *The New York Times* in August of that year, date-lined Kubishev, Russia, reported

> A campaign to help the Russians to become acquainted with their Allies is being undertaken by United Nations diplomats and scholars. In view of the fact that Russia has been virtually isolated from the outside world since the Bol-

shevik Revolution, some observers believe that books, pamphlets, and motion pictures portraying the United States and Great Britain are almost as urgent for the Soviets as planes, tanks, and guns. The United States, Britain, and Fighting France are assuming leadership in the task of improving understanding between their peoples and the Russians, with a view to strengthening co-operation, both during and after the war.

We may assume that Russia has continued one convention, which was to present annually a concert of American music on 4 July, which the American Ambassador always attended. Our last news about this was in 1946; a cable to Dr. Koussevitzky informed him that *Voks* had organized the program of American works by George Antheil, Aaron Copland, George Gershwin, and Elie Siegmeister. Ambassador Walter Bedell Smith attended in Moscow. No reciprocal copyright laws were in force, hence no royalties were paid.

During General Smith's years in Russia, he was strongly hopeful that he might effect reciprocal visits of Soviet and American cultural groups, including student and professorial exchanges, and other proposals of like nature. But, he concludes reluctantly in his book *My Three Years in Moscow*, 'There is complete and forceful evidence that Soviet participation in international culture is *impossible* under Soviet policy.' [2]

Our hope for continuity of an international policy for the League of Composers lay in adapting ourselves to the war effort. Cut off from Europe, Japan, and Russia, one dividend was the improvement of our relations with South America and with Canada.

We found a group of young Canadians who had been writing significant works and in January 1942 we decided upon a program. The event aroused great interest because it was probably the first time attention in the United States had been focused on an all-Canadian concert. The composers represented

---

2. J. B. Lippincott and Company, New York, 1949.

were from Winnipeg, Montreal, and Toronto; Barbara Pentland, Hector Gratton, Louis Applebaum, André Matthieu, Godfrey Rideout, and John J. Weinzweig. We received an enormous Canadian press about this event. The Canadian Trade Commissioner co-operated, publicizing the concert through a large list of Canadian organizations, and was personally represented at the concert. To my further surprise and pleasure, on the day of the event we received a telegram from Ottawa from the Canadian Prime Minister, Mr. W. L. MacKenzie King, to the effect,

> I am interested to learn of the concert to be given in New York City by a group of young Canadian composers under the sponsorship of the League of Composers. It is very gratifying to know that such a splendid opportunity is being given to our young artists and that their talents should receive this recognition. To the sponsors of the program and to the performers themselves I extend my very best of wishes, that the concert may be an unqualified success.

Our interest in Latin American music had begun in the early years of the League's history. Probably one of the first all-Latin American concerts in New York of contemporary music was the program we presented by Allende, Caturla, Chavez, Gonzalez, Ponce, and Villa-Lobos. We had exchanged music with several of the South American societies and had published many articles in *Modern Music* on Latin American subjects; too, our evenings honoring renowned South American visiting composers had been part of our platform.

The Division of Cultural Relations with Latin America in the Department of State had asked us in 1940 for American compositions to be sent to Buenos Aires. Charles A. Thompson, the acting chief, wrote, 'If the music is sent to this office, the Department will be willing to arrange for its transmission to the Buenos Aires Pro-Arte Quartet. . . . I feel sure that this generous co-operation will result in a valuable contribution to musical interchange between the United States and Argentina.'

A year later, we were invited to represent the Office of the

Co-ordinator of Commercial and Cultural Relations between the American Republics, and sponsor the tour through South America of a group of composer-instrumentalists. Nelson Rockefeller's committee at the time had consulted Aaron Copland, who recommended the League as the ideal sponsor for this undertaking, which was completely financed through the Co-ordinator's office. The policy for the project had been established in Washington.

The League, in co-operation with Carleton Sprague Smith, director of the New York Public Library Music Division, discussed the selection of a quintet of composer-artists, also the general plan of the programs to be presented on the tour; the quintet consisted of a flutist, an oboist, a clarinetist, a bassoonist, and a French horn player. It was understood that all these men would also play their own compositions while on tour. The manager chosen to book the quintet in South America was a Mexican of *mañana* temperament; accordingly there were many delays before all the arrangements were concluded.

The League's only request in being the sponsor-in-name for this project had been that we would retain control over the programs to be performed. But when the five composer-artists arrived in New York only a day before sailing, the sole assurance we were able to obtain from them was that they would play a contemporary work on each program.

At the very last moment we learned that several wives of the quintet members were accompanying their husbands at their own expense. We sensed that difficulties might arise out of the unexpected additions to this professional tour. Too, official receptions planned in many South American cities suggested some scope for personal intrigue.

Until the tour was over and the group reached Miami on its return three months later, we heard nothing. Meanwhile the League thought it would be a nice gesture to have the quintet close its good-will tour with a program in New York in honor of the Co-ordinator, Mr. Rockefeller, inviting representatives from all the diplomatic offices in New York and Washington.

We wired Miami to arrange a date convenient to the artists. To our astonishment we received a firmly negative reply to our suggestion. A second wire confirmed our uneasy suspicion that under no consideration would the quintet appear any longer as a group, no matter how many diplomats we intended to invite. The five planned simply to disband as quickly as possible.

In the next few months I received letters from one after another of the quintet, each giving his story and the reasons for the lack of harmony that had arisen during the tour. One of the wives also supplied an explanation, which only added more confusion. At that point we decided with the Co-ordinator in Washington that thereafter it would be simpler to send music rather than musicians with wives on any good-will tour!

I had been in touch with the Cultural Division also at the time Villa-Lobos was visiting in New York, and they had given the League financial assistance toward a program honoring the renowned Brazilian composer. Our treasurer, ever careful in his accounts, had been particularly meticulous in auditing the expenses for this musical occasion. I had, however, forgotten some of the details when, several years later, I paid a visit personally to the Washington offices of the Cultural Division, for the purpose of discussing a wartime matter.

One of the staff seemed unusually well informed about the League's activities, as well as about my name. I was puzzled by his smile throughout the early part of our discussion. When we reached a point of finances for the project of the moment, he revealed the reason for his good spirits, saying, 'You know, Mrs. Reis, you have made a lasting impression upon us here by returning $19.65 to the State Department! You remember that we assisted the League in order to give Villa-Lobos an evening. Actually we regarded it as part of our cultural relations activities.'

I remembered then, that we had made out a detailed statement of all the expenses of the occasion, returning to the State Department the unused small balance. Our contract specified the return of any balance, and we certainly intended to live up to it. I suppose the item of $19.65 had to be signed by innumerable State Department functionaries before it could officially be received, and it was therefore no wonder that it had made a lasting impression on him!

# 13

## On the Composers' Horizon

THE LAST concert of the League's twenty-fifth season was over.

Leaving the Museum of Modern Art with the audience, my ear caught fragments of comment about works which several European composers had written for this anniversary program. Actually I was more concerned with my own feelings; after twenty-five years in office I had resigned as chairman of the League of Composers, hence this had been the last program under my direction. There had been flattering protests from colleagues, but Serge Koussevitzky had urged me to hold to my decision. In his friendly and confidential manner he had said, 'My dear, I think you are quite right to resign. Keep your interest — you cannot help but do so after twenty-five such active years as chairman — but turn to doing other things too. Now I'm going to let you in on *my* secret. I, too, am going to resign soon, for I shall have been with the Boston Symphony for a quarter of a century. Yet both of us, you and I, will certainly go on "doing" for music.'

I felt assured that evening that the League of Composers would continue functioning to help the living composers. To some extent, at least, we had succeeded in our original aims, namely, to promote the composer and to help educate the public

232

in contemporary music. Yet, how many more composer needs were still to be fulfilled!

For example, merely because composers had banded together to present their own works, it was impossible to agree with those musicians who believed that 'The Helpless Period' was ended. Perhaps, rather, it was changing into a 'Helping Period.' I held to my conviction that there loomed on the horizon more than an ideological concept of a real composers guild.

Over the years I had listened to an endless variety of grievances over injustices suffered by musicians. Occasionally our organization had been able to inject itself into a composer's problem, particularly if the League had had any share in the situation. But often and often, I had wished for some well-defined court of arbitration, some neutral area, where a problem could be aired and wrong redressed in an atmosphere of objectivity!

One may learn many lessons in twenty-five years. Among those taught me by experience with the pioneering League, several had to do with unions. It was inevitable that we should come to recognize their practical protective powers. If only a similar mechanism existed for composers!

My first head-on encounter with unions came just before one of our earliest concerts in the Klaw Theater, and it was with a theater union.

It was the duty of the property man to place the piano and the music stands on the platform. On regular theater evenings, naturally his work was done with theatrical properties while the curtain was lowered. Although our concert was given in a theater it was not in the concert style to lower the curtain between numbers.

The property man, unaware of any such distinction, strolled onto the platform when the time came to do his duty, a disheveled figure in a crumpled gray suit, sporting a slouch hat on the back of a tousled head. If he was aware that he was an astonishing sight to an audience of experienced concertgoers, he gave no sign. There was nothing to be done at the moment, of course, but something had to be changed immediately; Alma Morgenthau, one of our directors, volunteered to have her nephews present for the next concert to do whatever was necessary on the platform; she suggested that not only would the boys enjoy the concert but they would also look neat and clean and more in keeping with the atmosphere of the concert hall.

And so it was arranged. At the appropriate moment the 'concert nephews' stepped out on the platform to place the violin stands for the next number. In a second one of them was seized by the regular theater property man and unceremoniously yanked off the stage to the accompaniment of a bellowed, 'Hey, you! You're no union men — get away from that platform — you can't touch a darn thing!'

The stands overturned with a clatter, the boys fled; in fact, in their excitement they kept right on going until they reached the street, quite forgetting that they were looking forward to hearing the remainder of the concert.

The property man again took up his duties, after making the small concession of removing his hat and brushing his hair before appearing again on the stage.

I was shortly to be confronted with more union rules. I engaged a neighborhood truckman to haul a load of theatrical material to Town Hall for a stage production of de Falla's marionette opera, *El Retablo de Maese Pedro*. To my dismay when I arrived at the 43rd Street entrance, I found all our properties plunked down on the sidewalk with no one in charge. I ran to find the building superintendent. 'What does this mean?' I cried, very upset because at that precise moment the great conductor Willem Mengelberg was due for the orchestra rehearsal. 'Why has the truckman left everything in the street? His job isn't finished!'

The superintendent sensed what was wrong. 'Lady, I guess you engaged a non-union truckman and he isn't allowed to deliver *into* the building. I'll help you this time, but next time you be sure to get a union truck driver, otherwise you'll always find your goods left on the pavement. Union rules are very strict, you know.'

Thus, I learned two important lessons about theater unions. A third was soon to be taught me, this time by the Musicians' Union. We happened to be broadcasting a series of League programs over NBC. We had invited the young American composer Harold Morris to play his own Piano Sonata. Fifteen minutes before the program went on the air the Musicians' Union called up the program director to demand that Morris be taken off, because he was not a member of Local 802. A vast flurry ensued and in the nick of time an exception was worked out for the composer for this one broadcast. But we were fully briefed on the fact that such a thing must never happen again.

After our baptism of fire, several years were to pass before we had any further union troubles. I found the next lesson particularly objectionable, personally.

A chamber orchestra rehearsal was scheduled for a League program to be conducted by Alexander Smallens, then conductor of the Philadelphia Civic Opera Company. While the rehearsal progressed, we observed that the percussion player seemed singularly uninterested in the whole proceeding. Soon he became downright troublesome to the conductor, who reprimanded him several times for using the wrong percussion instruments.

Suddenly there was a particularly loud noise; the percussionist's music stand clattered to the floor, followed by the flutter of his music sheets about the stage. Intermission was called. Glowering, Smallens called to the percussionist, 'What is wrong with you? Why don't you use the right instruments?'

Astonishingly, a surly, low voice replied, 'I don't like Stravinsky.'

I hurried to see if I could be of help in straightening out the wrangle and Smallens exclaimed to me, 'You'll simply have to call up the union and get me another percussion player.' He added excitedly, 'My patience is exhausted. It is impossible to rehearse with this man.'

I called up the Musicians' Union. They informed me that we could have another percussionist, certainly, but the first man could not be dismissed and we must therefore pay for *both* men. It was very important to us to give the best possible rendition to all new compositions; accordingly we paid for two percussionists. One played without animosity against Stravinsky, and the other, the obstreperous young man, sat by in bland idleness. Today he is the leading percussionist in one of our major orchestras, and he has played a great many Stravinsky compositions, swallowing his aversion and using the right instruments.

Obviously not all the difficulties of composers are related to unions nor would union action always be a successful means of remedying them. A large proportion of composers' problems are tied to their struggles to get a livelihood and to find a public which will take an interest in their work; many an instance of injustice has grown out of prolonged neglect or poor advice.

I recall a sharp retort some years ago by Louis Gruenberg when I asked him if he was interested in writing another opera. 'Why,' he burst out, 'should any animal on God's earth be stupid enough to write a work of the magnitude of *Emperor Jones* and receive practically nothing for it?' I could well understand why he felt so deeply and so bitterly about the general neglect of composers as people. His opera had been performed by the Metropolitan Opera Company six or seven times in one season, even attracting sufficient attention to make the front page of *The New York Times*, a rare occurrence indeed for a composer. Yet, as Gruenberg said, 'I went back to California a poorer man than when I left. My contract for royalties did not even cover the tremendous expenses I had for the copying of the parts, not to mention the hundreds of hours that went into writing the opera!'

As time passed, it was necessary to call together a group of League directors and members of the national composers committee to act as a kind of informal arbitration board to consider the unfortunate experience of one young composer.

A work by William Bergsma had been commissioned by Carl

Fischer, Inc., in honor of the League's twenty-fifth anniversary. Without consent of the composer or knowledge of the League, 170 measures had been cut from a 464-measure composition in a radio performance, with the result that in the broadcast the work was completely distorted.

In the course of the meeting, in the office of our public relations director, Herbert Barrett, we drew up a statement to the press, setting forth the facts as to the mutilation of Bergsma's score, declaring that this was not a matter of concern alone to the League but to every composer, every person interested in music, indeed, to the very status of the art itself. In this case the pressure of public opinion which we generated forced the radio station to give a complete broadcast of the uncut work a few weeks later.

As another case in point, Paul Nordoff, a young composer whose works have been played by leading conductors, recently came to ask for advice about an unfortunate experience of his.

'I was commissioned to write a dance composition for Miss X——.' he explained. 'We discussed the general idea, also the length of the work she wanted. Imagine my surprise when she later told me, after the performance had taken place, that she had cut the work in half because of the limited time in which to rehearse! What was even worse, it was cut so inartistically — without consulting me — that the music came off very badly; in fact it simply did not hold together. As a result my composition got very bad reviews. After all, as you well know, Claire, I've had a fair amount of success as a young composer; yet after those reviews that piece of music stands condemned.'

I felt as though my hands were tied. There was little advice to give, or help to offer, because so far as the composer was concerned, the damage was done. If a work is in manuscript, a composer has little opportunity for redress except through the courts, usually a prohibitively expensive process.

Talking one day with Ernest Bloch about some of his chamber music, he launched explosively into an irremediable situation involving him. Although one of his Quartets had been played many times *shortly* after it was published, in recent years it had been ignored, he said. 'I wanted to obtain a copy or two for myself,' he recalled, 'as I had given away my last one long ago.

'At the publishing house I was told there were no copies on their shelves. Finally I called upon the publisher personally. Without the slightest embarrassment he told me that there was simply no room on the shelves after a while to keep music that did not move; all the copies of my Quartet had been thrown out. I then asked for the plates, thinking, at least, I can have those! But those, I was told, had been destroyed at the printer's!' Obviously Bloch had not heard about Thoreau's experience. When his first book sold only 213 copies out of the thousand printed, the publisher told him he did not know where to house the surplus. Thoreau, thereupon, took a wheelbarrow to the publisher's and carted the remainder of his books home in it, remarking wryly, 'I now have a library of nearly 900 volumes — over 700 of which I wrote myself.'

An experience which has brought severe disappointment to many composers is failure of an outstanding conductor to put on a promised performance. When a work, announced months previously, is withdrawn ten days before a concert, it may often prove to have prevented another conductor from placing the work on his program during the same season. For example, in a recent situation, when Dmitri Mitropoulos found in all sincerity that in order to do justice to a very difficult composition he needed more rehearsals than the Philharmonic Symphony could afford, he was so genuinely apologetic in withdrawing the work that the composer told me, 'With all my bitter disappointment over my symphony being taken off the program a week before the concert, Mitropoulos was so profuse in his apologies that I really began to feel sorry for him instead of for myself!' Inevitably, however, the withdrawal of that work must have been a crushing disappointment to the composer.

If the American composer has a feeling of being neglected by musical groups he frequently has some justification. For example, how few names of composers appear on the boards of directors of music societies. In most cases a composer's musical bias is no greater than that of the general run of conductors. Actually the composer may prove far more objective in suggesting new compositions than will some of the orchestras' ladies committees, who have been known to work hysterically to promote a pet musician! Moreover, as a practical matter, who — other than conductors, composers, and a few critics — is even able to read scores and recommend works?

Gian-Carlo Menotti, the well-known composer, has made an eloquent plea for the creative artist. 'The indifference of the American public toward creative life,' he pointed out, 'is reflected even in its cultural institutions. . . . Relatively few artists have ever been granted academic recognition by a first-rank university.' He added, 'At the reception given for its 100th Anniversary by the New York Philharmonic Symphony — to which every Tom, Dick and Harry of the musical world was invited — I don't know of a single composer of note who received an invitation.' [1]

'Music Week' had been an annual event in the United States for several years before it came to my attention that contemporary music received no definite place in the setting aside of those seven days for music. Co-operating groups of all kinds celebrated with widely advertised convocations, conventions, and concerts; Boy Scouts, Girl Scouts, Rotary Clubs, Federations, and many varieties of concert organizations contributed to the week's events.

I paid a call on the executive secretary and insisted that the League of Composers be added to the roster of organizations, for there was no group on the long list representing contemporary music. The secretary seemed quite indifferent, and the plea fell on deaf ears. Finally, he did agree to include the League, when we promised to contribute a concert during that week, even though the schedule of events was overcrowded. 'I'm only

---

1. *The New York Times.*

surprised you didn't consider modern music when you began these large-scale celebrations,' I said, in parting. I really should not have been surprised; we had already been in too many struggles in our endeavor to promote the living composer.

The collaboration of composers with other creative artists in certain instances causes problems which demand ironing out by a third party; sometimes time alone can effect an improvement.

In the late 'twenties there were few instances in the United States wherein a composer collaborated with a dancer and vice versa. Reverberations from the great Diaghilev ballets undoubtedly had created a yearning in the souls of some of the American dancers to find a new form of expression; I had heard a little about the unfulfilled desires of young American dancers to work out new choreography with composers.

As a first step toward finding a forum for airing their problems, I invited a group of dancers to my home one afternoon to meet a group of composers. I hoped that we could find a formula for creating ballets that would interest equally both creative groups. Among the dancers present were Martha Graham, Doris Humphrey, Agnes de Mille, Edwin Strawbridge, Charles Weidman. The composers were members of the League's board of directors.

A dancer opened the session, complaining, 'I feel that a composer always has his own ideas about what a dancer would like. After all, I think I know more about dance movements than does the composer.'

Henry Cowell quickly jumped to the defense, saying, 'The trouble with most dancers is that the story they have to tell is usually too literary in quality.'

Richard Hammond supported this, adding, 'And when a dancer tries to discuss a movement for pantomime, it is usually such an abstract idea that they seem unable to explain the type of music needed.'

We held several protracted sessions, arguments weaving back and forth for several hours at a time, in the effort to find some basic ideas that would be acceptable to all. Although these round-table discussions were abandoned without any perceptible results, there was no doubt that the young talented dancers were on the lookout for contemporary works, eager to find composers who would accept a full partnership in a creative collaboration.

Today, however, there are ballets such as *Judith* which Martha Graham and William Schuman created; *Appalachian Spring* by Martha Graham and Aaron Copland; *Orpheus*, created by Igor Stravinsky and George Balanchine. There are other works in this category wherein the inspiration stems from a close collaboration between a choreographer, a composer, and sometimes, also, a designer. In a different category, the sensational list of works by contemporary composers produced for the New York City Ballet by Bernstein, Britten, Copland, Hindemith, Ives, Schoenberg, Stravinsky, Thomson, and others is adding enormous vitality to a new era of dance compositions.

Recently Norman Dello Joio told me about a dancer who wanted to find a composer to create music for a new ballet; she asked him to write it.

'First,' Norman recounted, 'this choreographer-dancer asked my ideas about the music for her ballet. Then she invited me to her studio to discuss it further. Imagine my surprise!' Norman then began to illustrate some of her dance movements. 'She moved across the floor step-by-step — like this — doing whole notes, quarter, and eighth notes. She had planned in detail every dance step for the music which *now* she wanted made to order for her ballet! In answer to my question "What about my creative share in this production?" the dancer replied airily, "Your inspiration will come from watching the dancers' motions, and you will fill in the necessary bars of music!" ' Norman laughed; 'I left then,' he said, 'I had had enough!'

Today there is wide searching for a means of collaboration between composer and librettist. Fortunate indeed are the few musicians who can write their own librettos. I discussed this problem with Gian-Carlo Menotti who has unique insight into the impact of drama needed for opera.

'What do you tell other composers when they want your advice about finding a libretto?' I asked him.

'I tell them "Write your own!"'

'But suppose one doesn't know how to write a libretto?'

'Then he must learn,' he answered firmly.

This subject was discussed long ago by Gioacchino Rossini and Richard Wagner. Rossini thought that few composers had sufficient literary knowledge or dramatic experience to be able to furnish their own texts. Wagner believed that composers of dramatic music should study history and legend as well as counterpoint, and learn which subjects were sympathetic to them. If they still lacked the talent to dramatize action, Wagner thought they should call upon some competent dramatist to work with them.

Many composers today are eager to write for the stage, but complain that they cannot find a good libretto, nor do they have any personal acquaintance with those who are good librettists. I had heard this discussed for a long time and decided to take up the subject and air it. A group of eminent composers and dramatists, also poets, was invited to join in a round-table conference; for this occasion the League of Composers obtained the collaboration of the City Center of Music and Drama, and the Metropolitan Opera Company.

The subject was 'Opera 1953; the Music and the Libretto.'

The composers were Leonard Bernstein, Marc Blitzstein, Aaron Copland, Douglas Moore, William Schuman, and Virgil Thomson. The writers were W. H. Auden, Russell Crouse, Howard Dietz, Chester Kallman, Arthur Miller, and Arnold Sundgaard. The late Professor Irwin Edman was moderator, maintaining the balance between the two groups by his skillful guidance, leading the composers and authors through various aspects of the discussion.

Although nothing was resolved, considerable light was thrown on a situation which is filled with immediate and important problems. It was evident that the poets — particularly W. H. Auden and Chester Kallman — had the most interest in collaborating on an opera, in contrast to other authors and playwrights, who seemed to feel no need of adding music to their plays to emphasize the dramatic impact. That a good playwright may have no interest in collaborating with a composer was indicated by one of those present, who asked whimsically, 'Why does my play need to be flattered by an oboe?'

Obviously, musical-dramatic collaboration needs many more hours of discussion; it is a subject which is of vital importance today to a great many composers — and perhaps even to playwrights, if they would but admit it. Time may help, as it did with the play *Liliom*. Although Puccini pursued Molnar for a long time, wanting his great play *Liliom* as a libretto for an opera, Molnar continually refused to give it to him. He was afraid that the acclaim that had come to it on the legitimate stage would be lost if it were turned into a libretto, possibly to be overshadowed by Puccini's music.

Puccini persisted, but all in vain.

Then, years later, Richard Rodgers asked to use *Liliom* with his music. Finally Molnar relented. *Carousel* was the result. Its great success emphasizes good libretto and good music even if *Liliom* in play form often eludes memory as the origin of *Carousel*.

Meanwhile composers in need of dramatists struggle along, alone, in their search for the right collaborator.

In the field of grand opera there is little place today for the living composer. In the Metropolitan Opera Company's repertoire, even the great Stravinsky's opera, *The Rake's Progress*, was not retained after two seasons. The New York City Center's Opera Company, struggling with a small budget to do its share, occasionally premieres contemporary works, such as Alban Berg's *Wozzeck*, Aaron Copland's *Tender Land*, Béla Bartók's *Blue Beard's Castle*, and Gottfried von Einem's *The Trial*.

A new repertoire of opera for television is in the making, due largely to the forward-looking Peter Herman Adler, conductor of the Opera Division of the National Broadcasting Company. Under his supervision, operas have been performed by Leonard Bernstein, Benjamin Britten, Lukas Foss, Vittorio Giannini, Bohuslav Martinu, Gian-Carlo Menotti; it would be a happy circumstance if other networks would add to opera for television in equal proportion.

The interest of many composers in writing opera in smaller form, without huge choruses or enormous casts of soloists, extends the list of works appropriate for the small opera companies, opera workshops, and summer festivals; why not for television? In this connection, it will be remembered that the opening performance of the Metropolitan Opera Company's seventieth season in 1954 was telecast over a closed circuit of audiences in theaters in thirty-two cities over the country. Acts from standard works comprised the program. How much more the Metropolitan could have accomplished, and thus widened musical horizons of this large audience, by including a one-act opera by a modern composer!

It may well be that we are moving — if away from certain phases of opera — toward a great new era, with formats simpler than those of an opera such as *Aïda* where elephants and camels appear, and the masses of people milling about on stage suggest Cecil B. de Mille in his most ambitious Hollywood style.

Today, four industries concerned with music — recordings, radio, television, and films — reflect varying conditions pertaining to contemporary music. There is reason to feel somewhat optimistic about new music in recordings, to feel uncertain — with few exceptions — about the status of contemporary music on radio, to feel cautiously hopeful as to television (particularly with opera, over NBC), and to feel pessimistic about the use of music by contemporary composers in the film industry.

'The concert hall no longer occupies the position it once held as a factor in determining musical tastes,' is the opinion of Goddard Lieberson, executive vice-president of Columbia Records. He says, 'It has relinquished that position, not through inertia, but because the phonograph allows repetitive playings, consequently greater familiarity with new musical experience.'

To this forward-looking statement about recorded music today, David Hall, music director of the Classics Division of Mercury Records adds, 'The picture becomes very impressive in the record world when we learn that just about every trend and tendency in America composition is represented today, from the most conservative to the most radically experimental.'

The new music appreciation record series launched by Thomas Scherman and the Book of the Month Club, with one side of the disc for the performance, the other side for analysis, could prove a great boon in the study of difficult contemporary music, and a wisely selected catalogue could be a great asset to educational institutions.

It is evident that the increase of contemporary records has added immeasurably to the broadcasts from several stations, in particular WQXR and WNYC. They have been the *avant-garde* in New York in recent years, in fact almost the only hope for the composer. Mrs. Elliott Sanger, program director of WQXR, says

> Contemporary music is playing a greater role on WQXR than ever before, without displacing any of the standard repertoire. Two reasons for this are that LP has produced an astonishing number of hitherto unrecorded modern works, and the Louisville Orchestra commissioned works, now being released with regularity, are being used by us almost immediately.

WNYC's broadcasts for the annual American Festival of Music has over the years become one of the most important series in contemporary music on radio. Moreover, an encouraging factor, on both WNYC and WQXR, is the increasing percentage of contemporary compositions performed by live artists on these stations' programs. Unfortunately, too many other

stations introduce new music only between the hours of mid-
night and dawn. Perhaps composers who write during those
quiet hours derive a modicum of needed satisfaction from the
opportunity of hearing their own works performed.

'The revolution has come . . . though most serious composers
are not aware of it . . . Composers today can, or could, reach
ten million listeners, not just a hundred, or a thousand, in one
concert.' Thus wrote Gail Kubik, an able composer and conductor who believes that the composer can and should popu-
larize his work on radio. This particular revolution, however,
does not depend only on discerning and energetic composers,
but more on co-operation by broadcasting officials. They, in
turn, are naturally influenced by fan mail. How then can we
best break the passive mood of complacency which envelops
some of the radio stations with respect to programs of contemporary music?

Judging from the tenor of recent surveys of music in the
United States, we might conclude that we are 'bustin' at the
seams with culture.' The rising number of organizations of every
type — symphonic orchestras, ensembles, recitals, opera companies — plus the phenomenal addition of opera workshops and
grass-roots opera — do lend a certain optimism to the general
musical scene. Percentage-wise, however, the performance of
contemporary works is still but a very small part of the whole.

A few years ago, in a vigorous attempt to increase the presentation of contemporary music, the League of Composers brought
together a group of music publishers [2] who, with artists and
composers, have worked together on a project to encourage
more modern music on all programs. Is it too much to hope that
every program should carry at least one composition, if not more,
by a man or woman of our own generation? Perhaps we may
hope that this propagandizing project, supported by publishers,
and also ASCAP and BMI, may eventually change the conventional pattern. The usual opening work on a program is a Haydn

2. See Appendix, 257.

or a Mozart or some other classic. Why not end the program *always* with a work by a Sessions or a Barber or a Carter?

Happily, a vital stimulus was given to contemporary music in the past several decades through consistent efforts by two pioneers, Dr. Howard Hanson and Dr. Serge Koussevitzky. Dr. Hanson created the annual American Festivals at the Eastman School of Music in Rochester, and brought young composers there as guests, to hear their works performed.

Dr. Koussevitzky gave unstinting encouragement to unknown young composers in whom he had faith, and whose works he continued to play with the Boston Symphony.

Once, when they were discussing the American composer, the great pioneer said to Dr. Hanson, with a twinkle in his eye, 'The real beginning of American music dates from twenty-five years ago, when you came to Rochester, and I came to Boston!'

Many conductors living in the United States have helped to advance the cause of American composition; among them, Leonard Bernstein, Carlos Chavez, Eugene Ormandy, Thor Johnson, Walter Hendl, Dmitri Mitropoulos, Pierre Monteux, Fritz Reiner, Leopold Stokowski, and a few others. These men have frequently risked the displeasure of the critics, the antagonism of the public, and often, with more serious results, the disapproval of their own boards of directors. When Theodore Thomas was told that his audience at the Chicago Symphony concerts did not like his introduction of Richard Wagner's music in this country, his famous reply was, 'Then I shall continue to play it until they do like it.' He set a noble example for all time.

A feeling exists today, however, that the young men of talent now in their late 20's and 30's are deprived of the encouragement which was given twenty-five years ago to the composers now in their 50's and 60's. Although more contemporary music is actually being performed today, and many more musical organizations exist to perform it, the tendency of the symphonic conductors, with a few exceptions, seems to be to play American works by men whose names are well known. Quite rightly, the champions of the young composers hold that American music may lose the impetus gained over the past quarter of a century unless the younger men in this era are encouraged by being performed by symphonic orchestras and other ensembles.

All in all, the most marked changes in the status of the composer in the last twenty-five years have been in educational fields. It is heartening to know that the chances of employment of a composer as teacher have multiplied ten times in a quarter of a century.[3] This may well account for the larger number of students finding inspiration to write music today under the direction of creative minds. Moreover, 190 educational institutions are now offering musical degrees or credits.

The late Irwin Edman of Columbia University, discussing the role of American colleges and universities in the stimulation of creative arts, urged that 'a student should receive a sense of the past, with his outlook aimed at the future.' Professor Edman wanted universities to seize their opportunities to 'create a climate of perception in which the potential artist who happens to be a student there is both nourished and freshened.'

Major adjustments, artistic, financial, and possibly legal are called for by new media for creative expression. Like radio and recording, tape recordings and television are according both advantages and disadvantages to the composer. When just principles are laid down with special reference to these recent inventions, advantages to the composer well may outweigh the losses.

A situation in television and radio was recently exposed by Howard Taubman, music editor of *The New York Times* in an article in that paper; Mr. Taubman believes that at present composers have good ground for complaints and refers to the composer as 'the victim — scarcely ever mentioned — who gets no credit for the wide use of piecemeal performances of his work for TV background music.' As an example, Henry Cowell has told me about his contract with *Omnibus*, the television program created by the Ford Foundation in 1954. For a year, a

3. These statistics are from a survey made by Fred Smith at the College of Music of Cincinnati, and with the co-operation of Dr. Felix Labunsky.

theme by Cowell from an orchestral suite has been used each week, and the duration is two minutes, a total of one hundred and four minutes in the year. Although the composer is paid for this music, no credit is ever given to his name. The negative reason he is told is that the Studio cannot cope with any more credits!

A great deal of contemporary music, taken from recordings, is in use. Thanks to the watchful eye of ASCAP and BMI, royalties are paid, yet no spoken or visual credit is given for any part or use of the composition. According to Mr. Taubman,

> Perhaps it is comforting to the composers to know that their works have such value. The chances are, however, that if they were consulted, most of them would not be too happy to sanction performance of shreds and patches of their scores. The problem as far as the performer is concerned has greatly troubled the Musicians' Union. For composer and performer no change is foreseeable until Congress amends the copyright laws so that the composer and performer will retain a proprietary share in every record, thus have some voice in whether the record should be used.

In Hollywood, several years ago a composers guild was started. It may prove helpful to certain musicians employed in motion pictures, radio, television, also in certain types of recording and transcription. Deems Taylor (one of its first representatives appointed in the East), has written me that 'this guild is concerned with the interests of composers who work on salary, or by the piece, and it has been set up exclusively to get better working conditions for background music for radio, movies, and television. It is not concerned with music for concert or opera!'

How can the composers for concert or opera protect themselves in situations calling for a new legal status? Even outside the court, in cases of grievances, is the individual composer able to bring sufficient pressure on public opinion?

I believe that there will be a new alignment of composers some day, a true guild. It could have, first, a grievance committee, where the composer may air his complaint. Bar associations have them for lawyers; the Academy of Medicine has its grievance committee. There is Actors Equity to handle a variety of actor problems. AGMA is concerned with singers and the people of the chorus. The Musicians' Union deals with orchestra players, instrumentalists, and conductors.

A disagreement — more severe than a grievance — to avoid the expense of litigation, could be arbitrated, if so planned. As an example, the American Federation of Television and Radio Artists requires that any dispute which may arise between their members and any network *must* be arbitrated by the American Arbitration Association.

Instances will arise when court proceedings become necessary, or when laws need to be framed or to be amended by Congress. In such circumstances, a guild or union would naturally have a more forceful voice than the individual, or the small group of composers. The three categories — grievance committees, arbitrated disputes, and the courts — then would become the three protective means to be utilized by a guild or union of composers.

It is true that autocratic labor leaders have severely prejudiced unorganized groups, engendering fear of union control by the too familiar Big Boss. It does not follow that all unions face this problem. In Webster's dictionary, the definition of a union or guild is 'An agreeing or leaguing together for mutual benefit.'

When the day arrives for composers to organize, there will be a myriad of difficulties to be worked out. Each one of the industries dealing with composers has its own angle, as each composer has his own point of view. Yet with the increase of difficulties being encountered by composers today — whether in the realm of copyright, tape recording, or other music industry problems — I can only envision a planned organization of composers, which will establish a new *modus operandi* to give composers the protection they require, and supplement the invaluable functions of ASCAP, BMI, and ACA on royalty situations. The composers must eventually organize a strong platform for many conditions and situations, now only partially taken care of through one or another of the existing composer associations.

On a few occasions the League of Composers has been able to sustain certain composer rights, as I have already outlined in some of the injustices to composers. It is possible that the strength and prestige resulting from the merger of the League and the International Society for Contemporary Music could be a major force to draw together the composers from many parts of the country, also from various associations, to organize a composers guild. Many have shared this dream.

Robert Edmond Jones worked for many years with musicians, and his attunement to all the arts made him a keen critic and guide. I recall that after one concert by American composers which we attended together he wrote me these discerning lines: 'I had a curious impression last night that American music is often not what the wine-makers describe as "full bodied" and that spiritually it seems to be full of grieving. . . . Where is what Walt Whitman called "the flaunt of the sunshine"?'

The average creative artist is a lonely person. This is especially true of the young composer today, often seeking for contact with men and women in the allied arts, and for more experience with interested colleagues.

I visualize a center for creative artists among other means of dispelling this loneliness, this apartness. A place where young artists may meet, acquaint themselves with each others' views, find sympathetic co-workers, on a level of equality. A center could provide a forum for discussions, prepare the right atmosphere for auditions, be a clearinghouse for promoting experimental nonacademic ideas. Such a center should include all the humanities; thus it might hasten a better understanding and collaboration between artists in allied fields and furnish that needed environment young artists crave and properly need for growth.

Innumerable times, composers have asked to be given some job to help the League's work, chiefly for the purpose of reviving their contacts after a period of absence from their group of colleagues; perhaps they have been abroad on a fellowship, often finding it difficult on their return to re-orient themselves.

I received a letter one day from a young composer living away from New York, who was beset by the feeling of being apart. 'As the years go on,' he wrote, 'I can honestly say that I grow quite lonely; too much of this feeling is not good for an artist. I have practically no sympathy whatsoever for the followers of either Schoenberg or Stravinsky who dominate the scene here.'

Another young composer wrote, 'There is nothing that I would welcome more than a close association with the League of Composers, if I can come to New York to live. I think that a composer is fortunate if he can give part of his time to working with his colleagues, and still be able to isolate himself when living through a creative period.'

Rejoining the League's activities after a period of intense creativity, a composer will frequently throw himself into the work with renewed energy and a visible desire to be part of a sympathetic circle. I believe that a large part of it is sheer relief after apartness, as simple and human as that.

> We are the music makers,
> We are the dreamers of dreams . . .
> For each age is a dream that is dying,
> Or one that is coming to birth.[4]

As matters stand, a true composers guild or union is still on the horizon. In art, as in science, we can only envision a better future if we can fashion the right present in which the creative mind can grow and thrive. A center for the creative artist is a spiritual need, for to stimulate and encourage talented youth is the responsibility and the privilege of each age.

---

4. From 'Ode' by Arthur William Edgar O'Shaughnessy (1844–81).

# Appendix

Ten commissions offered to the League of Composers for its twenty-fifth anniversary were from:

Boosey and Hawkes to Harold Shapero
Broadcast Music, Inc. to Robert E. Ward
Carl Fischer, Inc. to William Bergsma
Hargail Music Press to Peter Mennin
Edward B. Marks Corp. to Wallingford Riegger
National Federation of Music Clubs to Richard F. Goldman
Richard Rodgers and Irving Berlin to Samuel Barber
Mrs. Walter Rosen to Nicolai Berezowsky
Albert F. Metz to Dai-Keong Lee
Edwin Franko Goldman to Percy Grainger

Later, other organizations added commissions. Among them were The Elizabeth Sprague Coolidge Foundation at the Library of Congress; Samuel R. Rosenbaum; The Koussevitzky Music Foundation; Lado, Inc. Among the recipients were Arthur Berger, Peter Mennin, Pavel Börkovec, André Jolivet, Roman Palester.

Richard Rodgers and Oscar Hammerstein have since given League commissions annually; recipients have been Leon Kirshner, Irving Fine, Aaron Copland, Henry Cowell, Stefan Wolpe.

The conductors and the orchestras who celebrated the League of Composers' twenty-fifth anniversary by playing works commissioned for the League were:

| | |
|---|---|
| The New York Philharmonic Symphony | Leopold Stokowski |
| The Boston Symphony | Serge Koussevitzky |
| The San Francisco Symphony | Pierre Monteux |
| The Chicago Symphony | Artur Rodzinski |

| | |
|---|---|
| The Minneapolis Symphony | Dmitri Mitropoulos |
| The Cleveland Orchestra | George Szell |
| The Rochester Symphony | Erich Leinsdorf |
| The Cincinnati Symphony | Thor Johnson |
| The New York City Symphony | Leonard Bernstein |
| The St. Louis Symphony | Vladimir Golschmann |
| The Fort Wayne Philharmonic | Hans Schwieger |
| The Baltimore Symphony | Reginald Stewart |
| The Indianapolis Symphony | Fabien Sevitzky |
| The National Symphony, Washington, D.C. | Hans Kindler |
| The Vancouver Symphony | Jacques Singer |
| The Columbia Broadcasting Symphony | Bernard Herrmann |
| The Symphony Orchestra of Mexico | Carlos Chavez |
| The National Gallery of Art Orchestra, Washington, D.C. | Richard Bales |
| The Denver Symphony | Saul Caston |

A gesture of appreciation is due to all the musicians and the laymen who have served on the board of directors of the League of Composers. The composers have taken time from their own important creative preoccupations to determine ways and means to help in the struggles of their fellow composers.

The men and women (non-composers) who served as directors or officers of the corporation gave their best effort and support to develop the organization.

To all of them the League of Composers owes a debt of thanks.

Among the composers who have been members of the board of directors are:

| | |
|---|---|
| Milton Babbitt | Henry D. Cowell |
| Samuel Barber | Norman Dello Joio |
| Marion Bauer | Irving Fine |
| Nicolai T. Berezowsky | Donald S. Fuller |
| Arthur Berger | Lehman Engel |
| William Bergsma | Richard Franko Goldman |
| Leonard Bernstein | Louis Gruenberg |
| Arthur Bliss | Richard Hammond |
| Marc Blitzstein | Everett Helm |
| Elliott C. Carter, Jr. | Mary Howe |
| Theodore W. Chanler | Frederick Jacobi |
| Chalmers Clifton | Erich Itor Kahn |
| Aaron Copland | Ulysses S. Kay |

*Appendix* 255

Otto Luening
Jacques de Menasce
Peter Mennin
Darius Milhaud
Douglas S. Moore
Nicholas Nabokov
Leo Ornstein
Vincent Persichetti
Walter Piston
Quincy Porter

Lazare Saminsky
Mark Schubart
William Howard Schuman
Roger Sessions
Louise Talma
Randall Thompson
Vladimir Ussachevsky
Bernard Wagenaar
Robert E. Ward
Emerson Whithorne

Composers and critics who contributed to the magazine *Modern Music* were many. It is only possible to list a few names of those who frequently wrote for it. Among them were S. L. M. Barlow, Paul Bowles, Israel Citkowitz, Edwin Denby, David Diamond, Alfred V. Frankenstein, John Gutman, Lou Harrison, Irving Kolodin, Arthur Love, Goddard Lieberson, Colin McFee, Charles Mills, Lawrence Morton, Colin Nancarrow, Pitts Sanborn, Cecil M. Smith, Virgil Thomson, and also many members of the board of directors and other musicians. Mrs. Frani Muser, Joe Lifflander, and Donald Fuller actively aided the editor, Minna Lederman, in the publication of the quarterly magazine.

Directors who worked on the League's board (professional musicians and laymen) were:

Dr. Thaddeus H. Ames
Stephen Bourgeois
Edgar M. Church
Mrs. Frederick S. Crofts
Miss Sally Dodge
Mrs. Stephen Duggan, Jr.
Mrs. Samuel Dushkin
Irving Gittell
Miss Peggy Glanville-Hicks
Mrs. Ernest S. Heller

Mrs. D. V. Holman
Mr. Richard Leach
Mrs. Alma Morgenthau
Mrs. C. Mckim Norton
David Oppenheim
Lawrence Perry
Mrs. Carleton Sprague Smith
Mrs. Kenneth Simpson
Alexander Smallens
Pierson Underwood

The Auxiliary Board gave particular support to the stage presentations. Certain members became interested in the League's general activities and supported the seasonal work. Among those who served on this board for many years were:

Countess Marie Mercati,
Chairman

Mrs. W. Murray Crane,
Chairman

Mrs. Myron Taylor,
Chairman
Mrs. Robert Woods Bliss,
Chairman
Mrs. Eugene Meyer,
Chairman

Mrs. Otto H. Kahn,
Vice Chairman
Madame Olga Samaroff,
Vice Chairman
Mrs. Charles S. Guggenheimer,
Vice Chairman

Mrs. Henry M. Alexander, Mrs. John W. Alexander, Mrs. Paul Baerwald, Mrs. Sydney Borg, Mrs. William C. Breed, Miss Phyllis Byrne, Miss Louise Crane, Mrs. Henry Glazier, Mrs. Christian Holmes, Mrs. John P. Marquand, Mrs. Charles E. Mitchell, Mrs. John Parkinson, Jr., Mrs. John De Witt Peltz, Mrs. John Rogers, Jr., Mr. Edgar Rossin, Mr. Robert A. Shaw, Mrs. Frederick Steinway, Mrs. Theodore Steinway, Mr. Allen Wardwell, and others.

Following my resignation as chairman of the board of directors in 1948, Aaron Copland served as chairman for two years; Mrs. Nicolai Berezowsky was chairman for the following three years, and Miss Betty Bean for the following year. In 1954 the League of Composers merged with the International Society for Contemporary Music and Roger Sessions was elected the first chairman of the board for the two societies; Aaron Copland became the chairman of the Composers Committee, and I became honorary chairman. Mr. Robert S. Groban was made treasurer, and Mr. Claire S. Degner the executive secretary.

The present board of directors are:

Claus Adams
Milton Babbitt
Marion Bauer
Betty Randolph Bean
Elliott C. Carter, Jr.
Aaron Copland
Mrs. F. S. Crofts
Norman Dello Joio
Alexei Haieff
Mrs. Ernest S. Heller
Erich Itor Kahn

Douglas Moore
David Oppenheim
Frederick Prausnitz
Mrs. Arthur M. Reis
Gunther Schuller
Roger Sessions
Clara Steuermann
Louise Talma
Vladimir Ussachevsky
Robert Ward

The publishing houses and editors who have co-operated with the League of Composers are:

| | |
|---|---|
| Associated Music Publishers | Mr. Richard F. French |
| Boosey and Hawkes | Mr. David Adams and Mr. Robert Holton |
| Chappell and Company | Mr. Ralph Satz |
| Carl Fischer, Inc. | Dr. Gustave Reese |
| Leeds Music Corporation | Mr. Michael Stillman |
| Mercury Music Corporation | Mr. Milton Feist and Mr. Leonard Feist |
| Oxford University Press | Mr. Lyle Dowling |
| G. Ricordi and Company | Dr. Franco Colombo |
| Southern Music Publishing Company | Mr. Vladimir Lakond |

The Phi Beta Sorority, ASCAP, and BMI have contributed to this project.

**AUTHOR'S NOTE.** The following *Index* appears as it did in the original 1955 edition. It does not cover material in pages I-XVI of this 1974 reprint edition. C.R.R. February, 1974.

# *Index*